A Hidden Wisdom

A Hidden Wisdom

*Medieval Contemplatives on
Self-Knowledge, Reason, Love,
Persons, and Immortality*

CHRISTINA VAN DYKE

Great Clarendon Street, Oxford, OX2 6DP,
United Kingdom

Oxford University Press is a department of the University of Oxford.
It furthers the University's objective of excellence in research, scholarship,
and education by publishing worldwide. Oxford is a registered trade mark of
Oxford University Press in the UK and in certain other countries

© Christina Van Dyke 2022

The moral rights of the author have been asserted

First Edition published in 2022

Impression: 1

All rights reserved. No part of this publication may be reproduced, stored in
a retrieval system, or transmitted, in any form or by any means, without the
prior permission in writing of Oxford University Press, or as expressly permitted
by law, by licence or under terms agreed with the appropriate reprographics
rights organization. Enquiries concerning reproduction outside the scope of the
above should be sent to the Rights Department, Oxford University Press, at the
address above

You must not circulate this work in any other form
and you must impose this same condition on any acquirer

Published in the United States of America by Oxford University Press
198 Madison Avenue, New York, NY 10016, United States of America

British Library Cataloguing in Publication Data

Data available

Library of Congress Control Number: 2022942370

DOI: 10.1093/oso/9780198861683.001.0001

Printed and bound in the UK by
Clays Ltd, Elcograf S.p.A.

Links to third party websites are provided by Oxford in good faith and
for information only. Oxford disclaims any responsibility for the materials
contained in any third party website referenced in this work.

For Bob Pasnau,

my philosophical older brother, without whose prodding
*("Surely **you** can write something about medieval mysticism!")*
this book would never have begun, and

for David,

my favorite and only child, without whose prodding
*("Seriously Mom, **how** have you not sent that off yet?")*
this book might never have been finished.

Contents

Acknowledgments	ix
Preface	xv
List of Figures	xxvii

1. Mysticism, Methodology, and Epistemic Justice	1
1.1 Implicit Assumptions and the Case of 'Mystical Experience'	3
1.1.1 A standard contemporary definition of 'mystical experience'	4
1.1.2 Debates about mysticism in the twentieth century	6
1.2 Apophatic Self-Abnegation	11
1.3 Correcting via Complementing: Embracing Embodied Experiences	14
1.4 Philosophical Morals and Historical Narratives	19
1.5 Looking Ahead	21

Interlude One: Who Is This Book About?	25

2. Self-Knowledge	33
2.1 Putting the Self into Perspective	34
2.2 Recommendations for Developing Self-Knowledge	40
2.2.1 Look outside yourself to know yourself: the mirror of self-knowledge	40
2.2.2 Root down in humility to rise up in dignity: the tree of self	45
2.2.3 Use reason and imagination to overcome selfish pride	51
2.3 Self-Knowledge, Mystic Union, and Our Final End	56
2.3.1 Our final end as self-annihilation	56
2.3.2 Our final end as self-fulfillment	58
2.4 Conclusion	61

Interlude Two: What Is a Beguine?	62

3. Reason and Its Limits	67
3.1 The Nature of Reason	68
3.2 Taking Leave of Reason	70
3.3 Reason as Guide	77
3.4 Reason as Enhanced by Mystical Union	86
3.5 *Scientia* vs. *Sapientia*	90

viii CONTENTS

Interlude Three: When Did Reading Become a Sign of
Religious Devotion for Women? 93

4. Love and the Will 101
    4.1 The Will in Context 103
        4.1.1 Sensation and sense appetite 106
        4.1.2 Imagination 110
    4.2 Meditation and the Will 112
    4.3 Contemplation and Love 121
    4.4 Clear Eyes, Full Hearts: Women's Bodies and the Reception
        of Truth 126

Interlude Four: Where Does the Erotic Imagery of Medieval
Mystics Come from? 133

5. Persons 139
    5.1 Putting 'Person' in Perspective 140
        5.1.1 Grammatical and logical context 141
        5.1.2 Legal and political context 142
        5.1.3 Theological context 146
    5.2 Individuality, Dignity, and Rationality in Contemplative Texts 150
        5.2.1 Individuality and agency 154
        5.2.2 Dignity 157
        5.2.3 Rationality 161
    5.3 Personal Perspectives, Personification, and Introspection 165
    5.4 Looking Forward: Locke and Personalism 171

Interlude Five: Why Do Medieval Women Talk Like They
Hate Themselves? 174

6. Immortality and the Afterlife 179
    6.1 The Metaphysics of Immortality 181
    6.2 Transcending Matter, Becoming God 184
    6.3 Embodied Immortal Experience 190
    6.4 Intellective Union and the Scholastic Tradition 198
        6.4.1 Robert Grosseteste 200
        6.4.2 Thomas Aquinas 202
    6.5 Conclusion 204

    Afterword 206

Bibliography 209
Index 223

Acknowledgments

This book has been a long time in the researching and writing, and I've worked up quite a debt of gratitude in the process. If I should have included you and have somehow forgotten, I'm terribly sorry. I encourage you to tell all your friends to read this book so that they can see what you were a part of, and I promise that I'll start my acknowledgments list earlier in the process of my next book. First credit goes, as promised, to the person who helped me come up with a title that evokes exactly what I was hoping for, while also providing the perfect 'hook' for the grocery list of topics that make up the subtitle: Robin Dembroff, thank you! When the pandemic is over and/or we're both in the same place at the same time again, dinner's on me.

I also need to thank Bob Pasnau—not just for originally assigning me the chapter on mysticism in *The Cambridge History of Medieval Philosophy* but for cheering me on ever since then as I've delved further and further into the medieval contemplative tradition, and especially for providing me with a full set of very helpful comments on the entire manuscript. Ursula Renz also played a crucial role in this book's history, although I'm sure she doesn't know it; I had already gone back to writing about Thomas Aquinas when she invited me to write a chapter on self-knowledge in medieval mystics for an Oxford Philosophical Concepts volume she was editing, and it was that essay that made me realize that I needed to keep going with the contemplatives—I remain deeply grateful for that invitation and her encouragement of what I wrote. It is Christia Mercer, however, who can take direct credit for my actually writing this book. Not only did she tell me that I had a book in the making already in February 2016, but she then kept inviting me to give talks on relevant topics at workshops at her Center for New Narratives in the History of Philosophy at Columbia University. Those workshops introduced me to both people and ideas that have expanded and deepened my understanding of medieval mysticism and contemplativism in fantabulous

X ACKNOWLEDGMENTS

ways—I'm sure I haven't done them full justice here, but special thanks in particular go to Katie Bugyis, Holly Flora, and Lauren Mancia for being kick-ass theologians, art historians, and historians willing to hang out with this analytically trained philosopher.

Speaking of people who have worked to create vibrant communities of scholars with cross-disciplinary interests, many thanks also to Mike Rea and the crew of his Logos conferences. The Logos conferences may be a thing of the past, but their impact remains, and I appreciate being made to feel part of a group (viz., philosophers of religion and analytic theologians) I'd long felt on the outside of. Thanks also to Scott MacDonald for continuing to hold the Cornell Medieval Colloquia each year, even now that they're actually happening in Brooklyn (and, in 2020–2022, online). The chance to connect and reconnect there with stellar scholars and friends like Susan Brower-Toland, Peter King, Scott Williams, and Thomas Williams has made both my work and my life better in myriad ways I find it hard to quantify. I am also endlessly grateful to Thomas Williams for reading this entire manuscript and providing me with not only a host of useful comments but several much-needed laughs ("These people need to be beaten with a Jesus-stick") and any number of pep talks. I look forward to finding out with you exactly what level of snark is allowed in heaven.

General thanks go to Elizabeth Barnes and Ross Cameron for their relentless support and encouragement; to Sara Bernstein for such good advice about so many things and always having my back; to Molly Brown—Star to my Barb and mother of my godpuppy Elodie (whose adorableness kept me going during the darkest part of the pandemic); to Amber Griffioen and Lacey Hudspeth for encouragement, support, and a place to vent about the mysticism haters; to Amy Seymour, Julia Staffel, and Natalie Hart for being my writing partners at coffee shops in NYC, Boulder, and Grand Rapids; and to Laurie Paul for making me feel like it was *obvious* that I was going to write an amazing book and that the only real question was how to make sure the right people read it. A most particular thank you to Keshav Singh for making me the cootie-catcher that decided which versions of the names of medieval figures I was going to use in this book when I was going bananas trying to decide between things like Johannes and John, of Oingt or d'Oingt. The result may be a bit idiosyncratic, but it is at least consistent throughout. Many thanks as well to Peter Momtchiloff, who has been wonderfully encouraging of this project and who sent me a few crucial email nudges at just the right moment in the fall of 2021.

It's hard to know exactly what sort of gratitude I owe to Calvin College (now University). On the one hand, both the college and my department provided me with deeply appreciated support and encouragement when I was a full-time single parent and an assistant (and then tenured and then full) professor; on the other hand, after several truly stressful years, in 2020 continued budgetary shortfalls led the university to cut a number of tenured positions, including mine, and I'd be lying if I said that I missed being there. I do miss what Calvin used to be, however, and I have a deep appreciation not only for the mission it now seems to have lost but for the people I've been fortunate enough to have shared a department with there, particularly Lindsay Brainard, Terence Cuneo, Rebecca Konyndyk DeYoung, Ruth Groenhout (the next-door office mate than which none greater could be conceived), Matt Halteman (with only one 'n'!), Lee Hardy, Al Plantinga (who spent several 'victory lap' years there after retiring from Notre Dame), Del Ratzsch, and Kevin Timpe. The tireless work of first Donna Kruithof and then Laura McMullen and Corrie Bakker kept me (relatively) organized and (mostly) in the right places at the right times, and I can't thank them enough for that. I am also deeply grateful to the students who have passed through my life over the twenty years I spent as a faculty member at Calvin, many of whom I now count as friends. You taught me that the most effective way to communicate the importance and value of philosophy is to live what you say you believe, and I am the better for it.

The next two paragraphs are lists of places that supported my research financially and/or invited me to speak to them about aspects of this project, and I'm very self-conscious about the fact that they might read like me bragging about what I've been privileged to receive, but I am both obligated to list them and quite grateful for the opportunities they all represent. That said, feel free to skip ahead to the part where I start talking about my family. In chronological order from when I began seriously to work on mystical experiences and immortality in 2014 to the present, I owe thanks to John Hawthorne's *New Insights and Directions*

xii ACKNOWLEDGMENTS

for Religious Epistemology project for funding a Hilary Term fellowship at Oxford University, and to John Martin Fischer's *Immortality Project* for a year-long grant to support my project "(Ever)Lasting Happiness: Immortality and the Afterlife," which I amazingly got to combine with a year-long fellowship at Notre Dame's Center for the Philosophy of Religion. (Both projects thought they were funding me to write a book on Aquinas on the afterlife, but instead they actually supported much of the initial research for this book, and I'm extremely grateful.) Thanks also to the University of Colorado at Boulder for inviting me to be their inaugural Distinguished Visitor; to the *Aspects of Religious Experience* grant that Laurie Paul and Mike Rea administrated for their generous support of Robin Dembroff's and my "Embodied Religion: Social Structures and Religious Experience"; to the Calvin Alumni Research Grant for travel funding in 2017, which is when I took a number of the photographs that appear in this book; to Dean Zimmerman and the Rutgers Center for the Philosophy of Religion for a year-long fellowship there; and, finally, to Sidney Sussex College at the University of Cambridge for granting me the visiting fellowship I was only five weeks away from when the pandemic shut everything down in March 2020.

Here is a compressed list of places at which I've given talks related to the content of this book, and a far-too-truncated list of the wonderful people who have spent time talking to me about it there. I am deeply grateful to all these places and all the people who have worked to get me there—with special thanks to the administrative staff at various institutions who made my presence possible! Thanks to audiences at all three regional APAs for their feedback on various talks; the Epistemology Brownbag series at Northwestern University; the Cornell Colloquium in Medieval Philosophy; L'Abri Fellowship International; the University of Konstanz; the University of Leeds Centre for Philosophy of Religion, as well the Leeds School of Philosophy, Religion, and History of Science Mangoletsi Lecture Series in 2019—with a special shout-out to Mark Wynn and Robbie Williams for hosting me so wonderfully; Lingnan University and the University of Hong Kong; Boğaziçi University in Istanbul; the University of St. Thomas in St. Paul; the Society for Medieval Logic and Metaphysics; the Brooklyn College Minorities and Philosophy chapter; the Sheffield Religious Experience workshop; the

ACKNOWLEDGMENTS   xiii

Center for New Narratives in the History of Philosophy at Columbia University; the University of North Carolina at Asheville, St. Mary's Philosophy Department Retreat in South Bend; Creighton University; the 40th Anniversary Conference of the Society of Christian Philosophers; Shieva Kleinschmidt's California Conference in Metaphysics; the Society of Medieval and Renaissance Philosophy; Georgetown University; St Andrew's University; the Practical Philosophy Workshop + Women in Philosophy series at the University of Chicago; the Ayers Lecture in Philosophy and Theology at Furman University; the Ax:Son Johnson Foundation Seminar for the Concept of Self-Knowledge in Ancient and Modern Times; the University of Indiana at Bloomington; the Vrije University at Amsterdam; the American Academy of Religion; the Goliardic Society at Western Michigan University; the Medieval Philosophy Colloquium at the University of Toronto; the Rutgers Center of Philosophy of Religion; the Princeton Project in the Philosophy of Religion; the University of Trier; and Leiden University.

OK, and now to my family. Tolstoy famously begins *Anna Karenina* with the claim that "Happy families are all alike; each unhappy family is unhappy in its own way." I know that he's supposed to have meant that there is a list of common attributes that all families need in order to be happy, but if you've ever met my family you will understand why that sentence has always made me laugh. We are, in general, very happy and yet I can't image our hilarious, bizarre family being like any other family in the world. Mom and Dad—I'm more glad than I can put into words that you're still here to see this book come out, health scares of 2021 notwithstanding. I promise to write any number of other books if you promise to stick around to bug me about whether I've finished them yet! To my siblings, Jamie, Jon, and CarlaJoy, I love you excessively; our weekly Zoom family chats during the pandemic have made me feel closer to you than ever despite the physical distances between us, and have often left my stomach hurting from laughing so hard. Thank you also to Jamie and Robin and CarlaJoy and Steve for producing such excellent niblings—Jon and Aki, Max and Pepper have also been quite excellent catlings. I've already dedicated this book to David, but I want to make sure everyone knows that David's amazingness goes far beyond skeptical side-eye and effective prodding to finish book manuscripts.

xiv ACKNOWLEDGMENTS

My child, your presence in my life has made me happier than I could ever have expected or even desired. It may not have been *easy* to share a one-bedroom apartment with you during strict lockdown in 2020, but there's no one else I would have rather gotten irritated with under those circumstances.

No one, that is, except perhaps my beloved, Andrew Arlig. (Which is good, because I got to share *all* the lockdowns with you!) Andy, I have been working on this book the entire time that we have been together, and you have never been anything but supportive and encouraging about it. It's been a challenge in any number of ways combining our lives over the past five and a half years, but a challenge that is more than worth the effort. Our love is not a unicorn—magical and illusory; it is a narwhal—rare, weird, and extremely real. Here's to years and years of swimming together in the same direction.

Preface

In college and graduate school, I was taught that women didn't do philosophy in the Middle Ages. My teachers were clear that this was a shame, but they were also clear that their job was to teach me facts, and the facts were that 1) 'medieval philosophy' happened primarily in the cathedral schools and universities of something called the 'Latin Christian West' during the eleventh–fifteenth centuries, and 2) women weren't allowed to participate in these discussions.[1] This first 'fact' has been completely overturned in the past twenty years; it would be difficult to find a well-respected book about medieval philosophy published today that didn't acknowledge the importance of Greek, Islamic, and Jewish thought from the sixth century on, and new editions of old textbooks generally take pains to include a variety of these sources alongside the requisite Anselm, Abelard, Aquinas, Scotus, and Ockham.[2] The truth of the second 'fact', however, remains largely accepted, for women were generally no more welcome in medieval Greek, Islamic, or Jewish schools than they were in their Latin counterparts. On this view of the history of philosophy, women were essentially barred from contributing to philosophy between Hypatia's death in Alexandria in the fifth century and Descartes's correspondence with Princess Elizabeth of Bohemia in the seventeenth century.

I don't think what I was taught reflects badly on my teachers. At the time (I started college in 1990 and finished my PhD in 1999), this was not just the dominant narrative about women and medieval

---

[1] For a history of the development of these institutions, see Jon Marenbon's two-volume *Early Medieval Philosophy: 480–1150* (London: Routledge, 1983) and *Later Medieval Philosophy: 1150–1350* (London: Routledge, 1987).

[2] Marenbon's *Medieval Philosophy: An Historical and Philosophical Introduction* (London: Routledge, 2006), for instance, is meant to supersede the two-volume work mentioned in note 1 by addressing "all four main traditions of medieval philosophy that go back to the same roots in late antiquity: the Greek Christian tradition, the Latin tradition, the Arabic tradition, and the Jewish tradition (written in Arabic and in Hebrew)" (Preface, p. 1/i).

xvi PREFACE

philosophy—it was the *only* narrative. It didn't even bother me particularly. I wrote my dissertation on Thomas Aquinas's theory of individuation and identity for human beings, and I was tenured for my work on Aquinas's metaphysics and Robert Grosseteste's theory of illumination; I found this work both challenging and rewarding. I channeled my interests in gender and sexuality into side projects in the philosophy of gender, particularly projects that explored the relation between gendered eating and religion. Mentally, I compartmentalized my research as addressing either medieval philosophy (as characterized by 'fact' 1) or the philosophy of gender: I hadn't realized yet that the 'or' could be inclusive. I originally read Caroline Walker Bynum's monumental *Holy Feast and Holy Fast*, for instance, not because it was about the Middle Ages but because it was about women and the religious significance of food.[3] The bookshelves in my office were packed with Latin texts and secondary literature on Augustine, Boethius, Anselm, Aquinas, Scotus, and Ockham; my bookshelves at home started to fill up with titles like *Holy Anorexia* and *God and the Goddesses: Vision, Poetry, and Belief in the Middle Ages*.[4]

And then, in the academic year 2007–8, I spent my first sabbatical working with Bob Pasnau on *The Cambridge History of Medieval Philosophy*. At some point we had received all fifty-five commissioned chapters—over one thousand pages of state-of-the-art scholarship on medieval philosophy in the Greek and Latin Christian, Islamic, and Jewish traditions—and we realized that not a single chapter discussed texts authored by medieval women. You could read the entire manuscript and fairly form the impression that women had taken a collective pass on thinking in the Middle Ages. This was an unacceptable state of affairs, but how to address it? Adding a chapter called something like 'Women and Medieval Philosophy' struck us both as the worst sort of ad hoc maneuver; adding more mentions of women in the chapters on, say, poverty or religious orders or war didn't address the central issue, which

---

[3] Caroline Walker Bynum, *Holy Feast and Holy Fast: The Religious Significance of Food to Medieval Women* (Berkeley: University of California Press, 1988).

[4] Rudolph Bell, *Holy Anorexia* (Chicago: University of Chicago Press, 1985); Barbara Newman, *God and the Goddesses: Vision, Poetry, and Belief in the Middle Ages* (Philadelphia: University of Pennsylvania Press, 2003).

was that it seemed highly implausible that women had really not contributed anything of value to the ongoing practice of philosophy in the millennium we were covering in the volume. The question Bob and I ended up asking each other was "Where were women writing in the Middle Ages, and what were they writing about?"

As soon as we phrased the question that way, I realized I already knew the answer—I just hadn't connected the dots. My teachers had been right that women didn't participate in philosophy as it was practiced in scholastic contexts (that is, in the cathedral schools and universities), but women did author a vast number of mystical and contemplative texts in the later Middle Ages, and these women were hardly writing in a philosophical or theological vacuum: they were integral parts of the intellectual, theological, and cultural movements of their day.

My joint expertise in thirteenth-century philosophy and gender studies meant that it fell to me to explore the medieval contemplative tradition for its philosophical insights. As I rolled up my sleeves and went to work on what became the chapter in the *Cambridge History* titled 'Mysticism', I discovered that although mystics and contemplatives in the Middle Ages might not have thought of themselves as engaging in philosophy per se—and although what they wrote often tends not to fit neatly into our contemporary conceptions of philosophy—they have a wealth of insightful things to say about philosophical topics of perennial interest (such as self-knowledge, reason and its limits, will and love, persons, and immortality and the afterlife). Furthermore, the fact that women writing in these traditions didn't think of themselves as engaging in philosophy *per se* shouldn't prevent us from considering their works as philosophical, for in this respect they resemble most of the other figures we today study under the descriptor 'medieval philosopher': Augustine's *Confessions* was written as a spiritual memoir, for instance, and Anselm's Ontological Argument is presented as part of a prayer for understanding. Even the paradigms of scholastic philosophy—Thomas Aquinas, Duns Scotus, and William Ockham—were masters of theology (rather than philosophy) at their respective institutions.[5] If we shift our

---

[5] This has led to an ongoing heated (if not particularly productive) debate about whether these figures (especially Aquinas) should be thought of as philosophers at all. Personally,

xviii PREFACE

conception of medieval philosophy to include contemplative texts (as I argue we should in Chapter 1), we find a host of women doing philosophy in the Middle Ages—including any number of women not addressed in this book, which focuses on the 'Latin'[6] Christian tradition from the thirteenth to fifteenth centuries.

When my initial attempt to demonstrate the relevance of the contemplative tradition to the study of medieval philosophy appeared in the first edition of *The Cambridge History of Medieval Philosophy* (2010), however, my colleagues in the field didn't seem particularly interested. As I continued to argue for its importance and to discuss the contributions of women to this tradition, I started to wonder if I was trying to make the medieval philosophical version of 'fetch' happen. Then, just as I was giving up hope, there came a surge of interest in the topic—a surge due in large part, no doubt, to the successful efforts of scholars like Andrew Janiak, Marcy Lascano, Christia Mercer, Eileen O'Neill, and Lisa Shapiro to demonstrate the philosophical significance of women from the early modern period whose work had previously been downplayed or ignored.[7] I started being asked to give talks on the medieval contemplative tradition and the women writing within it and to contribute papers on the contemplative tradition to special journal issues and edited volumes; my fellow historians of medieval philosophy started to ask me which women-authored texts they should include on their syllabi and on what topics. And then, in February 2016, Christia Mercer told me almost off-handedly over breakfast at the Nassau Inn at Princeton that the work I'd already done on this topic basically amounted

---

I believe that we're better off expanding rather than defending philosophy's borders. For a similar view, see Peter Adamson's "If Aquinas is a philosopher then so are the Islamic theologians" (https://aeon.co/ideas/if-aquinas-is-a-philosopher-then-so-are-the-islamic-theologians>) and also his *Medieval Philosophy: a History of Philosophy without Any Gaps, Vol. 4* (Oxford: Oxford University Press, 2019).

[6] The reason for putting scare quotes around 'Latin' here is that although church, legal, and university authorities continue to write in Latin during this period, many of the women discussed in this book wrote or dictated in their native vernacular.

[7] See, e.g., Eileen O'Neill and Marcy Lascano's *Feminist History of Philosophy: The Recovery and Evaluation of Women's Philosophical Thought* (Cham: Springer Nature Switzerland, 2019); Christia Mercer's "Descartes' Debt to Teresa of Avila, or why we should work on women in the history of philosophy," *Philosophical Studies* 174/10 (2017), pp. 2539–55. See also the resources of Project Vox at https://projectvox.org/about-the-project/ and New Narratives in the History of Philosophy at https://www.newnarrativesinphilosophy.net/index.html.

to a book, and that I just should sit down and write it. And so, over the course of six very long and full years, I did.

Writing this book has been both challenging and exciting. It's difficult to highlight the philosophical insights of women-authored texts without coming across as essentializing their status as women, for instance, but I've done my best. In each chapter I discuss the range of contemplative views on a given topic in works by both men and women from the Rome-based Christian tradition of the thirteenth–fifteenth centuries; focusing only on women's contributions would produce as skewed a picture of the intellectual landscape as the traditional focus on scholastics has already produced. At the same time, I center the contributions of medieval women throughout this book, for even within the contemplative tradition the philosophical and theological insights of medieval male figures consistently receive more attention than their female counterparts. Take, for instance, the introduction to *Pseudo-Dionysius: the Complete Works*, in which Jean Leclercq traces Pseudo-Dionysius's influence in Western Europe through the fourteenth and fifteenth centuries as follows:

> The works of Dionysius provided a powerful contribution in the fourteenth and fifteenth centuries to the spirituality that flowered in the Rhine valley and elsewhere among theologians of the "abstract school," as historians have termed it. Master Eckhart (d. 1327) proved capable of adopting fundamentally Dionysian themes, "while changing the meaning substantially." Several other writers did more or less the same, each in his own way: Tauler (d. 1361); Ruysbroeck [*sic*] (d. 1381), Gerson (d. 1429), Nicholas of Cusa (d. 1464), Denis the Carthusian (d. 1471), Harphius (d. 1477), and Marsilio Ficino (d. 1499).[8]

Although this list includes several figures who are hardly household names, it excludes every single woman writing in the same tradition in this period—even those such as Marguerite Porete and Hadewijch who had an identifiable influence on Eckhart and Ruusbroec. This list also

---

[8] Jean Leclercq, *Pseudo-Dionisius: the Complete Works*, trans. Colm Luiheid (Mahwah: Paulist Press, 1987), p. 30.

xx   PREFACE

overlooks the centrality of Dionysian themes of unknowing, apophatic silence and divine darkness in works by any other number of women mystics at this time, such as Angela of Foligno.

Two more recent examples demonstrate the continued neglect of women in discussions of medieval philosophy and theology, and they represent merely the tip of the iceberg of scholarship that fits this bill. First, Stephen Boulter's 2019 *Why Medieval Philosophy Matters* includes as "good examples of important medieval figures who were not scholastics" the following list: "John Scotus Eriugena, the Cathari and Albigensians, Bernard of Tours, Amalic of Bene, Joachim de Floris, Witelo, Theodoric of Freiburg, Raymond Lully, Roger Marston, Meister Eckhart, Raymond of Sabunde, and Nicholas of Cusa."[9] Again, not a single woman makes the cut. Second, the 2020 *Oxford Handbook of Mystical Theology* devotes a great deal of attention to the Western Christian medieval tradition, and yet an entire chapter on Trinitarian indwelling fails to even *mention* Julian of Norwich, while the chapter on depth, ground, and abyss discusses Eckhart, Tauler, and others (again) without so much as paying lip service to Hadewijch's and Marguerite Porete's influence on those authors, much less their own original contributions; another chapter discusses theological epistemology and apophasis in both the 'intellectualist' and the 'affective' Christian mystical traditions without naming a single woman, despite the overwhelming number of medieval women who write about these topics.[10]

If I have leaned too far in this book towards prioritizing women's voices over those of their male contemporaries, it is in the spirit of Aristotle's advice in the *Nicomachean Ethics* 2.7 to steer towards the opposite extreme in attempting to reach the mean—in this case, the mean of justice.[11] Mysticism and contemplativism have traditionally

---

[9] Stephen Boulter, *Why Medieval Philosophy Matters* (London: Bloomsbury Academic, 2019), p. 161. Unfortunately (and egregiously), the book also neglects Greek Byzantine, Islamic, and Jewish contributions.

[10] *The Oxford Handbook of Mystical Theology*, ed. E. Howells and M. McIntosh (Oxford: Oxford University Press, 2020). For an argument that these omissions and those of similarly marginalized voices are actively (if unintentionally) pernicious, see my "Review of *The Oxford Handbook of Mystical Theology*" in *Faith and Philosophy* 38 (3) 2021, 396–402.

[11] The issue of epistemic injustice in particular has received a great deal of attention in the past fifteen years or so: who is believed when they speak, and in what contexts and on what subjects? Who is given the conceptual tools to make sense of their own situations and who

been some of the very few contexts in which people otherwise denied a voice by Christian institutions can speak truth to power and be heard. Their focus is not on intensive study of hierarchical systems of knowledge and texts available primarily to the elite but on accessible practices such as meditation and contemplative prayer, and on personal experience of God, which is available to anyone. Because the Christian tradition acknowledges mystical experiences and knowledge of God's hidden truths as granted by God via an act of grace, the philosophy and theology of mysticism and contemplativism can never be simply the purview of the powerful: they are available to anyone and everyone God chooses. (And, as Scripture teaches us, God consistently chooses the disenfranchised and overlooked.) One of the most important legacies of the medieval contemplative tradition is the way in which it creates space for people to connect directly with God and to claim to God's own authority in their love-filled striving to unsettle the unjust status quos of this world. (Consider Catherine of Siena, for instance, the twenty-fourth child of a Sienese cloth-dyer who becomes an influential political figure as well as a renowned spiritual teacher—and is not merely canonized by the Catholic church but eventually made one of its Doctors.) By giving the views of medieval women more than equal time in this book I hope to highlight (and contribute to) this legacy, at the same time that I work to contextualize those views in the intellectual and cultural contexts necessary for understanding them.

A few quick notes about the book as a whole before I start actually doing this work and not just talking about it. First, I use the terms 'mystical' and 'contemplative' more or less interchangeably throughout this book, with a preference for 'contemplative'. While fields outside philosophy are comfortable talking about medieval mystics and mysticism, philosophers tend either to be squeamish about those terms and their anti-rationalist connotations or to associate the terms with projects rather different from those medieval figures understood themselves to be undertaking. (See Chapter 1 for further discussion of this

---

lacks them? Two of the most influential books in this discussion have been Miranda Fricker's *Epistemic Injustice: Power and the Ethics of Knowing* (Oxford: Oxford University Press, 2007) and Jose Medina's *The Epistemology of Resistance: Gender and Racial Oppression, Epistemic Injustice, and Resistant Imaginations* (Oxford: Oxford University Press, 2013).

xxii PREFACE

phenomenon.) In addition, the label 'mystical' is sometimes taken to apply only to reports or accounts of actual mystical experiences, and 'mystic' to apply only to someone who has such experiences. The set of people who report such experiences, however, does not overlap neatly with the set of writings and people we today commonly think of under those descriptions—Meister Eckhart, for instance, is one of the very few figures familiar to contemporary philosophers as a medieval mystic, and yet he himself never reports having mystical experiences. Thomas Aquinas, on the other hand, does report having mystical experiences, and yet he is thought of today not as a mystic but as a paradigm of analytic thought. The term 'contemplative', on the other hand, doesn't quite connote the full range of relevant literature and experiences to most philosophers (or non-philosophers), who tend to associate contemplation with intellective activity, and so I use both terms. I do use the term 'contemplative' more often than 'mystical', however, both because I want people to start associating the medieval contemplative tradition with theories about feelings and love as well as cognition, and because I want to emphasize this tradition's connections to its ancient predecessors and to its early modern, modern, and contemporary successors.

Second, my treatment of topics and figures in this tradition is meant to be representative rather than exhaustive—a tasting menu, if you will, rather than a series of full courses. One of my goals while writing this book has been to keep each of its chapters relatively short and accessible in order to avoid overwhelming the reader with the sheer volume of primary texts still available (both in the original languages and in translation) and with the enormity of secondary literature on these texts available from outside philosophy. When confronted by seemingly endless shelves full of primary texts (there are at least forty separate volumes just of English translations in the 'Christian Pre-1501' section of Paulist Press's *Classics of Western Spirituality*, for instance), even well-motivated scholars of medieval philosophy might well throw up their hands and return to the equally voluminous but more familiar terrain of Thomas Aquinas. The fact that the best secondary literature on these texts tends to consist of densely written 600-plus-page tomes (or whole series of 600-plus-page tomes, like Bernard McGinn's magisterial seven-volume *Presence of God*) means that only people already committed to

PREFACE   xxiii

developing a specialization in this area are likely to get far enough in to appreciate what the tradition has to offer. For that reason, although I provide resources for further primary and secondary research in footnotes and in the bibliography, I try to provide representative samples of primary texts via relatively succinct quotes, and I generally avoid engaging secondary research in the main text.

Speaking of quotes, I have chosen to cite mostly primary texts for which there are high-quality, readily available English translations, and almost all my quotes come from those English translations. Texts from the later medieval contemplative tradition are written not just in Latin but in a host of vernaculars, including Old French, Middle Dutch, fourteenth-century Tuscan, Franco-Provençal, Middle Low and Middle High German, and Middle English; it is difficult to access many of these manuscripts, and even print versions of many of these texts in their original languages are hard to track down and/or lack critical editions. Since one of my central goals is to encourage people to engage with this tradition, I've stuck to translations and works which most people should be able to access without too much difficulty.

Finally, throughout this book I concentrate my attention primarily on mystics and contemplatives from Western Europe in the thirteenth–fifteenth centuries.[12] This focus is, on one level, arbitrary and porous: I include Richard of St. Victor (d.1173), for instance, but not Bernard of Clairvaux (d.1153). (Bernard's influence is nevertheless felt throughout, particularly via discussion of the late-thirteenth-century *Meditations on the Life of Christ*, which paraphrases a number of sermons from Bernard's commentary on the *Song of Songs*.) I also don't venture too far into the fifteenth century: Julian of Norwich and Christine de Pizan take us into the first half of the 1400s, and no discussion of medieval contemplative thought would be complete without Thomas à Kempis (d.1471), but the Italian Renaissance is in mid-swing by the fifteenth century.

---

[12] Unfortunately, both Hildegard von Bingen (1098–1179) and Teresa of Avila (1515–82) fall outside this scope. I highly recommend further examination of both, however, for their important philosophical and theological insights. See, for starters, Julia Lerius's "Hildegard von Bingen on Autonomy," in *Women Philosophers on Autonomy: Historical and Contemporary Perspectives*, ed. S. Berges and A. Sinai (New York: Routledge, 2018), pp. 9–23, and Christia Mercer's "Descartes' Debt to Teresa of Avila."

xxiv PREFACE

(Dante is dead already in 1321, a full half-century before Catherine of Siena is even born, and the contemplative works of Marsilio Ficino and Giovanni Pico della Mirandola in the second half of the fifteenth century display a Platonism that is more humanist than Augustinian.)

On another level, however, this focus is not arbitrary at all: it encompasses the height of the production of mystical and contemplative texts in the Rome-based Christian tradition, a period in which what Herbert Grundmann famously termed 'The Women's Religious Movement' is at its height.[13] As the number of lay religious movements focused on the contemplative life explodes, laypeople as well as ecclesiastical and scholastic authorities become engaged in the search for union with God and share their insights and personal experiences. The fact that so many women in this period not only speak but are listened to and taken as spiritual authorities (as testified to by the sheer number of extant manuscripts) is my primary reason for focusing on the Christian contemplative tradition over Jewish or Islamic mystical and contemplative traditions in the thirteenth-fifteenth centuries, in which women have less of a voice.

Scholastic discussions become increasingly specialized in the thirteenth century and beyond, leading to the infamous caricature of their being focused on minutiae such as "How many angels can dance on the head of a pin?"[14] The place where foundational questions about the life worth living—both theoretical and practical—continue to be asked and investigated in the later Middle Ages is the contemplative tradition. The resulting wealth of mystical and contemplative literature should engage anyone interested in the idea of philosophy as a Way of Life, whether or not you personally share their religious commitments, for these are people who tried their best to practice what they believed, to put *theoria*

---

[13] Grundmann's groundbreaking 1935 work has been translated and republished as *Religious Movements in the Middle Ages: The Historical Links between Heresy, the Mendicant Orders, and the Women's Religious Movement in the Twelfth and Thirteenth Century, with the Historical Foundations of German Mysticism* (Notre Dame, IN: University of Notre Dame Press, 1995).

[14] There is no historical record that this was an actual topic of discussion in the Middle Ages, but there are a number of discussions about whether or how angels move, and whether or how angels can occupy spatial location. See, e.g., Thomas Aquinas's treatise on angels in *Summa theologiae* Ia 50–64.

into *praxis*—and who see debates about who we are and how we should live as posing questions whose answers have potentially eternal consequences.[15]

* * *

Various bits of this book started life as parts of papers published elsewhere. In chronological order of publication, those papers are "Self-Knowledge, Abnegation, and Fulfillment in Medieval Mysticism," in *Self-Knowledge*, ed. U. Renz, Oxford Philosophical Concepts Series (Oxford: Oxford University Press, 2016), 131–45; "What has History to do with Philosophy? Insights from the Medieval Contemplative Tradition," in *Philosophy and the Historical Perspective*, ed. M. Van Ackeren, *Proceedings of the British Academy 214* (Oxford: Oxford University Press, 2018), 155–70; " 'Many Know Much, but Do Not Know Themselves': Self-Knowledge, Humility, and Perfection in the Medieval Affective Contemplative Tradition," in *Consciousness and Self-Knowledge in Medieval Philosophy: Proceedings of the Society for Medieval Logic and Metaphysics Vol. 14*, ed. G. Klima and A. Hall (Newcastle upon Tyne: Cambridge Scholars Publishing, 2018), 89–106; "The Phenomenology of Immortality (1200–1400)," in *The History of the Philosophy of Mind Vol. 2: Philosophy of Mind in the Early and High Middle Ages*, ed. M. Cameron. (London: Routledge, 2019), 219–39; "Medieval Mystics on Persons: What John Locke Didn't Tell You," in *Persons: a History*, ed. A. LoLordo, Oxford Philosophical Concepts Series (Oxford: Oxford University Press, 2019), 123–53; "The Voice of Reason: Medieval Contemplative Philosophy," *Res Philosophica* 99/2 (2022), pp. 169–85; "Lewd, Feeble, and Frail: Humility Formulae, Medieval Women, and Authority," in *Oxford Studies in Medieval Philosophy Vol. 10* (Oxford: Oxford University Press, forthcoming). My thanks to the relevant publishers for permission to reproduce material here.

---

[15] For the classic source of the idea of philosophy as a way of life, see Pierre Hadot's *Philosophy as a Way of Life*, ed. Arnold Davison; trans. by Michael Chase (Malden: Blackwell Publishing, 1995).

List of Figures

I1.1. *St. Francis*, Margaritone d'Arezzo, mid-thirteenth century, Vatican Museum   26

I1.2. *Bridget of Sweden*, Master of Soeterbeeck, 1470, Metropolitan Museum of Art, New York   30

I1.3. *Catherine of Siena*, Lorenzo di Pietro, mid-fifteenth century, Palazzo Pubblico, Siena   31

2.1. Lunette, anonymous, first half of the twelfth century, church of San Giusto, Volterra   36

2.2. *Prudence*, Piero del Pollaiolo, 1470, Uffizi Gallery, Florence   42

2.3. Detail of 'Sight' panel of the Lady and the Unicorn tapestries, Flemish workshop, *c*.1500, Musée de Cluny, Paris   45

2.4. *Esaltazione della Croce*, Maestro di Tressa, 1215, Pinacoteca Nazionale di Siena   53

2.5. *Lamentation over the Dead Christ*, Ambrogio Lorenzetti, 1342–4, Pinacoteca Nazionale di Siena   54

I2.1. Entrance into the beguinage of Antwerp, seen from inside   64

I2.2. Beguinage of Amsterdam, central courtyard, seen from church   65

3.1. Lady Reason with mirror and laying foundation with Christine, Cité des dames, *c*.1410–14, Harley MS 4431, f. 290r, British Library. Reproduced courtesy of the British Library   80

3.2. Detail of *Adoration of the Magi*, Andrea Mantegna, mid-fifteenth century, Uffizi Gallery, Florence   84

I3.1. Detail of *Saint Humility and Scenes from Her Life*, Pietro Lorenzetti, *c*.1335–40, Uffizi Gallery, Florence   93

I3.2. *Madonna of the Magnificat*, Sandro Botticelli, 1483, Uffizi Gallery, Florence   94

I3.3. Annunciation of Mary with reading tree and multiple books, Orsini Castle, Bracciano   95

I3.4. *St. Catherine of Alexandria*, workshop of Jan Crocq, *c*.1475–1525, Metropolitan Museum of Art, New York   96

xxviii LIST OF FIGURES

I3.5. *The Libyan Sibyl*, Guidoccio Cozzarelli *c.*1482–3, floor of
Siena Duomo   98

I3.6. The "Royal Portal," 1150–70, west transept, Chartres Cathedral   99

I3.7. Detail of statuary, *c.*1225–30, north portal, Reims Cathedral   99

4.1. *Saint Humility and Scenes from Her Life*, Pietro Lorenzetti,
*c.*1335–40, Uffizi Gallery, Florence   114

4.2. *The Holy Family*, attributed to Lux Maurus, *c.*1517–27,
Musée de Cluny, Paris   115

4.3. Detail of *Meditationes vitae Christi*; ms. Ital. 115, Bibliothèque
nationale de France. Credit: Johannes de Caulibus, *Meditatione
de la uita del nostro Signore Ihesu Christo*, XIV century.
National Library of France. Department of Manuscripts.   118

4.4. Detail of *Memorial Tablet of Hendrik van Rijn*, Johan Maelwael,
*c.*1363, Rijksmuseum, Amsterdam   128

4.5. Detail of *Virgin of the Rose Garden*, Master of the Saint Lucy
Legend, *c.*1475–80, Detroit Institute of Arts Museum   132

I4.1. Detail of side panel, "Attack on the Castle of Love," ivory casket,
*c.*1300–25, Musée de Cluny, Paris   135

I4.2. Mirror-case with "Attack on the Castle of Love," Paris workshop,
*c.*1320–40, Museo Nazionale del Bargello, Florence   136

I4.3. *St. Catherine of Siena Exchanging Hearts with Christ*, Guidoccio
Cozzarelli, late fifteenth century, Pinacoteca Nazionale di Siena   138

5.1. *Dittico del Beato Andrea Gallerani*, verso, detail showing four
mendicant pilgrims, Dietisalvi di Speme, *c.*1270, Pinacoteca
Nazionale di Siena   145

5.2. Detail of tapestry of Arithmetic, Flanders workshop, *c.*1520,
Musée de Cluny, Paris   152

5.3. Detail of *Allegory of Good Government* from *The Allegory of
Good and Bad Government*, Ambrogio Lorenzetti, 1338–9,
Palazzo Pubblico, Siena   169

I5.1. Personified figures of Humility and Pride from illumination
of *La Somme le Roi*, workshop of Honoré, *c.*1280   175

6.1. *The Last Judgment*, detail of *Paradise*, Giovanni di Paolo,
*c.*1460–5, Pinacoteca Nazionale di Siena   192

1

Mysticism, Methodology, and Epistemic Justice

Current efforts to expand the 'canon' of the history of philosophy present an exciting opportunity to reconceptualize how philosophy both has been and is currently practiced. In drawing attention to voices and methodologies that have previously been overlooked, these efforts present a vision of philosophy that more accurately captures its multi-faceted past and points the way towards a more interesting future. This book is presented in that spirit. Instead of volunteering ideological nuggets mined from ancient sources or explicating theories whose value stems in part from their very lack of connection to current interests, my primary methodological goal is to highlight a different, corrective and complementary, role that historically informed philosophy can occupy.[1]

What follows is *corrective* in that it challenges existing narratives about medieval philosophy by debunking the assumption that medieval philosophy in the 'Latin West' happened only in university settings and (thus) that women didn't do philosophy in the Middle Ages; it is *complementary* in adding to these existing narratives the wide range of philosophical insights contained in the Christian contemplative tradition from the thirteenth to fifteenth centuries. (See the Preface for an explanation of my choice of this particular time period, as well as religious and regional focus.) In engaging the work of men and women excluded by a narrow focus on scholastic disputations, moreover, this book also enhances our understanding of medieval philosophy as it has been traditionally understood, for the authors of those disputations did not live in

---

[1] For discussion of these two extremes, as well as a different alternative than the one I lay out here, see Dominik Perler's "The Alienation Effect in the Historiography of Philosophy," in *Philosophy and the Historical Perspective. Proceedings of the British Academy 214*, ed. M. Van Ackeren (Oxford: Oxford University Press, 2018), pp. 140–54.

2 MYSTICISM, METHODOLOGY, AND EPISTEMIC JUSTICE

isolated bubbles—they lived in complex societies full of political and religious intrigue and were deeply involved in conversations that extended far beyond the classroom, conversations that frequently included women.[2]

Focusing exclusively on the works of medieval women contemplatives and mystics would, of course, present as weirdly distorted a picture of these conversations as has been created by the 'traditional' focus on the works of scholastic men. It would also run the risk of essentializing the status of these authors *as women* and/or treating them as providing 'the feminine perspective,' whereas the truth is simply that the contributions of medieval women have often been overlooked because of their sex, while their contributions are shaped by their experiences as subjects occupying particular spaces in the societies in which they wrote.[3] As we'll see throughout this book, there is often more commonality (in views, methodology, and interests) between women and men of the same religious order and geographic region than between women of different religious orders or centuries; one of my aims is to undermine the idea that there is "a" way that women address questions of philosophical and religious significance. Thus, although I do prioritize women's contributions to contemplative philosophy in the thirteenth–fifteenth centuries—particularly in addressing conversations in which the voices of male contemplatives such as Meister Eckhart have already been relatively well represented—this book draws on texts authored by women and men from a variety of religious affiliations, social backgrounds, and geographical regions to address contemplative views on five topics of interest to both their scholastic counterparts and to contemporary philosophers: self-knowledge, reason and its limits, love and the will, persons, and immortality and the afterlife.

Before turning to these topics, however, I want to demonstrate the need for this book (and the advantages of this corrective and complementary method) by addressing contemporary philosophical conceptions of mysticism and what counts as a mystical experience.

---

[2] For a series of engaging bite-sized windows into this world, see Peter Adamson's *Medieval Philosophy: A history of philosophy without any gaps, Volume 4* (Oxford: Oxford University Press, 2019).

[3] For discussion of the tensions inherent in drawing attention to the work of under-studied women, see the Introduction to Sara Poor's *Mechthild of Magdeburg and Her Book: Gender and the Making of Textual Authority* (Philadelphia: University of Pennsylvania Press, 2004).

THE CASE OF 'MYSTICAL EXPERIENCE' 3

Many philosophers consider mysticism too eldritch to be the subject of serious inquiry and rational argumentation. While contemplative philosophy has a long and respected history (if one rather marginalized today), mysticism generally counts as philosophy to scholars in contemporary philosophy departments in the same way that the crystals and tarot cards in the 'metaphysics' sections of bookstores count as metaphysics—which is to say, it doesn't. Those philosophers who do take mysticism seriously as a philosophical topic tend also to work in other disciplines (such as religious studies, psychology, and cognitive science) and to operate with conceptions of mysticism and mystical experience that are heavily indebted to the early twentieth-century theories of William James and Evelyn Underhill. Yet, as we'll see in Section 1.1, those theories discount enormous swaths of reported mystical experiences on the basis of ideology that is deeply suspicious of embodiment. After laying out a contemporary definition of 'mystical experience' that has inherited these suspicions, I turn in Section 1.2 to look at the nature and range of mystic experiences reported in the Rome-based Christian tradition of the thirteenth–fifteenth centuries. The philosophical motivations given in favor of excluding physical and affective experiences from the set of "real" mystical experiences rest both then and now, as we will see, on highly controversial claims about the natures of both God and human persons. In fact, as I show in Section 1.3, standard views of mystical experiences in the thirteenth–fifteenth centuries enthusiastically include embodied and affective experiences in addition to those that involve non-sensory, selfless union. In Section 1.4 I explain how broadening contemporary philosophical conceptions of mysticism and mystical experience can help philosophers engage with scholars working on similar topics in other disciplines; I conclude in Section 1.5 by presenting an overview of the rest of this book.

1.1 Implicit Assumptions and the Case of 'Mystical Experience'

What it takes for an experience to count as mystical has been the source of significant controversy. Many current definitions of 'mystical experience' (particularly those found in analytic philosophy and theology)

4 MYSTICISM, METHODOLOGY, AND EPISTEMIC JUSTICE

exclude embodied, non-unitive states. In so doing, however, they exclude an enormous group of reported mystical experiences such as visions, auditions, and other somatic experiences. In the remainder of this section, I explicate the current standard philosophical conception of mystical experience in light of its twentieth-century influences, showing how prejudices against women, emotions, and the body have played a significant role in determining which sort of reported mystical experiences fall under the contemporary definition and which do not.

1.1.1 A standard contemporary definition of 'mystical experience'

To do this, I begin where everyone begins their philosophical inquiries these days: the *Stanford Encyclopedia of Philosophy*. As one might expect from the *SEP*, the entry on 'Mysticism' does an excellent job capturing current philosophical assumptions about mysticism. Jerome Gellman, its author, begins with two definitions of 'mystical experience.' First, he presents a "wide definition," as follows:

> A (purportedly) super sense-perceptual or sub sense-perceptual experience granting acquaintance of realities or states of affairs that are of a kind not accessible by way of sense-perception, somatosensory modalities, or standard introspection.[4]

Then he offers a 'narrow' definition, which is described as "more common among philosophers":

> A (purportedly) super sense-perceptual or sub sense-perceptual unitive experience granting acquaintance of realities or states of affairs that are of a kind not accessible by way of sense-perception, somatosensory modalities, or standard introspection.[5]

The only difference between these two definitions is the addition of the word 'unitive' in the one characterized as "suiting more specialized

---

[4] https://plato.stanford.edu/entries/mysticism/, section 1.1.
[5] https://plato.stanford.edu/entries/mysticism/, section 1.2.

THE CASE OF 'MYSTICAL EXPERIENCE' 5

treatments of mysticism in philosophy." As I discuss in Sections 1.2 and 1.3, however, this addition is crucial for understanding one of the main ways in which contemporary philosophical conceptions of mysticism rule out a great deal of reported mystical experiences.

Both definitions maintain that a mystical experience must be either 'super' or 'sub' sense-perceptual. To count as '*super sense-perceptual*,' an experience must have 'perception-like content of a kind not appropriate to sense perception, somatosensory modalities...or standard introspection.'[6] That is, although a mystical experience may accompany or even be occasioned by sense perception (of, for instance, a tremendous thunderstorm), this definition stipulates that a mystical experience must itself transcend the senses in a distinctive way. To count as '*sub sense-perceptual*,' in turn, an experience must go beyond the senses in the other direction, so that the experience contains little to no phenomenological content. (As I discuss in Section 1.2, such experiences are usually seen as the end achievement of a lengthy process of self-loss or self-annihilation en route to union with the divine.) Crucially, in insisting that a mystical experience be either super or sub sense-perceptual, this definition rules out embodied experiences in which a subject, say, hears God's voice (as Moses hears God in the burning bush), or sees visions (as John 'sees' the events he records in Revelations). Gellman is clear that this exclusion is intentional, on the grounds that this is common philosophical practice: "Generally, philosophers have excluded purely para-sensual experiences such as religious visions and auditions from the mystical."[7]

The emphasis on the inherently unitive nature of a mystical experience in the more 'philosophical' definition is also significant. Beginning at the outset of the twentieth century with William James's discussion of the 'four marks' of a mystical experience in *Varieties of Religious Experience*,[8] and continuing with Evelyn Underhill's influential 'five stages of the mystic path' in her *Mysticism: A Study of the Nature and*

---

[6] Text elided: "including the means for sensing pain and body temperature, and internally sensing body, limb, organ, and visceral positions and states," section 1.1.

[7] https://plato.stanford.edu/entries/mysticism/, section 1.1.

[8] *Varieties of Religious Experience: A Study in Human Nature.* Gifford Lectures held at Harvard, 1902.

6 MYSTICISM, METHODOLOGY, AND EPISTEMIC JUSTICE

Development of Man's Spiritual Consciousness,[9] modern scholars of mysticism have generally upheld a conception of selfless mystic union as the ultimate end of religious experience.[10] Thus, Underhill talks about a 'death of selfhood' in her depiction of the unitive life, which she describes as the highest and final stage of the mystic life,[11] while Gellman characterizes a unitive mystical experience as involving 'phenomenological de-emphasis, blurring, or eradication of multiplicity.'[12] This sort of union utterly transcends awareness of our bodies and our senses—it is what William Alston refers to as "extreme mystical experience" in which "all distinctions are transcended, even the distinction of subject and object."[13] Such union is taken by many philosophers today to be both necessary for an experience's being mystical and the (retroactive) sign of a "true" mystical experience. Yet, I argue, the requirements of this definition are overly rigid and exclusive.

1.1.2 Debates about mysticism in the twentieth century

The nature of mystical experience was a topic of interest throughout the twentieth century.[14] In the first half, influential scholars such as

---

[9] Underhill, for instance, describes the final stage of the mystic path (which she bases on John of the Cross's writings) as the 'unitive life.' See Underhill's *Mysticism: A Study of the Nature and Development of Man's Spiritual Consciousness* (Grand Rapids, MI: Christian Classics Ethereal Library, 1911) and *The Essentials of Mysticism and Other Essays* (New York: Dutton, 1920). The previous four stages are, respectively, 'awakening of self,' 'purgation of self,' 'illumination,' and 'the dark night of the soul.'

[10] Whether this loss of self should be understood metaphorically, ontologically, or phenomenologically is the subject of much debate. For our purposes, what is significant is merely that such union is understood to erase any distinction between the consciousness of the individual having the mystic experience and the divine.

[11] See Underhill, *Mysticism*, p. 444.   [12] https://plato.stanford.edu/entries/mysticism/.

[13] William Alston, *Perceiving God: The Epistemology of Religious Experience* (Ithaca: Cornell University Press, 1991), p. 24. Alston himself adopts a perceptual model of religious experiences that allows for a wider range of mystical experiences. As he writes: " 'Mystical experience' and 'mystical perception,' as we use those terms, do not imply absolute undifferentiated unity" (25). Yet even Alston excludes embodied, sensory mystical experiences from his examination of religious perception: "I am going to concentrate in this book on non-sensory mystical perception. It seems clear that a non-sensory appearance of a purely spiritual deity has a greater chance of presenting Him as He is than any sensory presentation" (20).

[14] For a detailed discussion of the history of the term 'mysticism' that also includes helpful references to further discussions, see Amy Hollywood's introduction to *The Cambridge Companion to Christian Mysticism.* (Cambridge: Cambridge University Press, 2012). For an

THE CASE OF 'MYSTICAL EXPERIENCE' 7

William James and Evelyn Underhill focused on the psychological and philosophical as well as religious aspects of mysticism, and there was a general post-Freudian and Jungian interest in psychologizing such experiences in order to uncover their true significance. This combined with the rise of medicine as a science and increased interest in identifying physical causes for altered mental states to produce working definitions of 'mysticism' and 'mystical experiences' from which physical and affective states were carefully ruled out—in part due to epistemological worries about how to distinguish genuine religious experiences from hallucinations or medical conditions such as epilepsy.

In the post-Auschwitz world of the second half of the twentieth century, the search for a universal divine that encompasses all outwardly conflicting world religions gained ground, popularized by works such as Joseph Campbell's *The Hero with a Thousand Faces* (originally published in 1949) and W. T. Stace's *Mysticism and Philosophy* (1960). This push towards religious pluralism, epitomized by John Hick's work in influential volumes such as *The Myth of God Incarnate* (1977) and *God Has Many Names* (1980), stressed the similarities in descriptions of selfless mystic union among different religious traditions in order to argue for a common basis for them all.

A common denominator in many of these modern discussions has been their dismissal of embodied experiences as inferior to (or even misleading or counterfeit versions of) "true" mystical experiences. In ruling out these sorts of experiences, however, treatments of mysticism have discounted many of the states reported as mystical experiences by women, a great number of which are embodied in some form or another.[15] The assumptions made by modern philosophers such as Nelson Pike and Steven Katz about the nature of those experiences worth attention

---

overview of the complex politics involved in the struggle to define mysticism in the twentieth century, see the first chapter of Sarah Beckwith's *Christ's Body: Identity, Culture, and Society in Late Medieval Writings*. (London: Routledge, 1993).

[15] See Grace Jantzen's *Power, Gender, and Christian Mysticism* (Cambridge: Cambridge University Press, 1995) and Monica Furlong's *Visions & Longings, Medieval Women Mystics* (Boston: Shambhala Publications, 2013) for book-length treatments of this topic. *Gendered Voices: Medieval Saints and Their Interpreters*, ed. Catherine Mooney (Philadelphia: University of Pennsylvania Press, 1999), is a collection of essays on the ways in which gender factors into how female mystics' reported experiences were recorded, altered, and/or understood.

8 MYSTICISM, METHODOLOGY, AND EPISTEMIC JUSTICE

have negatively influenced their approach (and the approach of those influenced by them) to the much broader range of experiences considered mystical prior to the twentieth century. As Grace Jantzen notes in *Power, Gender, and Christian Mysticism*, contemporary scholars who unquestioningly accept this 'philosophical' conception of mysticism err in not asking "whether this is the right focus, or whether it might seriously distort what the mystic herself considered to be essential."[16] It has also led to a disproportionate amount of attention paid to those contemplatives and mystics who emphasize self-loss and annihilative union, of whom Meister Eckhart is the classic example.

The dismissal and/or mistrust of female reports of embodied mystical experience has a long history. According to the widely accepted Aristotelian biology of the Middle Ages, women's mental acuity is compromised by their bodies, which are more sensitive to sensory perception and thus more susceptible to bodily passions and emotions.[17] Although this sensitivity makes women seem better candidates for certain sorts of religious experiences (such as visions and physical states such as stigmata and closure), the belief that their bodies consistently overpower their intellective capacities simultaneously calls into question their reports and judgments about such experiences.[18] Thus, after the surge in reported mystic experiences in the thirteenth and fourteenth centuries, the people whose reports church authorities were most likely to scrutinize closely and then condemn were predominantly female—a result, no doubt, buoyed by further persistent cultural and religious

---

[16] *Power, Gender, and Christian Mysticism*, p. 4. For examples of the sort of approach Jantzen is criticizing, see *Mysticism and Philosophical Analysis*, ed. S. Katz (New York: Oxford University Press, 1978), which contains essays by Pike and Katz, in addition to a number of others (all men).

[17] In *Discerning Spirits, Divine and Demonic Possession in the Middle Ages* (Ithaca: Cornell University Press, 2003), Nancy Caciola discusses how women were seen as more likely to experience divine visions, auditions, etc.—and more likely to be possessed by demons as well.

[18] For detailed discussion of the sorts of experiences being reported, the general increase in embodied mystical experiences in this time period, and their perceived relation to women and women's bodies, see 'The Female Body and Religious Practice' in Caroline Walker Bynum's *Fragmentation and Redemption: Essays on Gender and the Human Body in Medieval Religion* (New York: Zone Books, 1991), as well as Bernard McGinn's *The Flowering of Mysticism: Men and Women in the New Mysticism—1200-1350. Vol. III of The Presence of God: A History of Western Christian Mysticism* (New York: Crossroad Publishing Co., 1998).

THE CASE OF 'MYSTICAL EXPERIENCE' 9

beliefs that women are less trustworthy than men and prone to exaggerate their emotional and physical states.[19]

Although women and their bodies have been strongly associated both with each other and with the negative side of the dualistic binary of men/women, mind/body, reason/emotion, self/other, active/passive, etc. in Western culture since before the time of Plato, the role this association plays in the exclusion of embodied states from contemporary philosophical definitions of mystical experience has been left largely unacknowledged. In many cases, the association between bodies and women is left implicit, as when Evelyn Underhill dismisses reports of ecstatic union and other sensory and physical mystic states as a result of "the infantile craving for a sheltering and protecting love" that is "frequently pathological."[20] We should be seeking to transcend our bodies and ourselves, she writes, not wallowing in pleasures and pains that speak to our personal desires. Underhill claims that somatic visions and ecstatic experiences are not truly mystical, but instead are frequently accompanied by other "abnormal conditions" suffered by "emotional visionaries whose revelations have no ultimate characteristics."[21] Underhill's disdain for emotional and physical claims to mystical experience is clear; what is left unsaid is that the vast majority of these 'emotional visionaries' were women, and that the mystics whose experiences typify her portrayal of the superior unitive life—which possesses such 'ultimate characteristics' as self-abnegation and transcendence of physical experience—are almost exclusively male.

In other cases, however, the negative associations between emotion, bodies, and women are quite explicit. David Knowles, for example, describes the 'pure spirituality' of the early Middle Ages as "contaminated" by "a more emotional and idiosyncratic form of devotion...deriving partly from the influence of some of the women saints of the fourteenth century, women such as Angela of Foligno, Dorothea of Prussia, and

---

[19] This was one of the reasons the testimony of women was not accepted in court. Perhaps it is also one of the reasons why, in a recent volume on *The Spiritual Senses: Perceiving God in Western Christianity*, ed. P. Gavrilyuk and S. Coakley (Cambridge: Cambridge University Press, 2012), none of the fourteen historical figures who receive their own chapter are women.

[20] Underhill, *The Essentials of Mysticism*, p. 20.

[21] Underhill, *The Essentials of Mysticism*, p. 23.

10   MYSTICISM, METHODOLOGY, AND EPISTEMIC JUSTICE

Bridget of Sweden."[22] Like Underhill, Knowles associates purity of spirituality with an emphasis on transcendence of the particularities of the body and its affective states; unlike his predecessor, Knowles makes it clear that the sort of emotional and individual forms of religious expression which taint the appropriately dispassionate, universal modes of true mysticism are primarily the province of women.

Simone de Beauvoir draws the same negative connection between women, bodies, and emotional religious experiences in her ground-breaking work of feminist philosophy *The Second Sex*. In her chapter 'The Mystic,' Beauvoir is sharply critical of the reported experiences of the majority of female medieval mystics: "Not clearly distinguishing reality from make-believe, action from magic, the objective from the imaginary," she writes, "Woman is peculiarly prone to materialize the absent in her own body."[23] Women are more likely than men to report physical mystical experiences, she argues, because their disadvantaged status as Other has led them to become more susceptible to religious fervor and extreme emotional states. That is, having internalized being Other and Inessential, Woman is more likely to passively embody religious beliefs in physical and emotional suffering or ecstasy than she is to attempt concrete action in the world of men from which she has been excluded. In fact, Beauvoir maintains, Woman's acceptance of the promise of rewards for an earthly life of obedience in an eternal paradise is one of the central obstacles that keeps her from working towards transcendence and self-actualization.[24]

It seems clear, then, that prejudices against emotions, bodies, and women have influenced the development of current philosophical conceptions of what counts as a mystical experience. Jerome Gellman, the author of the working definition quoted above, himself admits that "the thinking that there is a common, unconstructed, essence to mystical experience has worked against the recognition of women's experiences

---

[22] David Knowles, *The Religious Orders in England* (Cambridge: Cambridge University Press, 1948–9), pp. 222–3.

[23] Simone De Beauvoir, *The Second Sex*, trans. H. M. Parshley (New York: Vintage Books, 1989), p. 672.

[24] See Beauvoir, *The Second Sex*, pp. 621ff.

as properly mystical."[25] It does not seem, however, that Gellman thinks this is a cause for particular concern, much less a signal that the definition he has offered might be faulty. As Grace Jantzen observes, "Contemporary philosophers are seduced by a particular picture of mysticism, inherited largely from William James, which involves them in a stately dance of claims and counterclaims about experience and interpretation, language and ineffability, credulity and doubt...what is hardly ever noticed is how little resemblance they bear to the things which preoccupied the medieval men and women whom they themselves would consider to be paradigm mystics."[26] Yet it seems to me that the way in which these problematic assumptions undergird contemporary conceptions of mysticism demonstrates the need for a serious re-examination of both the definition and how it is applied.

1.2 Apophatic Self-Abnegation

It would be convenient to think that the negative associations of body, emotion, and women have always worked against the inclusion of embodied, affective experiences in the mystical canon—we like to think of ourselves today, after all, as more enlightened and open-minded than our historical predecessors. It would be convenient to think this, yes, but it would be wrong. Although there is a strain within the medieval Christian contemplative tradition that excludes embodied experiences from what it considers 'true' mystical experiences—namely apophaticism, which focuses on the ineffability of the divine and the inability of language and thought to express any direct experience of that divine— this strain is only one among many. Cautions against physical and affective states from within this strain need to be understood in the larger context in which such embodied states were actually seen as the mystic norm. In addition, as I argue in Section 1.3, the reasons those states were accepted as the norm should be taken quite seriously.

The apophatic tradition in Western Christianity has a long philosophical lineage, arguably beginning with Plato's claims about the nature of

---

[25] https://plato.stanford.edu/entries/mysticism/, section 9.
[26] Jantzen, *Power, Gender, and Christian Mysticism*, p. 3.

12 MYSTICISM, METHODOLOGY, AND EPISTEMIC JUSTICE

the Good in the *Republic* and continuing in the early Middle Ages via figures such as pseudo-Dionysius and John Scotus Eriugena, and in relation to the Islamic and Jewish mystic traditions developing at the same time. In the thirteenth century and onward, medieval apophaticism is typified in the works of Marguerite Porete, Meister Eckhart, and the anonymous English *Cloud of Unknowing*; it continues post-Reformation most prominently in the writings of Teresa of Avila and John of the Cross. During the centuries in which mysticism flourished as a form of religious expression and in which it (arguably) found its fullest form, however, apophaticism was a non-dominant tradition, and one often seen as bordering on heresy. This fact, of course, makes no difference for the philosophical plausibility of the view; what is significant is that, in positing a selfless merging with an unknowable God as the ultimate end of human existence, apophatically minded contemplatives make highly controversial assumptions about both God and the ultimate goal of life.

Apophatic contemplatives tend to describe the spiritual life as a series of stages that we move through in a journey towards unknowing union with the unknowable divine. On this journey, one of the most important tasks is the process of cultivating self-abnegation, or radical self-loss. In *The Mirror of Simple Souls*, for instance, Marguerite Porete explains that union with God requires the complete elimination of the conscious self. In the perfect state of such union, "All things are one for her, without an explanation (*propter quid*), and she is nothing in a One of this sort." All the individualizing activities of the soul—thought, will, emotion—cease: "The Soul has nothing more to do for God than God does for her. Why? Because He is, and she is not. She retains nothing more of herself in nothingness, because He is sufficient of Himself, because He is and she is not." In the ultimate expression of annihilative union, "She is stripped of all things because she is without existence, where she was before she was created."[27] This stress on self-abnegation runs throughout Porete's work: annihilation of individuality is essential for the highest form of union with God.

---

[27] All quotes in this paragraph are from *Marguerite Porete. The Mirror of Simple Souls*, trans. E. L. Babinsky (Mahwah: Paulist Press, 1993), p. 218, translation slightly modified.

Meister Eckhart also frequently exhorts his listeners to detach themselves from all individual affections and desires, in preparation for the self-abnegation that allows God to be all. In Counsel 23, he states: "There is still one work [after the soul has detached itself from worldly concerns] that remains proper and his own, and that is annihilation of self."[28] It is often unclear in such texts precisely how to understand this self-abnegation (is it meant to be understood literally or metaphorically, ontologically or phenomenologically?), but the stress on removing any sense of self that might impede complete union with God is consistent throughout the apophatic tradition. In extreme cases, apophatic mystics even portray self-abnegation as allowing for an identity of the mystic with God; when no egoistic self remains, one can be filled with God to the point where one *becomes* God. (For further discussion, see Section 5.2.)

Given this emphasis on eliminating all sense of individual selfhood, it is not surprising that apophatic texts frequently caution their readers against taking physical and emotional states to be signs of mystic union. Such states may indicate a sort of spiritual progress, but they are not themselves either necessary or sufficient for attaining the goal of the contemplative life. The anonymous English *Cloud of Unknowing*, for instance, advises us to "Mistrust all consolations, sounds, gladness, and sweet ecstasies that come suddenly and externally."[29] In his late-four-teenth-century *The Scale of Perfection*, Walter Hilton also warns against accepting physical sensations as signs of true mystic union, whether "by sounding of the ear, or savoring in the mouth, smelling at the nose, or else any sensible heat like a fire glowing and warming the breast or any other part of the body." Such an experience, he writes, "though it be ever so comfortable and liking," is not itself true contemplation but is, rather, "simple and secondary" to the knowing and loving of God that accompanies the real thing.[30] This is a direct jab at Richard Rolle's earlier *Fire of Love*, which describes Rolle's mystical experiences as including

---

[28] *Meister Eckhart: The Essential Sermons, Commentaries, Treatises, and Defense*, eds. and trans. E. Colledge and B. McGinn (Mahwah: Paulist Press, 1981), p. 280.

[29] Anon., *The Cloud of Unknowing: with the Book of Privy Counselling*, trans. Carmen Acevedo Butcher (Boulder, CO: Shambhala Publications, 2009), ch. 48, p. 110.

[30] *Walter Hilton: The Scale of Perfection*, ed. Serenus Cressy (Monee, IL: Scotts Valley California, 2010), Book One, ch. 10, p. 8. *The Scale* contains repeated admonitions against accepting embodied experiences as signs of true mystical union.

14 MYSTICISM, METHODOLOGY, AND EPISTEMIC JUSTICE

physical warmth in his body (especially his chest), a sense of surpassing sweetness, and the sound of celestial music. *The Cloud of Unknowing* takes aim at Rolle's 'fire of love' as well, attributing such embodied experiences to novices who "mistake a high-strung excitement and warmth in their cheeks for the genuine fire of love kindled by the grace and goodness of the Holy Spirit deep within our hearts."[31] *The Cloud* even goes on to caution that such experiences might have sinister origins: "The devil has his own contemplatives, just as God does."[32] Meister Eckhart, in turn, "tartly condemn[s] those who want to see God with the same eyes with which they behold a cow."[33]

In all these cases, God is characterized as utterly unknowable and, at least for Eckhart and Porete, beyond being itself. Experience of such a God necessarily transcends physical and affective experience: for many apophatics, it entails the loss of individual experience altogether. On the view according to which human beings reach their ultimate end by perfecting the act of self-annihilation, the highest form of mystical union is one in which neither human beings nor God exist in standard ways. In part because of this, apophaticism was never the leading mystical tradition in the medieval period. Instead, the dominant tradition was a more body-friendly and affective mysticism—a mysticism embraced by a large variety of religious communities throughout Europe during the thirteenth–fifteenth centuries (the point at which Western Christian contemplative movements were at their height). I turn now to a closer examination of this tradition.

1.3 Correcting via Complementing: Embracing Embodied Experiences

As we saw in Section 1.1, affective mysticism has often been dismissed because of its association with the body and with emotions. Ruling out

---

[31] Anon., *The Cloud of Unknowing*, ch. 45, p. 103.   [32] Ibid.

[33] Bernard McGinn, Introduction to *Meister Eckhart: The Essential Sermons, Commentaries, Treatises, and* Defense, ed. Edmund Colledge, OSA, and Bernard McGinn (Mahwah: Paulist Press, 1981), p. 61. The sermon referenced is Sermon 16b in Meister Eckhart, *Die deutschen und lateinischen Werke. Herausgegeben im Auftrage der Deutschen Forschungsgemeinschaft* (Stuttgart and Berlin: W. Kohlhammer, 1936–?), p. 272.

affective experiences as properly mystical for this reason, however, is to miss the significance of such reported forms of connection with the divine. Human beings are physical and affective as well as intellective and volitional beings: our primary interaction with reality—created and divine—is physical. Whereas the apophatic tradition urges us to transcend those modes of interaction, the affective tradition encourages us to delve more deeply into them. Once we recognize the problematic prejudices that shaped the contemporary conception of mystical experience and the controversial philosophical assumptions underlying the apophatic exclusion of embodied experiences, we are in a position to see the rich history of embodied mystical experiences reported in the Middle Ages as offering a vital complement to the narrow range of religious experiences which currently serve as the main focus of analytic philosophers and theologians.

The medieval emphasis on embodied contemplative experiences developed in part as a response to twelfth-century gnostic movements that either denied or de-emphasized Christ's humanity and taught the need for purifying our immaterial souls from the inherently corrupt material realm. In other words, the push to transcend our bodies in apophatic mystical union was viewed as displaying an important misunderstanding of both God and human nature. In the mainstream contemplative tradition, figures as diverse in education, social status, and geographical location as Hadewijch (a Flemish Augustinian), Catherine of Siena (an Italian Dominican), Richard Rolle (an English hermit), Marguerite d'Oingt (a French Carthusian nun), and Angela of Foligno (an Italian Franciscan) viewed altered physical states such as mystic death or bodily 'closure,' emotional states such as uncontrollable weeping or laughter, and parasensory states such as visions and auditions not as distracting from true mystic union but as important ways of experiencing a direct connection with the God who had become incarnate for us.

One sign that this tradition understood the spiritual subject as a holistic union of body and soul (as opposed to a soul seeking to rise above the material realm) is its reliance on the imagination. In the thirteenth century and onward, the imagination was generally taken to be the faculty of the human soul that stores mental 'pictures' formed via

16 MYSTICISM, METHODOLOGY, AND EPISTEMIC JUSTICE

information collected by the external senses and then is able to combine those images in both familiar and unfamiliar ways. In a popular spiritual exercise of the time called 'meditation' (*meditatio*), contemplatives were encouraged to imagine themselves present at key moments of Christ's life, particularly his Passion; the explicit purpose of these exercises was to generate certain sorts of affective responses that would deepen the subject's devotion. (See Chapter 4 for further discussion of both the role of imagination and the medieval practice of meditation.)

This use of the imagination in spiritual exercises was also closely linked with the idea of 'spiritual vision' (*visio spiritualis*), a concept borrowed from the Augustinian Platonic tradition. In contrast both to the sort of material vision (via the eye) which is directed at physical objects and to the sort of intellective vision (via reason) which is directed at divine truths, spiritual vision is directed at images held in the imagination. As such, it mediates between our physical sense capacities and our intellective and volitional capacities; physical experiences and intellective experiences come together and are combined in significant ways in spiritual vision (also associated in this tradition with the 'inner senses' and the 'inner body'). In the affective mystical tradition, meditative exercises such as imagining oneself present at the birth of Jesus enable the inner senses to undergo spiritual experiences with transformative physical and intellective/volitional effects. Such meditation helps us to "construct an inner space that creates affectively embodied access to the divine."[34]

Because strong emotion was closely linked in the later Middle Ages both to bodies and to our ability to imagine things vividly (driving us to deeper devotion and closer communion with God), it was particularly welcomed in forms of religious expression that celebrated Christ's Incarnation. Rather than being discounted as the result of overexcited sensory capacities, the mystical visions, auditions, smellings, tastings, etc. associated with such emotions were generally understood to be

---

[34] Niklaus Largier, "Inner Senses – Outer Senses: The Practice of Emotions in Medieval Mysticism," in *Emotions and Sensibilities in the Middle Ages*, ed. C. Jaeger and I. Kasten (Berlin and New York: de Gruyter, 2003), pp. 3–15.

important spiritual experiences, and valued as such.[35] Embodied mystical experiences were seen as connecting the human subject to God in ways that enhanced rather than abnegated our distinctive humanity. In the words of Catherine Walker Bynum, "All Christ's members—eyes, breasts, lips and so on—were seen as testimony to his humanation, and the devout soul responded to this enfleshing with all its bodily capabilities."[36]

A striking example of this can be found in a vision of Hadewijch which she reports receiving during a celebration of the Eucharist—a particularly significant act in the medieval affective tradition, since it involves a connection between Christ and the worshiper that is both mystical and physical.[37] Hadewijch writes that Christ appeared to her "in the form and clothing of a Man, as he was on the day when he gave us his Body for the first time" (that is, at the Last Supper).[38] Christ then shares himself with Hadewijch, first via the elements ("he gave himself to me in the shape of the Sacrament, in its outward form, as the custom is; and then he gave me to drink from the chalice, in form and taste, as the custom is"), and then in human form: "After that he came himself to me, took me entirely in his arms, and pressed me to him; and all my members felt his in full felicity, in accordance with the desire of my heart and my humanity." This embrace is not the end of Hadewijch's experience, however. After she enjoys Christ's presence for a brief time, she writes that "I saw him completely come to naught and so fade and all at once dissolve that I could no longer recognize or perceive him outside

---

[35] As Patricia Dailey notes in "The Body and Its Senses": "The goal of affective mysticism is not to excite the outer body into a Bacchic frenzy, but to allow one's affective and thus embodied experience to stimulate the construction of the inner body and then to allow the heart, innards, or inner senses to speak and act through the outer body." *The Cambridge Companion to Christian Mysticism*, ed. A Hollywood and P. Dailey (Cambridge: Cambridge University Press, 2012), p. 269.

[36] Bynum, *Fragmentation and Redemption*, p. 91.

[37] Caroline Walker Bynum has written extensively on the significance the Eucharist takes on in the affective tradition; see, e.g., the chapters "The Body of Christ in the Later Middle Ages" and "Women Mystics and Eucharistic Devotion in the Thirteenth Century" in *Fragmentation and Redemption*, as well as *Holy Feast and Holy Fast: The Religious Significance of Food to Medieval Women* (Berkeley: University of California Press, 1988).

[38] All quotes from Hadewijch in this and the following paragraph are from Vision Seven, *Hadewijch: The Complete Works*, ed. and trans. Mother Columba Hart (Mahwah: Paulist Press, 1980), p. 281.

18 MYSTICISM, METHODOLOGY, AND EPISTEMIC JUSTICE

me, and I could no longer distinguish him within me. Then it was to me as if we were one without difference."

This account begins with not just one but two different sorts of embodied union with Christ, and it is significant that Hadewijch describes it as fulfilling the desire of her *humanity*. (See Chapter 5 for further discussion of this vision.) Even when she reports the later experience of being "one without difference," the metaphor at play is one of physical digestion: Christ has become one with her (and she with him) in the way that food and drink become one with us—part of our very being. Hadewijch also sometimes describes mystical union that involves a loss of self, but she consistently does so without downplaying the significance of affective and embodied experiences.[39]

This acknowledgment of the importance of physicality for human subjects is present in Hadewijch's letters as well. In one particularly striking depiction of union with the divine, for instance, she describes how mystical union can also involve eternal self-preservation:

> Where the abyss of his wisdom is, God will teach you what he is, and with what wondrous sweetness the loved one and the Beloved dwell one in the other, and how they penetrate each other in a way that neither of the two distinguishes himself from the other. But they abide in one another in fruition, mouth in mouth, heart in heart, body in body, and soul in soul, while one sweet divine nature flows through both and they are both one thing through each other, but at the same time remain two different selves – yes, and remain so forever.[40]

Another striking portrayal of physical and self-preserving mystical union can be found in Marguerite d'Oingt, who reports a vision in which she is a withered tree which is turned completely upside down and then renewed by a torrent of water rushing down from a nearby mountain. (See Subsection 2.2.3 for the medieval contemplative use of

---

[39] As Mary Suydam notes in "The Touch of Satisfaction: Visions and Religious Experience according to Hadewijch of Antwerp": "There is absolutely no indication, either here or anywhere else in Hadewijch's writings, that this embodied experience represents a 'lower' stage of religious experience." *Journal of Feminist Studies in Religion* 12 (Fall 1996), p. 16.

[40] *Hadewijch: The Complete Works*, Letter 9, p. 66.

'tree' metaphors to signify the self.) Having drawn the 'living water' (that is, Christ) into herself, Marguerite sees the names of the five senses written on her newly revived leaves.[41] The vision represents both union with God, as the water saturates every aspect of the tree, and the corresponding renewal of the tree of self—in body as well as in spirit.

The rest of this book has much more to say about apophatic and affective strains of medieval mysticism and contemplativism. Just this brief discussion should make it clear, however, that ongoing debates concerning the nature and role of religious and mystical experiences would benefit from considering the entire range of reported mystical experiences rather than focusing exclusively on super- or sub-perceptual experiences. Indeed, as Hadewijch's vision demonstrates, even a focus on unitive mystical experiences need not rule out consideration of embodied and affective mystical states.

1.4 Philosophical Morals and Historical Narratives

To this point, I have focused on the corrective and complementary roles that historically oriented approaches can play in philosophical discussions, and on the particular ways in which this book offers both complement and correction to existing scholarship in medieval philosophy. There is an additional benefit to including the contemplative tradition in discussions of medieval philosophy, however, that it is far from unimportant—namely, the way in which taking a more inclusive approach to what counts as a mystical experience opens exciting avenues of engagement with scholars working in other disciplines.

Consider again the contemporary philosophical understanding of mystical experience discussed in Section 1.1, which is specifically characterized as "suiting more specialized treatments of mysticism in philosophy" in its focus on unitive experiences. What is it about the addition of the word 'unitive' that makes this definition particularly suited to *philosophical* examination? The answer, I think, is just that it helps pick

---

[41] *The Writings of Margaret of Oingt, Medieval Prioress and Mystic (d. 1310)*, trans. with an introduction, essay, and notes by Renate Blumenfeld-Kosinski (Cambridge: D. S. Brewer, 1990).

20 MYSTICISM, METHODOLOGY, AND EPISTEMIC JUSTICE

out the particular range of super- or sub-sensory experiences that analytic philosophers became interested in over the course of the twentieth century. And, as we saw in Section 1.1, philosophical interest in that particular range of experiences is impacted by negative associations with affective and embodied experiences and with women. Furthermore, as we saw in Section 1.2, the strain of medieval mysticism and contemplativism that seems to share the perspective of those analytic philosophers most closely (namely, apophaticism) was the exception rather than the rule in its own day. Claiming that this narrow range of perspectives represents how mystical experiences have 'always been understood' ignores the vast majority of reports of such experiences. Think of that as the corrective stick. Here, then, is the complementary carrot: enlarging the scope of what philosophers include under their mystical umbrella would allow us to engage in meaningful and productive conversations with scholars in a variety of other disciplines.

Any number of other fields already include embodied experiences in their working conceptions of medieval mysticism and contemplativism, including political science, history, religious studies, sociology, medieval studies, theology, art and art history, gender and women's studies, English, French, and Italian literature, and more. In the remainder of this book, I follow their example, adopting Nicholas Watson's characterization of mystical experiences as generally *phenomenological* ("concerning individual felt experience in addition to systems of knowledge or belief") and *transcendent* ("involving an encounter— whether direct or mediated, transformatively powerful or paradoxically everyday—with God").[42]

The fact that philosophers have set their parameters so narrowly in their discussions has in turn led to the exclusion of philosophers from most of the ongoing inter- and intradisciplinary conversations about mysticism. *The Cambridge Companion to Christian Mysticism*, for instance, contains essays by twenty-two scholars who represent thirteen distinct disciplines—but there is not a single philosopher among them. The reason for this is simple: the standard conception of mystical

---

[42] See Nicholas Watson's Introduction to *The Cambridge Companion to Medieval English Mysticism*, ed. S. Fanous and V. Gillespie (Cambridge: Cambridge University Press, 2011), p. 1.

experience that philosophers are working with corresponds so poorly to what everyone else is talking about that there is almost no point in trying to engage in a common conversation.[43] Philosophers excel at biting bullets, and this complete lack of engagement with other disciplines might be one on which some would happily clamp down. One of the central goals of this book, however, is to show what philosophy would lose out on as a result.

1.5 Looking Ahead

The remainder of this book is divided into five chapters and five interludes. Each chapter focuses on a topic of enduring philosophical interest (respectively, self-knowledge, reason and its limits, love and the will, the nature of persons, and immortality and the afterlife). Each interlude focuses on a question the answer to which provides an important piece of historical, artistic, and/or literary context for subjects discussed in the main chapters. Each of the chapters and interludes is framed so that it can stand on its own, allowing readers to jump in (and out) according to their particular interests and needs. That said, each successive chapter builds on the previous one(s) in a way that allows the whole to be much greater than the sum of its individual parts. What follows is an overview of the remaining five chapters.

One of the very few theses on which there was widespread contemplative agreement in the twelfth–fifteenth centuries is that self-knowledge constitutes the grounds or precondition for our future moral and spiritual growth—everything from the development of individual virtues to achievement of our final end as human beings. The centrality of self-knowledge for the contemplative project raises the practical questions, though, of both what it is and how we are meant to attain it. Chapter 2 addresses the range of answers medieval mystics and contemplatives provide to these questions. After establishing a general sense of what

---

[43] This isn't simply conjecture on my part: I asked Amy Hollywood (the primary editor) why there weren't any philosophers among the authors of the essays, and this was the essence of her reply.

22 MYSTICISM, METHODOLOGY, AND EPISTEMIC JUSTICE

self-knowledge is and why we want it, I lay out three of the most common recommendations medieval contemplatives give for how to acquire it: 'look outside yourself to know yourself,' 'root down in humility to rise up in dignity,' and 'use reason and imagination to counter selfish pride.' Although contemplatives agree about the importance of self-knowledge, they disagree sharply about the final purpose of introspection and self-examination; I thus conclude the chapter by laying out the differing ends towards which contemplatives advise applying this knowledge— ends that range from relinquishing any individual sense of self to merge with God to preparing us for complete self-fulfillment via union with God.

Self-knowledge relies on our ability to reason, but the continued use of reason within the contemplative life is highly controversial, with some contemplatives—particularly those in the apophatic tradition— arguing that we need to abandon reason entirely to reach our final end. This has contributed to the perception that reason is inimical to medieval mystical and contemplative projects; it has also created the impression of an unbridgeable rift between the projects of medieval scholastic philosophy and of medieval mysticism. In Chapter 3 I argue that this perception is misleading in at least two important ways. First, even contemplative texts which ultimately advocate abandoning reason and knowledge (such as Porete's *Mirror*, Meister Eckhart's *Counsels*, and the anonymous *Cloud of Unknowing*) affirm intellect's role in getting the mystical project off the ground and progressing to the point where reason can be transcended. Second, any number of contemplatives portray reason not as something to be overcome or relinquished but as one of the most important ways in which we resemble or 'image' God and, thus, as a crucial point of connection between human beings and the divine.

At the same time that reason plays a much more important role in the medieval mystical and contemplative tradition than usually acknowledged, the increasingly specialized and technical nature of university discussions in the thirteenth century, together with earlier religious reforms that took a great deal of religious authority from lay members of the church, leads to widespread frustration with formal education and *scientia* (knowledge gained via natural reason and argumentation). Partly in response, love—which is available to everyone—becomes identified as the central component of the contemplative life in the fourteenth and fifteenth centuries.

A primary question in many contemplative texts from this period thus becomes 'How we can train our wills to love the right things in the right way?' In Chapter 4 I address the will's general role in human life in relation to our soul's other relevant faculties: intellect, imagination, and sensation and sense appetite. The spiritual exercise of imaginative meditation becomes particularly important to contemplative practice in this period, for it is seen as inspiring love, encouraging virtue, and increasing knowledge. Meditation also serves as a bridge between our ordinary experience of the material world and our transcendent experience of the immaterial God in higher levels of contemplation. Importantly, as I discuss at the end of the chapter, this focus on imaginative meditation and love also creates space in which women, who are seen as better at loving and more closely connected with embodiment, can speak with authority about their religious experiences. As the highest form of contemplation is increasingly identified as union with God via love, women become increasingly accepted as contemplatives.

In Chapter 5 I take a step back to look at what, exactly, "we" are understood to be in this tradition—not just as human beings, but as persons, a category that includes all rational beings, including God. By the outset of the thirteenth century, the term 'persona' already had a long history in logical, legal, and theological contexts. The overlapping but distinct connotations the word 'persona' assumes in those contexts boil down to three central concepts: individuality, dignity, and rationality, understood broadly to include the full range of rational capacities. These three concepts combine in the contemplative tradition with the use of first- and second-person perspectives, personification, and introspection to yield a complex and rich understanding of who we are and what it is to be a person. As I discuss at the end of the chapter, this concept of person also prefigures both Locke's famous seventeenth-century definition and influences the development of the philosophical theory of personalism.

Scholastic and mystical/contemplative traditions during this time share a common focus on the final or ultimate end for human beings. While scholastic discussions tend to focus on metaphysics and mechanics,

24 MYSTICISM, METHODOLOGY, AND EPISTEMIC JUSTICE

however, contemplative and mystical works contain a wealth of first-person speculations about and reports of union with God. Those reports ground a set of expectations for experiences of immortality and the afterlife that range all the way from a transcendent merging with the divine that involves a complete loss of sense of self and individuality to a deeply intimate experience that nevertheless preserves a sense of self. In Chapter 6 I argue that we can understand these views as forming the extreme endpoints of what I call an 'experiential continuum of immortality.' This continuum proves useful not only for understanding the range of views medieval contemplatives hold about immortality and the afterlife but also for situating scholastic accounts of immortality, as I demonstrate at the close of the chapter, using the cases of Robert Grosseteste and Thomas Aquinas.

A single book can only begin to explore the wealth of philosophical resources contained in the Christian contemplative tradition of the thirteenth–fifteenth centuries. In the Afterword, I spell out some directions for future research on this topic, suggesting further ways in which traditional narratives can be enhanced and corrected by drawing on medieval contemplatives.

Interlude One

Who Is This Book About?

A timeline of major figures and works, organized by approximate date of death.

1150

Richard of St. Victor (d.1173): Augustinian monk of the Victorines, a renowned twelfth-century school of mysticism begun by Hugh of St. Victor (d.1141). Most influential contemplative works are the *Mystical Ark* (also known as the *Benjamin Major*) and the *Twelve Patriarchs* (also known as the *Benjamin Minor*).

1200

Francis of Assisi (1182–1226): founder of the Franciscan mendicant order. His emphasis on radical poverty, humility, and love for all of God's creatures sets the standard for Franciscan piety. Best-known work is perhaps *The Canticle of the Sun*, although his *Regulae* (which includes the Earlier Rule in 1221 and Later Rule in 1223) and Testament are foundational documents for the Franciscan Order. Usually shown with the stigmata, as in Figure I1.1.

Clare of Assisi (1194–1253): founder of the Poor Clares, the order of Franciscan nuns. Stalwart champion of the right to poverty for her nuns; her most influential contemplative writings are her four letters to Agnes of Prague.

1250

Hadewijch (active mid-thirteenth century): Flemish author (and likely beguine) known as the first great 'love mystic' of the Middle Ages.

Figure I1.1 *St. Francis*, Margaritone d'Arezzo, mid-thirteenth century, Vatican Museum.

Influences Jan van Ruusbroec and Meister Eckhart, among others. Her writing reveals familiarity with a number of Latin philosophical and theological works (including those by Augustine, Bernard of Clairvaux, and Hugh and Richard of St. Victor), although she herself is one of the first authors to write in Middle Dutch. Extant work includes letters, poetry, and visionary literature.

Bonaventure (*c*.1217–74): Italian Franciscan friar, Master of Theology at the University of Paris, and eventually Minister General of the Franciscan order. Author of numerous scholastic as well as contemplative texts; influential contemplative works include *The Mind's Journey to God*, *The Three-fold Way*, and *The Tree of Life*.

Thomas Aquinas (1224/5–74): Italian Dominican friar, Master of Theology at the University of Paris; best-known works are the massive

Summa theologiae and *Summa contra gentiles*. Account of the Beatific Vision greatly influences later contemplative conceptions of the afterlife and is immortalized in Dante's *Paradiso*.

Mechthild of Magdeburg (*c*.1207–82): controversial German beguine with Dominican affiliations who eventually settles at the convent of Helfta, Germany, where she influences Mechthild of Hackeborn and Gertrude the Great. Although she appears to have been known Latin, she writes *The Flowing Light of the Godhead* in Middle Low German and incorporates a variety of different genres across its seven books, including prayers, dialogues, poetry, and visionary literature.

Mechthild of Hackeborn (*c*.1241–98): German nun at the famous convent of Helfta (associated today with both the Cistercian and Benedictine Orders; by Mechthild's day, the convent had Dominican spiritual directors). Her *Book of Special Grace*—a book focused on her visions and revelations, many of which were collected and written down by her sisters (including Gertrude the Great)—is composed in Latin and translated into a number of vernaculars. Although widely read in its own time, *The Book of Special Grace* has less long-term influence than the works of Gertrude.

1300

Gertrude the Great (1256–1301/2): German nun at the convent of Helfta. Influential in her own time, her writing receives renewed interest in the sixteenth–seventeenth centuries. Most famous works are *The Herald of Divine Love* (composed of five books, some of which appear to be written by her fellow nuns, as with Mechthild of Hackeborn's *Book of Special Grace*) and her *Spiritual Exercises*, both written in Latin.

Angela of Foligno (*c*.1248–1309): originally a wealthy woman in Foligno, Umbria (near Assisi), Angela experiences a radical conversion following the death of her husband and children and devotes the remainder of her life to Franciscan poverty and religious devotion, living as a tertiary (that is, a member of the 'Third Order' of Franciscans, composed of non-cloistered laypeople). She dictates her highly influential *Memorial* and *Instructions* in her native Umbrian to a monk from

28 MYSTICISM, METHODOLOGY, AND EPISTEMIC JUSTICE

Assisi, who transcribes and edits them in Latin. (This monk is identified in manuscripts only as 'Brother A' but traditionally identified as her cousin, Brother Arnauld.)

Marguerite d'Oingt (*c*.1240–1310): extremely rare example of a medieval Carthusian nun whose writings have survived. A well-known French mystic and contemplative in her own time, she dwelt on the common human experiences of Christ as a means of connecting more deeply with God. She writes her *Page of Meditations* in Latin and her remaining works (a number of letters, the *Life of the Blessed Beatrice of Ornacieux*, and her *Mirror*) in Franco-Provençal.

Marguerite Porete (d.1310): French religious woman (likely a solitary beguine) burnt at the stake for heresy on June 1, 1310, after a lengthy imprisonment and trial by the Dominican Inquisitor William of Paris. Her controversial *Mirror of Simple Souls* (which states that the noble soul has no need of the mediation of the Church once it has reached a certain stage of spiritual purification) influences what's often referred to as 'Rhineland mysticism' via Meister Eckhart, who resided at the Dominican house in Paris during her imprisonment and trial.

Meister Eckhart (*c*.1260–1327/8): Dominican friar known as the greatest of the 'Rhineland mystics'; Eckhart serves as Master of Theology at Paris and also ministers in Strasbourg to Dominican convents and beguines. Writes both scholastic and contemplative texts and preaches both Latin and German sermons; many of the German sermons remain extant today because they were written down by beguines and nuns for later study and transmission.

Richard Rolle (*c*.1300–49): English hermit whose works are written in the vernacular and widely read through the fourteenth and fifteenth centuries, particularly *The Form of Living* and *Fire of Love*, which celebrates embodied mystical experiences such as hearing music, smelling sweet things, seeing light, and feeling warmth of love in the chest.

1350

Margaret Ebner (*c*.1291–1351): German Dominican nun at the Monastery of Maria Medingen near Dillingen who influences Johannes Tauler and other 'Rhineland mystics.' Her surviving works, written in Middle High German, include her *Revelations*, a journal, and extensive correspondence with Henry of Nördlingen (a central figure in the Friends of God [*Gottesfreunde*] movement).

Johannes Tauler (*c*.1300–61): German Dominican friar and one of the 'Rhineland mystics' who preached regularly to beguines and other holy women in Strasbourg as part of the *cura monialium* that became part of the pastoral duty of the friars in the mid-thirteenth century. Deeply influenced by his teacher, Meister Eckhart, Tauler was himself influential as a leader in of the Friends of God (*Gottesfreunde*) movement, which emphasized attention to the inner person over outer works.

Henry Suso (*c*.1295–1366): Swiss-German Dominican follower of Meister Eckhart and—together with Eckhart and Tauler—one of the most influential 'Rhineland mystics.' Writes the tremendously popular *Little Book of Eternal Wisdom* in Middle High German; subsequently reworks and translates this into Latin as the *Clock of Wisdom* (*Horologium Sapientiae*), whose popularity becomes even more widespread in the following century.

Bridget or Birgitta of Sweden (*c*.1303–73): Swedish Franciscan tertiary and mother of eight (her second daughter is also sainted in the Roman Catholic church), who affiliates herself with the Franciscan order after the death of her husband. Founds the Brigittine Order, which involves a 'double monastery' in which men and women live in separate cloisters but work together. Works zealously for church reform in Rome and is often represented writing her major work, the massive Latin *Revelations*. (See Figure I1.2.)

Catherine of Siena (1347–80): the twenty-fourth child of a Sienese cloth-dyer, Catherine dedicates herself to religious devotion at an early age, refusing to marry and fighting for the right to join her local *Mantallate* (part of the Dominican 'Third Order'—a group of religious women who wore the habit of Dominican nuns but lived in their own homes under the direction of a prioress). Spends much of her short life mediating between various political and religious factions (most notably interceding with the pope to end the Avignon papacy and then working to heal the Western Papal Schism). Dictates over 300 letters to various political and religious figures in her vernacular Italian and

30 MYSTICISM, METHODOLOGY, AND EPISTEMIC JUSTICE

Figure I1.2 *Bridget of Sweden*, Master of Soeterbeeck, 1470, Metropolitan Museum of Art, New York.

dictates (and then edits) her enormously influential *Dialogue*—a conversation between her soul and God—in 1377–8. She is one of only four women recognized today as a Doctor of the Catholic Church. Usually shown in a Dominican habit and with the stigmata, as in Figure I1.3.

Jan van Ruusbroec (1293–1381): Flemish mystic (often grouped with the 'Rhineland mystics') whose best-known work is *The Book of Spiritual Espousals*, written in Middle Dutch. Influenced by Hadewijch and Meister Eckhart, van Ruusbroec is influential in turn for his Trinitarian theology and emphasis on the transformation of the inner person rather than external works.

The Cloud of Unknowing (*c*.1349–*c*.1395): anonymous Middle English contemplative text that stresses an apophatic approach to the spiritual

Figure I1.3 *Catherine of Siena*, Lorenzo di Pietro, mid-fifteenth century, Palazzo Pubblico, Siena.

life; typically paired with *The Book of Privy Counselling* and thought to be composed by the same author as *The Pursuit of Wisdom* (a much-abbreviated translation/paraphrase into Middle English of Richard of St. Victor's *The Twelve Patriarchs/Benjamin Minor*).

Walter Hilton (*c*.1340–96): English Augustinian mystic and author of the popular *Scale of Perfection* (written in Middle English) as well as perhaps *The Epistle on the Mixed Life*. Probably best known for his emphasis on transcending physical sensations to reach apophatic union with God and critique of Richard Rolle's celebration of embodied mystical experiences.

1400

Julian of Norwich (1342/3–*c*.1416): English anchorite whose given name has been lost ('Julian' comes from the church to which her cell was attached). Writes her famous *Vision Showed to a Devout Woman* and *Revelation of Divine Love* in Middle English. Sometimes grouped together as the *Showings*, Julian's writing includes both a "short text," written soon after the formative vision she has in 1373, and a "long text," written in the twenty years or so following the initial vision (and which expands on and explains the revelations of the shorter text). Likely influenced by Birgitta of Sweden and by Catherine of Siena, whose works were translated into Middle English at a nearby convent; Julian's emphasis on God's love and Trinitarian theology is important for the development of later English spirituality.

Christine de Pizan (1364–*c*.1430): born in Venice but a resident of Paris for the majority of her life; widowed at an early age, she becomes one of the first women authors known to have earned a living writing under her own name. Most influential work is *The City of Ladies* (written in French and published by 1405), which draws on a number of philosophical and literary sources in making its case for the equality of women, including Boethius's *Consolation of Philosophy* and Boccaccio's *On Famous Women*.

1450

Thomas à Kempis (*c*.1380–1471): German-Dutch member of the 'Devotio Moderna' movement, which stressed humility, obedience, and simple living based on the model of the life of Christ; influenced by the Brethren of the Common Life movement, having studied at their school in Deventer (as did Nicholas of Cusa and Erasmus). Wrote the enormously popular *De Imitatione Christi* in Latin in the first half of the fifteenth century.

Giovanni Pico della Mirandola (1463–94): Italian nobleman and humanist whose most famous work is the *Oration on the Dignity of Man*.

Marsilio Ficino (1433–99): Italian Platonist and humanist, translates Plato's complete works into Latin and writes the *Theologia Platonica*.

2

Self-Knowledge

The importance of self-knowledge is a truth universally acknowledged in the contemplative philosophical tradition: it is typically portrayed as a precondition for both the best sort of human life and knowledge of the divine.[1] The self is the lens through which we view the world, after all, and we cannot clearly see the truth about anything else—the world, our neighbors, God—until we see ourselves clearly. The oracle at Delphi's injunction to 'know thyself' takes on particular importance in the Western Christian tradition in the twelfth–fifteenth centuries: scholastic (that is, university-based) discussions tend to focus on the mechanics involved in knowing oneself and how those mechanics fit into broader metaphysic and epistemic frameworks, inquiring about 'what' we are and how we can come to know this, while contemplative and mystical discussions tend to focus on 'who' we are and to emphasize the significance of self-knowledge for the ethical and religious life.

Contemporary treatments of medieval perspectives on self-knowledge typically draw on scholastic sources, and thus skew toward the metaphysical and epistemological.[2] While contributing importantly to our understanding of medieval views on such important topics as the problem of universals and knowledge of singulars, however, this focus fails to address overarching questions such as why we should seek to know ourselves in the first place, and what the lasting effects of such knowledge might be; it also ignores practical concerns about how we are supposed to acquire self-knowledge. To find answers to these questions, we must look to contemplative texts—and so it is to these texts that I turn now.

---

[1] For a history of the philosophical concept of self-knowledge, see *Self-Knowledge*, ed. U. Renz, Oxford Philosophical Concepts Series (New York: Oxford University Press, 2017).

[2] For an excellent discussion of scholastic views on self-knowledge, see Therese Scarpelli Cory's *Aquinas on Human Self-Knowledge* (Cambridge: Cambridge University Press, 2014) and Dominik Perler's "Self-Knowledge in Scholasticism," in *Self-Knowledge*, ed. Renz, pp. 114–30.

34 SELF-KNOWLEDGE

As I explain in Section 2.1, most medieval contemplatives understand self-knowledge as a necessary condition for becoming virtuous and for achieving our final end as human beings; the first step towards this is a basic awareness of the self as an agent with various desires, fears, and dispositions. In Section 2.2 I lay out three of the most common recommendations given for moving from a basic awareness to the sort of self-knowledge necessary for true moral and spiritual progress: look outside yourself to know yourself, ground yourself in humility, and use reason and imagination to counter selfish pride. Section 2.3 describes the ultimate ends towards which contemplatives advise applying this knowledge, which range from knowing God via intellective union with God's essence to annihilating oneself in Love.

2.1 Putting the Self into Perspective

Although medieval contemplatives disagree with each other about the relative roles reason and will should take in human life (see Chapters 3 and 4, respectively), what it is to be a person (see Chapter 5), and expectations for immortality and the afterlife (see Chapter 6), virtually all medieval contemplatives agree that introspection is essential to ethical and spiritual growth. *The Pursuit of Wisdom*, for instance, dismisses the person who tries to do theology without self-knowledge as wasting their time,[3] while Julian of Norwich writes: "We cannot come to a complete understanding of God unless we come to truly know ourselves."[4] (This seems to presuppose both that there is a coherent 'self' and that human beings have access to it—ideas that today are highly controversial. In the Middle Ages, however, it was taken for granted that there is an inner center of consciousness that connects us to the external world and to the divine; the earlier Platonic, Stoic, Jewish, Islamic, and Christian sources

---

[3] *The Pursuit of Wisdom and Other Works by the Author of the Cloud of Unknowing*, ed. and trans. James Walsh (Mahwah: Paulist Press, 1988), p. 34. The *Pursuit of Wisdom* is an anonymous fourteenth-century Middle English translation and adaptation of Richard of St. Victor's twelfth-century *The Twelve Patriarchs* (also known as the *Benjamin Minor*).

[4] *The Showings of Julian of Norwich: A new translation*, trans. Mirabai Starr (Charlottesville, VA: Hampton Roads Publishing Co., 2013), p. 155.

on which medieval discussions drew were also united in this belief. Radical skepticism about the existence of this center of consciousness and/or our ability to access it comes later.[5]) The supposition that there is a conscious core at the center of our moral and spiritual efforts does not, however, entail that accessing this center is an easy matter. As virtually everyone has experienced, we are not transparent to ourselves. Knowing oneself in the way needed for moral progress requires hard and rigorous work: we tend to focus on incidental flaws and ignore the ones that actually sabotage our lives; we relax into self-complacency just when we should be pushing towards real change.

For this reason, the first step in a contemplative life is developing a basic awareness of the self. As Hadewijch writes, "If you wish to experience [spiritual] perfection, you must first of all learn to know yourselves: in all your conduct, in your attraction or aversion, in your behavior, in love, in hate, in fidelity, in mistrust, and in all things that befall you."[6] Meister Eckhart counsels introspection as a way of acquiring "a clear apprehension of our own inwardness"—a "lively, true, prudent and real knowledge"[7] of our tendencies and dispositions—while *The Book of Privy Counselling* states starkly that if one wishes to make moral or spiritual progress, "I bid thee first gnaw on the naked blind feeling of thine own being."[8] The image of animals gnawing on naked human bodies was sometimes used in this period to remind the viewer of their mortality and warn against the potentially eternal effects of sin (see Figure 2.1); here, a similar image is used to motivate us to lay bare the raw reality of our innermost selves.[9]

---

[5] For more on this development, see Bob Pasnau's *Metaphysical Themes 1274–1671* (Oxford: Oxford University Press, 2011) and *After Certainty* (Oxford: Oxford University Press, 2017).

[6] Letter 14, *Hadewijch: The Complete Works*, ed. and trans. Mother Columba Hart, OSB (Mahwah: Paulist Press, 1980), 77.

[7] Counsel Six in *Meister Eckhart: The Essential Sermons, Commentaries, Treatises, and Defense*, ed. E. Colledge, OSA, and B. McGinn (Mahwah: Paulist Press, 1981), p. 253. Here and throughout I have modified the translation to the plural both for stylistic consistency and to provide gender neutrality.

[8] *English Mystics of the Middle Ages*, ed. Barry Windeatt (Cambridge: Cambridge University Press, 1994), p. 94.

[9] C. S. Lewis's *The Voyage of the Dawn Treader* contains a striking metaphor for this process in Eustace's report of Aslan's peeling away Eustace-the-transformed-dragon's skin to get to Eustace-the-boy: "The very first tear he made was so deep that I thought it had gone right into my heart. And when he began pulling the skin off, it hurt worse than anything I've ever felt.

36 SELF-KNOWLEDGE

Figure 2.1 Lunette, anonymous, first half of the twelfth century, church of San Giusto, Volterra.

We tend to keep our guard up against this raw reality, however, distracting ourselves with food, drink, sex, and mindless entertainment—and then later, as Catherine of Siena observes, with the "delightful recollections" of those things. Unfortunately, as Catherine also notes, this sort of self-avoidance tends to result in the sort of selfish love for our own perceived good that in turn leads to "hatred and contempt for [our] neighbors."[10] Not only do we resent our neighbors when they have things we want but don't have (material goods, fame, attractiveness, etc.), but when we don't see ourselves clearly, we often become disproportionately frustrated or angry at others for precisely the behaviors and habits that we (unknowingly) hate the most in ourselves. We mistrust our neighbors' motives because we can't trust our own; we misinterpret what they do because we don't understand why we're doing what we do;

The only thing that made me able to bear it was just the pleasure of feeling the stuff peel off...And there was I as smooth and soft as a peeled switch and smaller than I had been." (New York: HarperCollins, 1994), 115–16.

[10] *Catherine of Siena: The Dialogue*, trans. Suzanne Noffke, OP (Mahwah: Paulist Press, 1980), ch. 4, p. 32.

PUTTING THE SELF INTO PERSPECTIVE   37

we mask our fears and insecurities in an ungrounded and precarious sense of superiority over those around us. Furthermore, as recent literature on epistemic injustice and moral epistemology demonstrates, these tendencies generate a variety of injustices on systemic and individual levels—injustices that cause particular harm to individuals and groups we see as "Other," since our prejudices shape what (and who) we hear when people speak, whose testimony we trust and on which subjects, etc.[11]

Training ourselves to confront the "naked blind feeling" of our own being thus requires dedication and willpower, and it is no easy feat. Catherine, for instance, describes our innate selfishness as a "cloud of disordered love" that prevents us from knowing our true nature.[12] Later, she writes that "selfish love of oneself" (the hallmark of the vice of pride) is the ground of evil, and that this love "blots out the light of reason."[13] We can't develop morally or spiritually if we live shadowed from reason (as we'll see in more detail in Chapter 3), but staying out from under this cloud requires vigilance. As Hadewijch writes in a letter of advice to one of her sisters, we need to stay strong in the task of honest self-investigation, for if our will falters, "We fall back…into our own self-complacency; we no longer grow and no longer make progress."[14]

If the first step towards awareness of self is overcoming basic self-avoidance, the second step is learning how to examine oneself in a way that is both deep (penetrating beyond our superficial sense of self) and broad (moving past examination of particular actions towards our general underlying dispositions). Medieval contemplatives are often quite specific about what sorts of activities are involved in this process. In *The Mind's Journey into God*, for instance, Bonaventure encourages us to turn inwards and "re-enter ourselves—that is, our minds—in which the

---

[11] In addition to the sources on epistemic justice mentioned in footnote 11 of the Preface (namely, Fricker 2007 and Medina 2013), see also Emmalon Davis's "Typecasts, Tokens, and Spokespersons: A Case for Credibility Excess as Testimonial Injustice" in *Hypatia* 31/3 (2016), pp. 485–501; Jennifer Lackey's "False Confessions and Testimonial Injustice" in *The Journal of Criminal Law and Criminology* 110/1 (2020), pp. 43–68; and Robin Zheng's "What is My Role in Changing the System? A New Model of Responsibility for Structural Injustice," in *Ethical Theory & Moral Practice* 21 (2018), pp. 869–85.

[12] Catherine, *Dialogue*, ch. 44, p. 90. "But they, blinded as they are by the cloud of disordered love, know neither me [God] nor themselves."

[13] Catherine, *Dialogue*, ch. 50, p. 102.

[14] Hadewijch, *The Complete Works*, Letter 30, p. 117.

38 SELF-KNOWLEDGE

divine image [*imago*] shines forth."[15] Meditating on the triune powers of understanding, memory, and will within us, we begin to see God, albeit "through a mirror darkly [*in aenigmate*]." Hadewijch recommends a more prosaic approach: "Examine yourselves as to how you can endure everything disagreeable that happens to you, and how you can bear the loss of what gives you pleasure... And in everything pleasant that happens to you, examine yourselves as to how you make use of it, and how wise and moderate you are with regard to it."[16] That is, we need not just to remember how we have acted on (and reacted to) situations in the past, and pay attention to what we currently enjoy, dislike, fear, and desire—we also need to imagine good and bad things happening to us in the *future* and observe what sorts of emotional reactions we have to those prospects. We must also learn from our experiences when how we *think* we will respond to a situation differs from how we *do* respond: if our projected happiness at a friend's success actually turns out to include an unexpected amount of self-loathing at what we perceive as our own failures, for instance, we need to pay attention and be responsive to this fact. Furthermore, because our behaviors, feelings, and attitudes fluctuate, this process of self-assessment needs to become a regular discipline.

Meister Eckhart compares learning how to engage in this process to learning how to write: at first it requires "attentiveness and a careful formulation within the self, like schoolchildren preparing themselves to learn."[17] At first, "we must indeed memorize each single letter and get it firmly into our minds," but repeated practice gradually internalizes the process: "Then, when we have the art, we will not need to think about and remember the letters' appearance; we can write effortlessly and easily." In the same way, self-reflection eventually becomes second nature to us, replacing our old habits of self-avoidance and complacency.

The prevailing assumption throughout these injunctions to examine ourselves is that we won't often be pleased with what we find; looking

---

[15] Translation mine; the Quaracchi edition of the Opera Omnia S Bonaventura, Vol V, 1891, http://faculty.uml.edu/rinnis/45.304%20God%20and%20Philosophy/ITINERARIUM.pdf (accessed July 18, 2019).

[16] Hadewijch, *The Complete Works*, Letter 14, p. 77.

[17] *Meister Eckhart: The Essential Sermons, Commentaries, Treatises, and Defense.* ed. and trans. Edmund Colledge and Bernard McGinn (Mahwah: Paulist Press, 1981), p. 254.

straight on at what we try to avoid about ourselves is likely to be both painful and humiliating (in the literal sense of 'producing humility,' as discussed in Subsection 2.2.3). In her *Flowing Light of the Godhead* Mechthild of Magdeburg memorably describes the process of preparing for this sort of self-examination in terms of getting dressed and then looking in the mirror:

> I put on the shoes of the precious time that I wasted day after day. I gird myself with the suffering I have caused. Then I put on a cloak of the wickedness of which I am full. I put on my head a crown of secret shameful acts that I have committed against God. After this, I take in my hand the mirror of true knowledge. Then I look at myself and see who I really am.[18]

As we'll see in Subsection 2.2.2, the metaphor of the mirror of self-knowledge runs throughout the medieval contemplative tradition and is typically associated with seeing ourselves the way that God sees us. Although the sort of self-knowledge in which medieval contemplatives are most interested is inherently humbling, then, it is important to note that gaining an awareness of the 'naked blind feeling' of our own being is *not* meant to be the beginning of a downward spiral of revulsion or self-loathing. Rather, when we arrive at an accurate self-assessment and acknowledge what that self looks like, we 'hit bottom'—in a rather literal sense. We reach the 'ground' of our being, "a receptive dimension, as bottomless and infinite as God," in which we can root ourselves and begin to grow.[19] According to medieval contemplatives, we can't relate to the world from a place of love until after we have stripped away our conceits and pretenses, for true love flourishes only in the presence of truth.

---

[18] *Mechthild of Magdeburg, The Flowing Light of the Godhead*, trans. Frank Tobin (Mahwah: Paulist Press, 1998), Book VI, pp. 226–7.

[19] "The Concept of Ground" in Ineke Cornet's *The Arnhem Mystical Sermons: Preaching Liturgical Mysticism in the Context of Catholic Reform* (Leiden: Brill, 2019), 271. The concept of the 'ground of being' is an important one in the contemplative tradition, with roots running back to its earliest texts. In the thirteenth-fifteenth centuries, it appears in a number of contemplative texts (including Hadewijch and Jan van Ruusbroec), growing in significance and becoming a central concept in Meister Eckhart and his followers (particularly Johannes Tauler).

40 SELF-KNOWLEDGE

2.2 Recommendations for Developing Self-Knowledge

Gaining an awareness of our innermost self is challenging, but it is also necessary for moving from toxic selfishness to the knowledge of self that yields radical compassion and clear-sighted love of both others and ourselves. Because this sort of love is viewed as an essential component of happiness in this period (see Chapter 4), acquiring this deeper sort of self-knowledge is considered one of the most important things we human beings can do. We thus find a wealth of practical advice for accomplishing this task in contemplative texts, which are typically written both by and for people committed to moral and spiritual development. In this section, I distill and explain three of their most common recommendations for making the shift from self-centered love to the *caritas* grounded in genuine self-knowledge: 1) look outside yourself to know yourself; 2) root yourself in humility (which, as we'll see, is also essential for recognizing our inherent dignity); and 3) use reason and imagination to overcome selfish pride.

2.2.1 Look outside yourself to know yourself: the mirror of self-knowledge

Contrary to the stereotype of desert hermit, most medieval mystics and contemplatives lived embedded in spiritual and intellectual communities.[20] Their experiences in these communities led them to recognize that, no matter how good we might be at solitary introspection, there are things about ourselves that we simply cannot know without rubbing elbows (emotional, intellectual, spiritual, and/or physical) with others. I might think, for instance, that I've achieved patience via meditation and

---

[20] By the thirteenth century, the Franciscan, Dominican, and Augustinian orders had joined the earlier Carthusian, Cistercian, and Benedictine orders in establishing monasteries, convents, abbeys, priories, etc., which housed men and women who took lifelong vows and lived in community. By the fourteenth century, lay religious movements that involved communal living were also spreading rapidly across France, Germany, and the Low Countries. Even anchorites, who lived in strict enclosure, received visitors and corresponded with spiritual brothers and sisters. See Mari Hughes-Edwards's *Reading Medieval Anchoritism: Ideology and Spiritual Practice* (Cardiff: University of Wales Press, 2012).

RECOMMENDATIONS FOR DEVELOPING SELF-KNOWLEDGE   41

readings until an hour in traffic with a screaming toddler makes me realize how much farther I have to go. Or I may hope that I've overcome my envy of a successful friend, but not know for certain until I see her win a well-deserved award and find myself genuinely rejoicing for her. As Catherine of Siena remarks, "Virtue cannot be perfected or bear fruit except by means of your neighbors... And I say the same of vice: Every one of them is committed by means of your neighbors."[21] The way people around us bring out both our worst and our best is also one of the reasons communities dedicated to personal growth stress the importance of accountability relations: not only does it take experiences with others to help us realize where we are, morally and/or spiritually, but those closest to us can frequently see aspects of ourselves more clearly than we can. In short, we serve as mirrors for each other in ways vital for developing and deepening self-knowledge.

The metaphor of the mirror becomes synonymous with self-knowledge in art and literature in this period.[22] Already in Section 2.1, we saw Mechthild of Magdeburg look at herself in "the mirror of true knowledge" as a way of building self-awareness.[23] In Christine de Pizan's *City of Ladies*, Lady Reason holds a mirror in lieu of a scepter, explaining: "No one can look into this mirror, no matter what kind of creature, without achieving clear self-knowledge." Reason goes on to link self-knowledge both with knowledge more broadly and with practical wisdom (also called prudence) in particular: "Thanks to this mirror, the essences, qualities, proportions, and measures of all things are known, nor can anything be done well without it."[24] Representations of practical

---

[21] Catherine of Siena, *Dialogue*, ch. 11, p. 45. Catherine, who left a period of extreme isolation in her early years to live the rest of her life in closely knit (and often tumultuous) religious communities, is speaking from experience here. See Karen Scott's "'This is why I have put you among your neighbors': St. Bernard's and St. Catherine's Understanding of the Love of God and Neighbor," in *Atti del Simposio Internazionale Cateriniano-Bernardiniano*, ed. D. Maffei and P. Nardi (Siena: Accademia Senese degli Intronati, 1982), pp. 279–94.

[22] As Nancy Frelick notes, mirrors become associated in this period with both "self-improvement (moral edification or spiritual purification) and vanity (excessive pride and preoccupation with the self or worldly goods)"; *The Mirror in Medieval and Early Modern Culture: Specular Reflections*, ed. Nancy Frelick (Turnhout: Brepols Publishers, 2016), 1–30, p. 1.

[23] See also Mechthild's *Flowing Light of the Godhead*, Book V, p. 186, in which God praises the loving soul as a "mirror of inward contemplation."

[24] Christine de Pizan, *The Book of the City of Ladies*, trans. Earl Richards (New York: Persea Books, 1982, rev. 1998), p. 9. Christine follows the *City of Ladies* with a book of advice written to women of various social stations; although the original title of this book is *Le trésor de la cité*

42   SELF-KNOWLEDGE

wisdom/prudence in this period often portray the virtue as a woman holding a mirror which symbolizes the self-knowledge necessary for making wise judgments.[25] (See Figure 2.2.) Self-knowledge's particular link with prudence also underscores the importance of introspection in the virtuous life, for practical wisdom straddles the line between intellective and moral virtues and was seen as crucial for the development and regulation of the moral virtues.[26]

Figure 2.2 *Prudence*, Piero del Pollaiolo, 1470, Uffizi Gallery, Florence.

des dames (*The Treasure of the City of Ladies*), it is published in English with the title *A Medieval Woman's Mirror of Honor* because it was written in the mirror genre (trans. Charity Cannon Willard, New York: Persea Books, 1989).

[25] Earlier representations of practical wisdom/prudence, particularly in manuscripts, often depict the virtue as a woman holding a book and teaching a group of women (other virtues); by the fifteenth century, however, the mirror of self-knowledge and the snake of wisdom become Prudence's iconographic symbols.

[26] See Anthony Celano, *Aristotle's Ethics and Medieval Philosophy: Moral Goodness and Practical Wisdom* (Cambridge: Cambridge University Press, 2015); Bonnie Kent, *Virtues of the*

RECOMMENDATIONS FOR DEVELOPING SELF-KNOWLEDGE   43

The Middle Ages in fact sees the development of an entire genre of literature called 'mirrors,' texts which present a model of a virtue, social role, or set of desired qualities, serving as a sort of instruction manual meant to help the reader by reflecting to them an ideal version of what they're aspiring to. Although mirrors are also written for any number of secular roles (Machiavelli's sixteenth century *The Prince*, although hardly a standard example of the genre, followed on a number of earlier medieval and renaissance mirrors for princes), mirrors become particularly prominent in the contemplative tradition from the mid-twelfth through fifteenth centuries. William of Saint Thierry and Aelred of Rievaulx write mirrors of faith and charity, respectively, more than a century before Marguerite Porete's *Mirror of Simple Souls* becomes the talk of Paris in the early 1300s. Such mirrors were meant to spark greater self-awareness while simultaneously encouraging moral and spiritual improvement: they functioned like a particularly wise and honest advisor or mentor.

People were also described as mirrors in this sense: in the 1253 papal bull canonizing Clare of Assisi, for instance, Pope Alexander IV describes her as a "a clear mirror given to the entire world."[27] Clare's own testament uses the same language to acknowledge the importance of moral and spiritual models, stating that "the Lord Himself set us as an example and mirror for others"; she warmly encourages the newer sisters in her order, saying that they will, in turn, "be a mirror and example to those living in the world."[28] The ultimate mirror in this sense, though, is of course Christ—the only human being to live a perfect, sinless life.[29] Clare of Assisi thus also encourages her protégée, Agnes, to place herself before "before the mirror of eternity," embracing the "blessed poverty, holy

---

Will: The Transformation of Ethics in the Late Thirteenth Century (Washington, D.C.: Catholic University of America Press, 1995); Pierre Payer, "Prudence and the Principles of Natural Law: A Medieval Development," Speculum 54/1 (1979), 55–70.

[27] Alexander IV, *Clara claris praeclara, Bullarium Franciscanum* 2 (Rome, 1761), 81, as quoted on p. 169 of *Francis and Clare: The Complete Works*, trans. Regis Armstrong and Ignatius Brady (Mahwah: Paulist Press, 1986).

[28] *Francis and Clare*, pp. 227–8. The authorship of the Testament of Saint Clare is unclear: it's likely that it was composed after her death based on things she said to the Sisters at San Damiano. See the lengthy discussion of the manuscript tradition in note 1 on p. 226.

[29] Indeed, one of the most widely circulated English texts of the fifteenth century is Nicholas Love's *Mirror of the Blessed Life of Jesus Christ* (an English translation and adaptation of the popular fourteenth-century *Meditations on the Life of Christ*).

44 SELF-KNOWLEDGE

humility, and ineffable charity," which we find there in Christ.[30] Clare goes on to tell Agnes to "Look upon that mirror each day, O queen and spouse of Jesus Christ, and continually study your face within it, so that you may adorn yourself within and without with beautiful robes and cover yourself with the flowers and garments of all the virtues." The noble-born Clare is here drawing on a trope familiar from the courtly love poems of her day (the lady dressing in finery and looking at herself in a mirror, which we also saw Mechthild of Magdeburg employ; see also Interlude 4) to illustrate the process of self-examination and improvement.

The metaphor of the mirror of Christ also provides a vital point of connection between knowledge of self and knowledge of God. As the fourteenth-century *Pursuit of Wisdom* notes, "When [a mirror] is clean, everything can be seen [in it] clearly. But when the mirror is dirty, you can see nothing clearly in it. It is just the same with your soul; when it is dirty, you know neither yourself nor God."[31] Catherine of Siena makes the same connection in her *Dialogue*, stating that, "As the soul comes to know herself, she also knows God better, for she sees how good God has been to her. In the gentle mirror of God, she sees her own dignity: that through no merit of hers but by his creation, she is the image of God."[32] (See Figure 2.3, in which a noble lady holds a mirror that reflects not her own face but the face of the unicorn next to her; unicorns symbolize purity in this period, but they also symbolize Christ.[33]) Julian of Norwich also links knowledge of self with knowledge of God quite definitively in the long text of her *Showings* or *Revelations of Divine Love*: "Whether we are moved to seek God or our own souls, we are led through grace to know them both as one."[34]

The ongoing process of self-examination and introspection that yields this deeper sort of knowledge of self is one that connects us to, rather than separates us from, those around us. As the early fourteenth-century Flemish Jan van Ruusbroec writes, "We must go out to God and to

---

[30] *Francis and Clare*, third letter to Agnes of Prague, p. 200.
[31] *Pursuit of Wisdom*, p. 34.
[32] *Dialogue* ch. 13, p. 48. See Section 4.2 for more on the concept of dignity as it relates to persons, especially in the fourteenth–fifteenth centuries.
[33] See Jane Beal's "The Unicorn as a Symbol for Christ in the Middle Ages," in *Illuminating Jesus in the Middle Ages*, ed. J. Beal (Leiden: Brill, 2019), pp. 154–88.
[34] Julian of Norwich, *Showings*, ch. 56, p. 154.

Figure 2.3 Detail of 'Sight' panel of the Lady and the Unicorn tapestries, Flemish workshop, c.1500, Musée de Cluny, Paris.

ourselves and to our neighbor, and this must be done with charity and righteousness." If we approach everyone (including ourselves) in this way, "charity and righteousness [will] lay a foundation in the kingdom of the soul in which God is to dwell; this foundation is humility."[35] As I discuss in Subsection 2.2.2, humility is both a natural consequence of self-knowledge and a necessary ground for moral and spiritual growth.

2.2.2 Root down in humility to rise up in dignity: the tree of self

Understood as a spiritual discipline, self-knowledge has an inherently humbling effect. Indeed, according to this tradition, one of the main effects of self-knowledge is humility, a virtue central to both the moral and religious life. Medieval expressions of such humility often sound to

---

[35] *John Ruusbroec: The Spiritual Espousals and Other Works*, ed. and trans. J. Wiseman, OSB (Mahwah: Paulist Press, 1985), p. 55.

46   SELF-KNOWLEDGE

our modern ears more like self-loathing—we instinctively recoil when Clare of Assisi refers to herself as an "unworthy servant" and "useless handmaid" of Christ, for instance, or when Mechthild of Magdeburg describes herself as a "filthy puddle"[36]—but it would be a mistake to reduce this to the familiar historical narrative that medieval religious movements encouraged self-hatred and that it took the 'Enlightenment' for human beings to regain a sense of dignity and self-worth. Rather, it is important to understand the contemplative emphasis on humility in its larger context, where rooting ourselves in the humble ground of our own being is a necessary condition for growing into our full potential as human beings and God-imagers. Gazing at ourselves in the eternal mirror of God is both humbling and uplifting: we see any number of ways in which we (both individually and as members of the human species) fall short of what we should be, but at the same time we see our own inherent dignity as image bearers of the divine. As Lady Conscience observes to Lady Knowledge in Mechthild of Magdeburg's *Flowing Light of the Godhead*, "When I examine myself in [my fine mirror], I experience both pleasure and pain. Pleasure, because God comes to me as a flowing goodness; pain, because I am so feeble in good works."[37]

Feelings of unworthiness are consistently portrayed in this period as appropriate attitudes to adopt *when comparing ourselves with God*. This exercise is meant to reduce our inclination towards inflated self-worth, but the ultimate end of the rigorous work of introspection is experiencing God's love in the most perfect way. Introspection highlights our fragility and leads us to recognize our dependency, but that dependency is on a God who loves us: we can't fully appreciate that love in the absence of accurate self-appraisal. It would be equally inappropriate in this context to loathe ourselves insofar as we are beings capable of

---

[36] The paradox of women using humility formulae to claim religious authority is real; I discuss this is more detail in Section 3.4 and Interlude 5, as well as in my "Lewd, Feeble, and Frail: Humility Formulae, Medieval Women, and Authority," in *Oxford Studies in Medieval Philosophy* 10 (Oxford: Oxford University Press, forthcoming). See also Amy Hollywood's "Suffering Transformed: Marguerite Porete, Meister Eckhart, and the Problem of Women's Spirituality," in *Meister Eckhart and the Beguine Mystics: Hadwijch of Brabant, Mechtild of Magdeburg, and Marguerite Porete*, ed. B McGinn (New York: Continuum, 1994), pp. 87–113; also Grace Jantzen's *Power, Gender, and Christian Mysticism*. (Cambridge: Cambridge University Press, 1995).

[37] *Flowing Light of the Godhead*, Book VII, p. 288.

RECOMMENDATIONS FOR DEVELOPING SELF-KNOWLEDGE 47

spiritual growth and union with the Divine or as beloved by God. Self-knowledge may inevitably lead to humility, but humility is, in Hadewijch's words, "the worthiest and purest place in which we receive love."[38]

The idea that self-knowledge puts the subject in a better position to love and be loved runs throughout the medieval contemplative tradition. Catherine of Siena, for instance, depicts the relation between self-knowledge, love, and knowledge of God as a sort of upwards spiral. She opens the *Dialogue* with an autobiographical account of this interplay:

> A soul rises up, restless with tremendous desire for God's honor and the salvation of souls. She has for some time exercised herself in virtue and has become accustomed to dwelling in the cell of self-knowledge in order to know better God's goodness toward her, since upon knowledge follows love. And loving, she seeks to pursue truth and clothe herself in it.[39]

On this view, greater self-knowledge means greater knowledge of God— and, in so doing, it kindles greater love for God in light of God's goodness, which in turn creates a greater desire to know more about God. In this way, humility is explicitly conceived as the starting point in a dynamic journey towards union with God.

Experience of this unitive state in earthly life is then described as a foretaste of the everlasting union that the blessed experience in the afterlife. As Angela of Foligno says, "In that state [mystic union] I see myself as alone with God, totally cleansed, totally sanctified, totally true, totally upright, totally certain, totally celestial in him."[40] It is the humility generated by true self-knowledge that, paradoxically, also generates the confidence that we are capable of being united with God's perfection, whatever our current state.

To illustrate the complex relation between self-knowledge, humility, and dignity, medieval contemplatives frequently draw on the ancient

[38] Hadewijch, *The Complete Works*, Letter 12, p. 72.   [39] *Dialogue*, Prologue 1, p. 25.
[40] *Memorial* IX, in *Angela of Foligno: Complete Works*, trans. Paul Lachance, OFM (Mahwah: Paulist Press, 1993), p. 215.

48   SELF-KNOWLEDGE

metaphor of the tree of self.[41] In Hadewijch's first vision, for instance, an angel shows her a series of trees, the first of which the angel calls the "tree of self-knowledge," and which has a rotten root, symbolic of fallen human nature.[42] The decay of the root indicates human nature can't flourish on its own—a fact that we learn about ourselves via knowledge of self. Marguerite d'Oingt, in turn, relates a vision in which she is a dry tree with withered leaves, who is miraculously revived by "great stream descending with a force like that of the sea," which represents God's love and mercy.[43] Similarly, Gertrude the Great describes herself in *The Herald of Divine Love* as a "frail little plant" that withers "hour to hour through her faults and negligences" until she is watered with the water and blood that flow from Christ's wound, at which point the little plant grows into a green tree which is literally rooted in Christ's side.[44] Mechthild of Hackeborn, meanwhile, relates a vision in which she sees the Virgin Mary in the form of "beautiful tree, higher and broader than the whole earth. This tree was just as transparent as a luminous mirror, and its golden leaves made the loveliest sound. In its crown was a delicious flower [Christ] that shaded the whole world and spread abroad an extraordinary fragrance."[45] Mary serves here as a model—a literal mirror—for how humble roots (humility being one of the traits most associated with her) can support extraordinary moral and spiritual growth.[46]

---

[41] Psalm 1:3–4, for instance, compares the righteous person with a flourishing tree, "planted near running waters," in marked contrast with the wicked, who will be dry and withered, "like dust." Such metaphors become particularly prominent in the thirteenth–fifteenth centuries; see Sara Ritchey, "Spiritual Arborescence: Trees in the Medieval Christian Imagination," *Spiritus: A Journal of Christian Spirituality* 8/1 (2008), pp. 64–82.

[42] Hadewijch, *The Complete Works*, Vision One, p. 263.

[43] *The Writings of Margaret of Oingt, Medieval Prioress and Mystic (d. 1310)*, trans. with an introduction, essay, and notes by Renate Blumenfeld-Kosinski (Cambridge: D. S. Brewer, 1990), pp. 66–7.

[44] *Gertrude of Helfta: The Herald of Divine Love*, trans. and ed. Margaret Winkworth (Mahwah: Paulist Press, 1993), p. 176. Trees also feature prominently in the spiritual life of fourteenth-century Adelheid of Langmann , a nun at the Dominican monastery at Engelthal. See Leonard Hindsley's *The Mystics of Engelthal: Writings from a Medieval Monastery* (New York: St. Martin's Press, 1998), p. 130.

[45] *Mechthild of Hackeborn: The Book of Special Grace*, trans. Barbara Newman (Mahwah: Paulist Press, 2017), 1.29. Significantly, this vision occurs on the Feast of the Nativity of Mary.

[46] The explicit reference to all five senses here and in Marguerite d'Oingt's vision indicate redemption of the human body via Christ's Incarnation. The connection between the need for restoration of the tree of self and our need for restoration in Christ is a common theme in the

RECOMMENDATIONS FOR DEVELOPING SELF-KNOWLEDGE   49

In general, the deeper our roots of humble self-knowledge delve, the higher we can reach towards God.[47] As Johannes Tauler (a fourteenth-century disciple of Meister Eckhart) explains: "In order to gain the crown of perfection, there is nothing more important than to sink down into the deepest ground and into the root of humility. Just as a tree's height comes out of its deepest root, so too everything that is high in this life comes from the ground of humility."[48] Catherine of Siena in turn offers a lengthy tree-related metaphor of the relation between self-knowledge, humility, and God. She invites us to "imagine a circle traced on the ground" with a tree in the center of the circle.[49] The tree represents the human soul, "made for love and living only by love," and planted in the soil of humility. In fact, the circle on the ground (which represents the interwoven knowledge of the self and of God) extends only as far as humility does.[50]

By the time Julian of Norwich completes the long text of her *Showings* at the turn of the fifteenth century, the metaphor of the tree of self (watered by God) is so familiar that she can reference it without explicit

thirteenth–fifteenth centuries, often linked to Christ's human lineage via the Tree of Jesse—an extremely popular subject in art of this period. Jesse is typically shown sleeping (reminiscent of Adam in representations of Eve's creation) with a tree growing up from his side on whose branches significant descendants such as Kings David and Solomon sit; Christ appears in the crown of the tree.

[47] Many contemplative texts reference Colossians 2:7 when using this metaphor: "Therefore, just as you received Christ Jesus as Lord, so walk in him: being rooted and built up in him." In the Vulgate: "*Sicut ergo accepisti Christum Iesum Dominim in ipso ambulate, radicati et super-aedificati in ipso.*"

[48] V 57, trans. McGinn, *The Harvest of Mysticism in Medieval Germany (1300–1500)*, Vol. 4 of The Presence of God: A History of Western Christian Mysticism (New York: Crossroad Publishing Co., 2005), p. 276.

[49] All the quotes in this paragraph are from *Catherine of Siena: The Dialogue*, ch. 9, p. 40.

[50] The whole passage reads: "The circle in which this tree's root, the soul's love, must grow is true knowledge of herself, knowledge that is joined to me, who like the circle have neither beginning nor end. You can go round and round within this circle, finding neither end nor beginning, yet never leaving the circle. This knowledge of yourself, and of me within yourself, is grounded in the soil of true humility, which is as great as the expanse of the circle (which is the knowledge of yourself united with me, as I have said). But if your knowledge of yourself were isolated from me there would be no full circle at all. Instead, there would be a beginning in self-knowledge but apart from me it would end in confusion. So the tree of charity is nurtured in humility and branches out in true discernment. The marrow of the tree (that is, loving charity within the soul) is patience, a sure sign that I am in her and that she is united in me. This tree, so delightfully planted, bears many-fragranced blossoms of virtue. Its fruit is grace for the soul herself and blessing for her neighbors." Later in the *Dialogue* (see chapter 93 for the fullest description) Catherine contrasts this "tree of love" with the "tree of death," rooted in pride and selfishness.

50   SELF-KNOWLEDGE

mention. In explaining the relation between human beings and God, for instance, she simply writes: "Mercy and grace spring from God's essential nature and flow into us, penetrating our souls and accomplishing everything needed for the fulfillment of our greatest joy. This is the soil in which our being, our growth, and our fulfillment are planted."[51] For Julian, knowledge of both self and God develops in organic relationship; neither can occur in separation from the other. "Our soul is so deeply rooted in God," she observes, "that we cannot come to know it until we have first come to know God, who is the Creator and to whom our soul is one-ed... [Yet] we cannot come to a complete understanding of God unless we come to truly know ourselves."[52] These understandings are so intimately connected that she concludes: "Whether we are moved to seek God or our own souls, we are led through grace to know them both as one."[53]

The ultimate end of self-knowledge, then, is the knowledge and love that unites us with God. As *The Pursuit of Wisdom* notes, if we "exercise ourselves diligently and for a long while in those spiritual works by means of which we are taught to know ourselves," we can be "lifted up to the knowledge and contemplation of God."[54] Self-knowledge enables us to reach from earth to heaven; self-knowledge allows us to spread from love of ourselves to love of neighbors to love of God.[55] The intimate experience of divine union is a far cry from self-abasement, and yet it is made possible by the humility that results from self-knowledge.[56]

---

[51] *The Showings of Julian of Norwich: a new translation*, trans. Mirabai Starr (Charlottesville, VA: Hampton Roads Publishing Co., 2013), ch. 56, p. 155.

[52] Ibid., p. 155.   [53] Ibid., p. 154.

[54] *The Pursuit of Wisdom*, p. 34. See also chapter 3 of Catherine of Siena's *Dialogue*, where God says to her, "If you would come to perfect knowledge and enjoyment of me, eternal Life: Never leave the knowledge of yourself" (p. 29).

[55] See Catherine of Siena, *Dialogue*, ch. 11, pp. 44–5: "Discernment [earlier described as "the knowledge one ought to have of oneself and God"] has a prudence that cannot be deceived, a strength that is invincible, a constancy right up to the end, reaching as it does from heaven to earth, that is from the knowledge of me [Truth/God] to the knowledge of oneself, from love of me to love of one's neighbors."

[56] See also Hadewijch's Letter 2, in which she explains that the end result of the hard and humbling work of introspection is perfection via union with God: "To this end [i.e., experiencing God's perfecting love] you must remain humble and unexalted by all the works you can accomplish, but wise with generous and perfect charity to sustain all things in heaven and earth.... Thus you may become perfect and possess what is yours!" (p. 52).

2.2.3 Use reason and imagination to overcome selfish pride

Developing the humility in which self-knowledge can flourish requires rooting out pride—the 'deadliest' of the deadly vices. Because pride is typically portrayed as disordered love (love of self above love of God and others), medieval contemplatives often recommend using reason and imagination to identify love's proper object (the good, which every being possesses but which God—the Highest Good—possesses to the greatest extent) and to guide love's attention back towards that object when it strays. The disciplines of coming to terms with the 'naked blind feeling of our own being' and seeing ourselves as reflected in and by others can make us aware of the desires and dispositions that are interfering with the growth and maturation of our selves, but it takes the careful application of reason and will for us to change. Catherine of Siena puts this in characteristically vivid terms when she writes that self-knowledge allows us to "find humility and hatred for [our] selfish sensory passions," at which point we then must "crush those desires firmly under the foot of reason."[57] It's an important step when we realize that our jealousy of a friend's amazing success stems from our deep-seated worry that we'll never measure up, but figuring out how to become someone whose sense of self isn't based on how others are doing—and then actually putting that into practice—is a much larger project. The goal is to eliminate the harmful inclinations that introspection has uncovered so that better desires and affections can flourish, and to amplify reason's efforts in guiding the development of these better desires, medieval contemplatives tend to advocate the careful application of imagination.

Imagination was seen in this period as reason's servant, or handmaiden.[58] One of its main functions is to store the sensory impressions

---

[57] Prologue to the *Dialogue*, 7, p. 36. As I discuss in more detail in Section 3.1, the key word here is 'selfish.' Catherine is not denigrating sensory passions as such.

[58] The language of imagination as reason's handmaiden appears to stem from the elaborate allegory of various mental faculties and virtues which Richard of St. Victor offers in his *Twelve Patriarchs*: reason and the will are Rachel and Leah, respectively, each of whom gives birth to various virtues, and each of whom has a handmaiden who assists them—imagination is reason's servant, and sensuality is the will's. See Sections 2.1 and 3.1 for further discussion. For a

52 SELF-KNOWLEDGE

(also called phantasms) that we draw on when we're thinking. When we're trying first to form and then later to refine an abstract concept like 'dog,' for instance, we need to be able to call to mind—in medieval terms, *imagine*—various experiences we've had with four-legged furry creatures with tails in order to separate the ones who meow or squeak from the ones who bark, and to connect the tiny yappy barking creatures with the large woofy barking creatures. In fact, a standard medieval line about human knowledge is that "without imagination, reason can have no knowledge," for phantasms are the building blocks of cognition.[59]

According to this tradition, imagination also allows us to take various sense impressions we've had in the past and combine them in new ways, as when a coach encourages you to picture yourself winning a race before you run it. Using imagination in this way gives us further insight into ourselves: when we picture ourselves winning, for instance, how do we feel? How do the people around us act, and how do we behave towards our fellow runners? Imagination thus plays an important role in moral self-improvement: if we notice that we regularly continue arguments in our heads long after an actual conversation has ended, for example, and get increasingly angry with people who aren't even there, the careful use of reason and imagination can help us refocus our mental energy towards generating more constructive responses to the situation and imagining how we might put those strategies into practice.

Medieval contemplatives also stress the importance of the joint work of reason and imagination for making spiritual progress. One of the most widely read devotional books of the fourteenth and fifteenth centuries, the anonymous *Meditations on the Life of Christ*, is specifically devoted to helping its audience engage imagination via reason, to deepen and develop participation in the contemplative life.[60] As it notes, "There

---

detailed discussion of the role imagination plays in medieval thought, see Michelle Karnes's *Imagination, Meditation, and Cognition in the Middle Ages* (Chicago: University of Chicago Press, 2011).

[59] *The Pursuit of Wisdom and Other Works by the Author of the Cloud of Unknowing*, ed. and trans. James Walsh (Mahwah: Paulist Press, 1988), p. 21.

[60] For more on the role the *Meditations* plays in bringing women's voices into contemplative conversations, see my "From Meditation to Contemplation: Broadening the Borders of Philosophy in the 13th–15th Centuries," in *Pluralizing Philosophy's Past—New Reflections in the History of Philosophy*, ed. A. Griffioen and M. Backmann (London: Palgrave Macmillan, forthcoming).

RECOMMENDATIONS FOR DEVELOPING SELF-KNOWLEDGE 53

are two things in us we must cleanse, namely our intellect and our feeling: our intellect that it may know; our feeling that it may will."[61] In order to do this, the *Meditations* alternates excerpts from sermons by Bernard of Clairvaux with a series of homely vignettes from the life of Christ meant to serve as 'mirrors'—and in which the audience is invited to place themselves. The whole medieval genre of meditations generally encourages its readers to imagine and then engage with the events in Christ's life, most particularly Christ's Passion and death. (For more on these meditations and their intended effects, see Section 4.3.) Representations of such events also become much more personal and engaging in this period. Thus, for instance, depictions of the Passion tend to shift from displaying Christ as nobly dispassionate in the eleventh and twelfth centuries (see Figure 2.4, in which both Christ and the onlookers seem relatively unaffected by his crucifixion) to more expressive scenes in the thirteenth century and onward in which Christ and

Figure 2.4 *Esaltazione della Croce*, Maestro di Tressa, 1215, Pinacoteca Nazionale di Siena.

---

[61] *Meditations on the Life of Christ*, trans. Francis X. Taney, Anne Miller, and C. Mary Stallings-Taney (Asheville, NC: Pegasus Press, 2000), p. 175.

54 SELF-KNOWLEDGE

Figure 2.5 *Lamentation over the Dead Christ*, Ambrogio Lorenzetti, 1342–4, Pinacoteca Nazionale di Siena.

his viewers openly suffer (see Figure 2.5, in which the Marys grieve over Christ's dead body—and in which nuns from the convent for whom the painting was created are portrayed mourning on the far right.)

The exercise of meditation was viewed as an important method of countering selfish pride and further grounding the self-knowledge in which love (*caritas*) flourishes. As the prologue to the *Meditations* explains, "From frequent meditation our hearts are set on fire and animated to imitate and lay hold of these virtues [i.e., the virtues Christ's life displays]. Then we are illuminated by divine virtue in such a way that we both clothe ourselves with virtue and distinguish what is false from what is true."[62] In other words, developing virtues via this imaginative engagement also makes us wiser. If we meditate regularly, we generate affection and love "enough for us to warm our whole self in it" as we move into higher realms of intellective contemplation.[63]

We see this interplay between imagination, virtue, and reason in a variety of contemplative texts. Catherine of Siena, for example, notes in

---

[62] Prologue to the *Meditations*, p. 3.   [63] *Meditations*, ch. 107, p. 330.

RECOMMENDATIONS FOR DEVELOPING SELF-KNOWLEDGE 55

her *Dialogue* that "There are, then, two aspects to yourself: sensuality and reason. Sensuality is a servant, and it has been appointed to serve the soul, so that your body may be your instrument for proving and exercising virtue."[64] The word translated here as 'sensuality' (*sensualitas*) doesn't correspond neatly to the contemporary English word 'sensuality': it's a broad term that includes all of our sensory capacities (sight, hearing, taste, etc.), imagination, and our sense appetites (inclinations towards things perceived as pleasant and away from things perceived as unpleasant, plus fear and anger towards things perceived as dangerous). (For more on medieval conceptions of *sensualitas*, see Chapter 4.1.1.) Reason is the means by which we put these things to good use and gain virtue, knowledge, and wisdom. As I discuss in more detail in Chapter 3, our faculty of reason is integrally tied up with our physicality. It is thus vital for us to use this faculty well, so that our bodies help rather than hinder us in our moral and spiritual pursuits. Our wills are also guided by reason in important ways. For instance, as Hadewijch notes, our desire to do good things falters when we don't use reason well: "When reason is obscured, the will grows weak and powerless and feels an aversion to effort, because reason does not enlighten it."[65]

On the other hand, if we use reason and imagination to guide our affections and develop virtue, we can combat the prideful love of self that wants everything for its own. To be truly effective in its guidance, though, our reason needs to be 'enlightened'—a concept that harks back to Plato and Plotinus and that is brought into in the Latin Christian tradition by Augustine and other advocates of illuminationist theories.[66] For many contemplatives (especially those in the Augustinian tradition, such as the Victorines and Hadewijch) reason that has been illuminated by God is perhaps our most important ally in deepening and developing the self-knowledge that undergirds moral and spiritual progress. Richard of St. Victor even goes so far as to claim that "through the illumination of our reason by the grace of God we come to perfect knowledge of

---

[64] *Dialogue* ch. 51, p. 105.   [65] Letter 4, *Hadewijch*, p. 53.
[66] See Steven Marrone's *The Light of Thy Countenance: Science and Knowledge of God in the Thirteenth Century. Volume 1: A Doctrine of Divine Illumination* (Leiden/Boston: Brill Academic Publishers, 2001).

56 SELF-KNOWLEDGE

ourselves and of God," before quickly adding "at least as far as is possible in this life."[67]

So much, then, for what it is possible with respect to knowledge of ourselves and knowledge of God in this life. But what about the next?

2.3 Self-Knowledge, Mystic Union, and Our Final End

Although virtually all mystics and contemplatives in the thirteenth–fifteenth centuries portray self-knowledge as a necessary step towards our final end, they present a wide range of differing views about what our final end is and how self-knowledge factors into it. Some maintain that our ultimate goal is merging with God in selfless union, and that self-knowledge's most important role is helping us release attachment to the self. Others hold that everlasting union with God will perfectly restore and fulfill the embodied self; self-knowledge remains important on this view insofar as it helps us recognize and appreciate this connection to God. (For more about contemplative expectations regarding immortality and the afterlife, see Chapter 6; in the remainder of this chapter, my aim is merely to map out the role self-knowledge is given in attaining those differing ends.)

2.3.1 Our final end as self-annihilation

As we saw in Chapter 1, some medieval contemplatives hold that the final end of human beings involves extinguishing awareness of individuality to merge with an unknowable God. This view is typically associated with 'apophatic' contemplativism; *apophasis*, which means 'denial' or 'negation' in Greek, is the view that language and thought are incapable of capturing or revealing positive truths about the Divine.[68] Union with a God who transcends not just matter but also thought—and possibly

---

[67] *Twelve Patriarchs*, pp. 33–4.
[68] For a detailed treatment of this topic, see Denys Turner's *The Darkness of God: Negativity in Christian Mysticism* (Cambridge: Cambridge University Press, 1995).

SELF-KNOWLEDGE, MYSTIC UNION, AND OUR FINAL END   57

being itself—cannot be attained as long as we hold onto any of those things ourselves.

On this framework, self-knowledge's ultimate function is identifying and rooting out any lingering self-orientation. As Meister Eckhart observes, "There was never anyone in this life who forsook himself so much that he could not still find more in himself to forsake. But as much as you go out in forsaking all things, by so much, neither less nor more, does God go in."[69] On this view, God cannot enter into us fully until we empty ourselves fully. Knowledge of ourselves is essential for this process—but even this knowledge must eventually be transcended; the more we detach from the self that introspection reveals, the more we can lose ourselves in the hidden darkness of God. In *The Mirror of Simple Souls*, Marguerite Porete describes this as a state in which "The whole is one to her without an explanation [*sine propter quid*], and she is nothing in such a one...God is and she is not."[70] Meister Eckhart echoes this idea, writing that "[After detachment] there is still one work that remains proper and his own, and that is annihilation of self."[71] This process of self-annihilation involves both intellect and will: to the extent that the intellect clings to its knowledge, it remains apart from God's truth; to the extent to which the will continues to want things for itself, it holds itself apart from God's will.

The paradox of using self-knowledge to annihilate the self is not lost on apophatic contemplatives. Nevertheless, they claim that there is no other way to reach our final end. Johannes Tauler, Eckhart's friend and follower, entreats us to "turn in to yourself with self-knowledge"[72] so that we may reach the state in which "everything brought there [namely, to the ground of the soul]—its humility, its intention, its very self—loses its name, and there is only a bare, silent, mysterious unity without any distinction."[73] In this state, Tauler says, a person "neither knows, nor

---

[69] *Meister Eckhart*, Counsel 4, p. 250.
[70] Marguerite Porete, *The Mirror of Simple Souls*, trans. E. L. Babinsky (Mahwah: Paulist Press, 1993), ch. 135, p. 218. For the Old French text, see *Le Mirouer des simple ames*, ed. Romana Guarnieri (Turnhout: Brepols, 1986).
[71] *Meister Eckhart*, Counsel 23, p. 280.
[72] V 57, trans. McGinn, *Harvest of Mysticism*, p. 276.
[73] Tauler V 7, trans. McGinn, *Harvest of Mysticism*, p. 290. The spirit united with God in this way "is so submerged in the divine abyss that it knows nothing, feels nothing, tastes

58 SELF-KNOWLEDGE

feels, nor experiences himself."[74] Although it is unclear from the texts whether such union ultimately involves a loss of being, the phenomenological experience of such union is certainly one in which any sense of self is lost.

This emphasis on self-abnegation also appears in the *Cloud of Unknowing* and *The Book of Privy Counselling*, anonymous fourteenth-century English works. Even the 'naked blind feeling' of our own being that we were instructed to gnaw on at the outset of the development of self-knowledge must be relinquished in order for us to attain our final end. "Your awareness of everything else is contingent on your awareness of yourself," counsels the *Cloud*. "When you succeed in forgetting all creatures and their works and even your own life and all you've done, you will be left alone with God to experience a stark awareness of your own existence. But even this must go. Yes, you must lose the naked feeling of who you are. It must be destroyed, if you wish to experience the perfection of contemplation, or love."[75]

2.3.2 Our final end as self-fulfillment

Although (as I discuss in Chapter 1) the conception of self-annihilating union as the final end of human beings is dominant in philosophical discussions of mysticism today, in the Middle Ages this view was the exception rather than the rule. The majority of medieval contemplatives saw self-knowledge not just as a step towards union with God but as a lasting feature of such union. Sometimes referred to in contemporary discussions as 'affective' mysticism, this tradition emphasizes Christ's humanity, viewing the human body and material world as in need of restoration, not annihilation.[76] The Incarnation—literally, the

---

nothing but a single, pure, empty, unified God" (Tauler V 21, trans. McGinn, *Harvest of Mysticism*, p. 264.

[74] Tauler V 47, trans. McGinn, *Harvest of Mysticism*.

[75] *Cloud of Unknowing*, ch. 43, p. 98. Chapter 44 goes on to tell the prospective contemplative that losing this basic awareness of self ultimately requires a combination of God's grace and our disposing ourselves to receive that grace.

[76] Karma Lochrie, for instance, characterizes affective spirituality precisely in terms of "its corporeality and the imitation of Christ's suffering humanity" (*Margery Kempe and Translations of the Flesh*, Philadelphia: University of Pennsylvania Press, 1991), p. 14.

SELF-KNOWLEDGE, MYSTIC UNION, AND OUR FINAL END 59

'enfleshment'—of God takes on central importance for many contemplatives in this period because it gives human beings a tangible connection to the divine. On this view, self-knowledge is essential for engaging in the work of restoration via love (*caritas*), which Christ literally embodies in his life on earth, Passion, and resurrection. In the thirteenth–fifteenth centuries, contemplatives use Christ's model to reconceptualize the relationship between human beings and God in a fresh, "bodily and emotionally laden way."[77]

Knowing ourselves as bodily subjects thus becomes a way of knowing Christ, who is simultaneously fully human and fully divine. Julian of Norwich, for instance, portrays the Incarnation as the key to restoration of creation as a whole, and fallen human beings in particular. Human nature possesses what she calls 'higher' and 'lower' parts: the higher part is the spiritual, intellective part which we have in common with immaterial beings such as God and the angels (see Chapter 4), and the lower part is the sensory part, which we have in common with other animals. Both parts are inherently good, but both have been corrupted by sin and thus need to be redeemed. The act of Christ taking on human nature is what allows both parts of our nature to be restored. As she writes:

Because of the glorious unity God forged between the soul and the body, humanity will inevitably be raised from the double death (physical and spiritual). This restoration would not be possible if it had not been for the Second Person of the Holy Trinity who took on the lower part of human nature, which has always been united to the higher part.[78] Both the higher and the lower aspects of human nature, enfolded in Christ, are elements of a single soul.[79]

For contemplatives in this tradition, sensory experiences are essential for the formation and development of the self; they serve as "vehicles for

---

[77] Nicholas Watson, "Introduction" to *The Cambridge Companion to Medieval English Mysticism*, ed. S. Fanous and V. Gillespie (Cambridge: Cambridge University Press, 2011), p. 2.

[78] In ch. 57, Julian explains that this happens in creation: "The higher part of our human nature is knit to God in creation, and by taking flesh, God is knit to the lower part of our human nature. And so our twofold nature is unified in Christ" (pp. 157–8).

[79] Julian, *Showings*, ch. 55, p. 152–3. See also ch. 57.

60 SELF-KNOWLEDGE

religious knowledge: knowledge of God, and of the human person in relation to God."[80]

The belief that human beings are most closely joined with Christ's divinity through his corporeity also makes the ritual of partaking in that body in the Eucharist especially prone to sensory mystical experiences.[81] As Caroline Walker Bynum notes, in this period "the fundamental religious goal was seen to be union with the physical body Christ took on in the Incarnation and daily in the mass"[82]—a union often experienced mystically as a fulfillment of the embodied self. The vision of Marguerite d'Oingt mentioned in Subsection 2.2.3 beautifully characterizes the idea of physical and sensory restoration of the self, and so I quote it here in full:

It seemed to her that she was in a large deserted open space where there was only one high mountain, and at the foot of this mountain there stood a marvelous tree. This tree had five branches which were all dry and were bending down. On the leaves of the first branch there was written "sight"; on the second was written "hearing"; on the third was written "taste"; on the fourth was written "smell"; on the fifth was written "touch"...And after she had looked attentively at the tree, she raised her eyes towards the mountain, and she saw a great stream descending with a force like that of the sea. This stream rushed so violently down onto the bottom of this tree that all its roots were turned upside down and the top was stuck in the earth; and the branches which had been bent downwards were now stretching towards heaven. And the leaves which had been dry were all green, and the roots which had been in the earth were all spread out and pointing towards the sky; and they were all green and full of leaves as branches usually are.[83]

---

[80] Susan Harvey, *Scenting Salvation: Ancient Christianity and the Olfactory Imagination* (Berkeley: University of California Press, 2006), p. 157.

[81] See Caroline Walker Bynum, *Fragmentation and Redemption: Essays on Gender and the Human Body in Medieval Religion* (New York: Zone Books, 1992) as well as her *Holy Feast and Holy Fast: The Religious Significance of Food to Medieval Women* (Berkeley: University of California Press, 1987).

[82] Bynum, *Fragmentation and Redemption*, p. 66.

[83] *The Writings of Margaret of Oingt*, pp. 66–7.

Such a depiction of the flourishing self, turned upside down and now rooted in Christ, is in sharp contrast to Marguerite Porete's vision of complete self-abnegation: a state in which she is 'nothing.'

2.4 Conclusion

There was general agreement among medieval mystics and contemplatives in the Rome-based Christian tradition that unflinching introspection is the first step towards moral and spiritual progress. We need self-knowledge in order to move from unthinking, prideful love of self to a reflective and clear-sighted love of self—a love that can support radical compassion and self-sacrifice, and that can also ground love for God and our neighbors. This second sort of love (*caritas*) is our ultimate goal, but we cannot simply will it into being. Thus, after we take unflinching stock of our 'inner being,' contemplatives recommend looking outside ourselves for models of this love; coming to know ourselves in a morally and spiritually useful way thus becomes a sort of community project. Grounding this sense of self in humility is also consistently portrayed as essential for perceiving our inherent dignity, and we are instructed to put reason and imagination to creative use in combating selfish pride. Medieval contemplatives differ widely in their understanding of the final goal of human life, however, and so they differ in their understanding of the role self-knowledge should play in attaining this goal. Self-knowledge is vital for us to open ourselves to God, but such knowledge of self can be used both to root out traces of oneself for self-abnegating union with the divine and to restore the self in relation to the God who became human without ceasing to be divine.

62 SELF-KNOWLEDGE

Interlude Two

What Is a Beguine?

Inspired by the life of Christ's apostles (the '*vita apostolica*'), a host of lay religious movements flourished in Western Europe in the thirteenth through fifteenth centuries—and chief among these were the beguines.[84] Part of the pre-Reformational shift towards lay personal piety and away from religious lives mediated via increasingly complex (and corrupt) levels of ecclesiastical hierarchies,[85] beguines were lay religious women who devoted their lives to prayer, teaching, penance, contemplation, and service. Usually living in communities of like-minded women (but sometimes alone, often in a room of their family's house), beguines taught school, ministered to the poor, and nursed the sick; unsupported by the Church, beguines maintained financial independence by sharing inheritances and selling their embroidery, lacework, and other products.[86]

Although the exact rise of the movement remains shrouded in mystery, it's easy to see why the life would have constituted an attractive option for medieval women.[87] Becoming a beguine meant avoiding the perils of childbirth and arranged marriages; at the same time, the beguine lifestyle offered more autonomy than that of a nun. While most convents at the time cloistered women, for instance, and all required lifelong celibacy, beguine communities were open to women who

---

[84] Herbert Grundmann's groundbreaking 1935 study is still authoritative; it is translated from the original German and published as *Religious Movements in the Middle Ages: The Historical Links between Heresy, the Mendicant Orders, and the Women's Religious Movement in the Twelfth and Thirteenth Century, with the Historical Foundations of German Mysticism* (Notre Dame, IN: University of Notre Dame Press, 1995). For more on the role of women in these movements, see Bynum, *Fragmentation and Redemption*, and Barbara Newman's *From Virile Woman to Woman Christ: Studies in Medieval Religion and Literature*. (Philadelphia: University of Pennsylvania Press, 1995).

[85] For a discussion of the development of these movements in the thirteenth century, see André Vauchez's "Lay People's Sanctity in Western Europe," in *Images of Sainthood in Medieval Europe*, ed. R. Blumenfeld-Kosinski and T Szell (Ithaca: Cornell University Press, 1991) pp. 21–32. See also Bernard McGinn's *The Flowering of Mysticism: Men and Women in the New Mysticism—1200–1350* (New York: Crossroad Publishing Co, 1998) and *Varieties of Vernacular Mysticism: 1350–1550* (New York: Crossroad Publishing Co., 2016).

[86] Ernest McDonnell provides a comprehensive overview in *The Beguines and Berghards in Medieval Culture: with Special Emphasis on the Belgian Scene* (New York: Octagon Books, 1969).

[87] See Carol Neel's "The Origins of the Beguines," in *Signs: Journal of Women in Culture and Society* 14/2, pp. 321–41.

WHAT IS A BEGUINE? 63

wanted to dedicate themselves to religious devotion but who were either not willing or not able to 'take the veil': unlike nuns, beguines remained actively involved in their broader communities, could leave at any time to get married (or for any other reason), and accepted anyone who was willing to live by their rules. Many convents also required dowry payments for entrance, particularly as space in existing communities became scarce, while—unrestricted by the tight rules governing the foundation of a convent, which had to be affiliated with and supported by a particular religious order—the number of beguinages simply increased to meet demand. And the demand in the thirteenth and fourteenth centuries was high, particularly in France, Germany, and the Low Countries (modern-day Belgium, Luxembourg, and the Netherlands). By 1300 there were at least two hundred beguinages in Strasbourg, where Eckhart and Tauler were preaching, and in Cologne "as many as fifteen hundred women lived in more than 150 beguine houses."[88]

The physical space of a beguinage was typically designed to reflect the needs of a group of single women living in community: a number of dwellings and other buildings were arranged around a central courtyard, surrounded by a high wall with an entrance that could be closed and/or guarded. In some ways, beguinages were similar to modern co-ops or condo associations: the women shared responsibility for and access to common courtyards and communal gardens, and collectively owned the property in which they all lived. The fact that their houses and land were owned not by the Church but by individual beguines meant that the those with enough resources to purchase property would often rent out rooms or houses at low rates to those with fewer resources; if a land-owning beguine left the beguinage for any reason, she would sell her house to someone else in the community. Although modified to meet changing needs, the basic configuration of beguinages remains the same over the centuries, with the main entrance that could be closed off (see Figure I2.1) and houses arranged around a central courtyard (see Figure I2.2.).

---

[88] Daniel Bornstein, "Women and Religion in Late Medieval Italy: History and Historiography," in *Women and Religion in Medieval and Renaissance Italy*, ed. D Bornstein and R. Rusconi, trans. Margery Schneider (Chicago: University of Chicago Press, 1996) pp. 1–27, p. 8.

Figure I2.1 Entrance into the beguinage of Antwerp, seen from inside.

WHAT IS A BEGUINE? 65

Figure I2.2 Beguinage of Amsterdam, central courtyard, seen from church.

Larger beguinages often had their own chapels, their own libraries, and sometimes even their own scriptoriums (as did some convents); not surprisingly, such beguinages were the source of a great deal of contemplative and mystical literature.[89] The Great Beguinage of Ghent, for instance, "constituted a city within the city, with its walls and moats, two churches, eighteen convents, and hundred houses, its brewery and infirmary."[90] Beguinages were also frequently located near Dominican houses, for that Order's focus on preaching and teaching meant that many Dominican friars served as confessors, spiritual advisors, celebrants, and preachers for beguines. (Many of Meister Eckhart's and Johannes Tauler's German sermons survive, for instance, because the communities of women to which they were preached wrote them down to study and to share.)

---

[89] See Anne Winston-Allen's *Convent Chronicles: Women Writing about Women and Reform in the Late Middle Ages* (University Park, PA: University of Pennsylvania Press, 2004) and Gertrud Jaron Lewis's *By Women, for Women, about Women: the Sister-Books of Fourteenth-Century Germany* (Toronto: Pontifical Institute of Mediaeval Studies, 1996).

[90] Bornstein, "Women and Religion in Late Medieval Italy," p. 8.

66   SELF-KNOWLEDGE

The Rome-based ecclesiastical hierarchy soon became uncomfortable with (and suspicious of) a massive movement of unmarried lay women who, although dedicated to a religious life, were not subject to the Rule of any particular Order. Already in 1311, the Council of Vienne aims one bull (*"Cum de quibusdam mulieribus,"* Clem. 3.11.1) specifically at beguines. The papal document criticizes 'certain women' for "discussing the Holy Trinity and for offering opinions to others regarding the sacraments."[91] (Note that this implies that there were enough women involved in debates about philosophical theology for the highest levels of the Church to worry about what they were saying.) Although the document officially forbids the founding of more beguinages, it allows women already living an "upright life" in such communities to remain, and the beguine movement continues to flourish throughout the Low Countries and France throughout the fourteenth century and well into the fifteenth. (It also enjoys a substantial revival in the seventeenth century.) The movement has left a permanent mark on cities throughout northern Europe, many of which still have beguinages that now serve other functions (some preserved as museums or tourist sites, some converted into housing for the elderly or low-income families, etc.) and/or streets named for the beguinages that used to be there (such as the Rue des Beguines in Chartres and the Wijde Begijnestraat in Utrecht).

---

[91] Robinson, *Nobility*, 31.

3
Reason and Its Limits

The perception that reason is somehow intrinsically opposed to mystical and contemplative projects is as widespread as it is mistaken. Reason famously occupies a central role in medieval university discussions of the twelfth–fifteenth centuries; although contemplatives in this period remain decidedly more ambivalent than their scholastic counterparts about the role of reason and our intellective capacities—particularly insofar as they relate to the final end of human life—the idea that mysticism and/or contemplativism is hostile to rationality is misleading in (at least) two important ways. First, even figures who ultimately advocate abandoning reason and knowledge affirm intellect's role both in getting the mystical project off the ground and in progressing to the point where reason can be transcended. Second, any number of contemplatives portray reason not as something to be overcome or relinquished but as one of the most important ways in which we resemble or 'image' God, and, thus, as a crucial point of connection between human beings and the divine.[1]

In Section 3.1, I establish common ground between scholastic and contemplative attitudes towards reason, identifying key assumptions university-based and contemplative texts share concerning human rational faculties (most importantly, intellect and will). In Section 3.2, I begin my examination of contemplative attitudes towards reason, beginning with the tradition that advocates abandoning reason in order to unite with God in love; in Section 3.3, I turn to contemplatives who instead portray reason as an essential guide towards God. In this tradition, reason is seen as capable of deepening love, as an essential

---

[1] As this chapter demonstrates, this holds true both for contemplatives who advocate a more intellective path towards God (for instance, the Victorines) and for contemplatives known for their emphasis on love (such as Hadewijch and Julian of Norwich).

68 REASON AND ITS LIMITS

component of faith, and as a characteristic we share with Christ (in virtue of his humanity) and which in turn connects us with his divinity. Section 3.4 addresses how medieval contemplatives often experienced mystical union as strengthening their rational abilities, granting them authority to instruct and counsel others, and providing insight into God's nature. At the same time, as I discuss in Section 3.5, over the course of the thirteenth and fourteenth centuries, formal education and specialized knowledge (*scientia*) become increasingly portrayed as extraneous to the contemplative life.

3.1 The Nature of Reason

No mere overview could hope to do justice to the complex space reason (*ratio, resoun, raison,* etc.) occupies in either scholastic or contemplative texts, much less both: it is central to discussions of epistemology, metaphysics, philosophy of mind, moral psychology, logic, ethics, theology, and more. Because reason plays so many roles in so many sorts of conversations, it would be an error to try to pin the concept down too narrowly; instead, I will follow the lead of my medieval subjects in respecting reason's nuanced and complex nature. At the same time, scholastics and contemplatives in the thirteenth-fifteenth centuries share a general understanding of what reason is and how it works.

First and foremost, reason is understood in the Middle Ages as one of the chief powers among the 'rational capacities'—capacities that were viewed as setting the human being apart from other animals. Medieval discussions followed their ancient predecessors in dividing the sets of capacities found in living beings into three basic and hierarchically ordered categories: vegetative, sensory, and rational. Plants, for instance, can take in nutrition, grow, and reproduce, while animals are able to do these things and also perceive, desire, and move around things in the world around them. Plants were thus described as having 'vegetative' or 'nutritive' capacities, while animals were described as having 'sensory' or 'sensitive' capacities. Human beings possess not only vegetative and sensory capacities, but also the ability to make second-order judgments about those perceptions, desires, and movements, to engage in

THE NATURE OF REASON   69

reasoning and argumentation, and to desire and choose things under abstract labels such as 'the good' and 'the true'. These were then described as 'rational' capacities and divided into two categories according to how closely related they were to material and sensory concerns. Imagination and sensory memory were seen as dependent on matter (because they require sensory input to function), while reason, intellect, will, understanding, and intellective memory were seen as transcending matter (because they deal first and foremost with universal concepts rather than particulars).

'Reason' and 'rational' are used in this period to refer both to the whole set of intellectual capacities (as when angels are described as rational beings; for more on rationality generally, see Chapter 5) and to a particular power among those capacities. In this second, narrower sense, reason is the power to make judgments, construct arguments, and gain knowledge of concrete and abstract truths. Reason is both a discursive and dialectical power, meaning that reason's investigations proceed in stages, moving from one premise to another in order to arrive at conclusions (as opposed to grasping a priori truths in their essence or grasping entire arguments at a glance, which is what the faculty of understanding does). In contrast to the will—an appetite for the good, linked with desires—reason is a 'logical' faculty in the Greek sense of *logos*: it is intrinsically linked with human linguistic abilities.

Its discursive and dialectical nature makes reason a popular subject in medieval literature with a contemplative or moralistic bent, particularly texts written in dialogue form. Augustine's *Soliloquies*, for instance, feature a dialogue between Augustine and Reason, and Philosophy herself famously appears to Boethius in the *Consolation of Philosophy* (as he sits in his prison cell composing sad poetry) in order to encourage him to think rationally about his fate and to instruct him about the nature of true happiness.[2] Following these literary and philosophical precedents, reason is—as we'll see in Section 3.2—frequently personified in later medieval texts as a conversational foil for protagonists grappling with

---

[2] Boethius's *Consolation* remains popular throughout the Middle Ages and is a source of continuing literary and artistic inspiration. Hrotsvit of Gandersheim draws on the *Consolation* in several of her plays (particularly *Sapientiae*), for example, while Christine de Pizan models the beginning of her *City of Ladies* on the beginning of the *Consolation*.

70   REASON AND ITS LIMITS

moral and/or spiritual questions. (See Chapter 5 for further discussion of personification in medieval contemplative literature.)

This personification is also used to clarify the role of reason in relation to the other faculties of the soul, particularly the will. The same debate about the relative roles of knowledge and love that occupies scholastic texts (namely, whether knowledge or love is the primary act in our union with God) also appears in contemplative texts in this period.[3] Yet, while scholastic discussions of reason are written in Latin, appeal frequently to authority, and are aimed at presenting the truth in the systematic, objective manner of a classroom, contemplative discussions are composed in the emerging vernaculars as well as Latin, expressed in a variety of genres (including dialogues, poetry, mirrors, letters, and visionary literature), and tend to be more dynamic.[4] In this way, contemplative discussions of the topic provide an important complement to scholastic sources on the question of what reason is and what role it plays in the ultimate end of human life. As we'll see, reason (taken in the narrower sense outlined above) is consistently understood as a faculty essential for negotiating the material world, for gaining knowledge of abstract truths, and for knowing ourselves (see also Chapter 2). Yet the faculty of reason cannot itself get us all the way to our final end, whether that end be understood as intellective union with God or as selfless union with Love.

3.2 Taking Leave of Reason

Contemplative and mystical philosophy and theology are often thought to be anti-rational—committed to the view that reaching our ultimate

---

[3] Thomas Aquinas's intellect-centered and John Duns Scotus's will-centered accounts become the foci for this debate, which is sometimes taken to epitomize the difference between Dominican and Franciscan spirituality. For an overview of the debate, see Tobias Hoffman's "Intellectualism and Voluntarism" in the *Cambridge History of Medieval Philosophy*, pp. 414–27.

[4] We can see that this is a feature of the genre rather than simply the writing style of the authors in cases where we can compare an author's scholastic treatises with their less technical works. Bonaventure and Eckhart are good examples of this: they express the same general ideas quite differently in their theological writings and their more mystical writings and/or sermons.

TAKING LEAVE OF REASON 71

end requires abandoning reason (and the knowledge it produces) in the journey towards a Divine that transcends thought and experience. Although this is hardly the whole story (as we've seen already in Chapters 1 and 2 and will see further in Sections 3.3 and 3.4), it is true that there is at least an apophatic bent in much medieval contemplative writing. By the end of the thirteenth century, frustration with the elitism of the university system and its increasingly specialized discussions was leading a number of contemplatives to downplay and/or criticize the usefulness of reason in attaining theological ends, and this tendency increases throughout the fourteenth century.[5] In reason's place, these contemplatives emphasized the primacy of love and, in some cases, a loss of self so radical that its proponents spoke of emptying themselves so completely that only God remains.[6] Yet even in the most extreme of these cases, reason has a role to play in helping the text's audience understand what the journey to God both does and does not entail.

We find a simple example of this in Book Two of Mechthild of Magdeburg's late-thirteenth-century *Flowing Light of the Godhead*. Drawing on the popular literary tropes of *fin'amor* (today often called 'courtly love') epitomized by the Arthurian legends of Lancelot and Guinevere and Tristan and Isolde, Mechthild presents a dialogue between Lady Soul and Lady Knowledge in which Lady Knowledge asks the Loving Soul—praised as the image of God and depicted as a bride with "noble longing" and "boundless desire" for God—to say something to her about the "ineffable intimacy" that exists between her and God.[7] In response, Lady Soul replies:

---

[5] As Bernard McGinn notes in *The Harvest of Mysticism in Medieval Germany (1300–1500)*, Vol.4 of *The Presence of God: A History of Western Christian Mysticism* (New York: Crossroad Publishing Co., 2005), "In the course of the fourteenth century, the professionalization of scholastic theology and its increasing obsession with technical debates concerning epistemology and language had clearly come to seem counterproductive for believers who sought more than just discourse about God" (p. 248). For more on the history of *scientia* in this period, see Robert Pasnau's "Medieval Social Epistemology: *Scientia* for Mere Mortals," *Episteme* 7.1 (2010), pp. 23–41.

[6] This is what is typically meant when mystics or contemplatives talk about 'becoming God.' To date, Meister Eckhart's discussions of this have received perhaps the most attention. See, e.g., Ben Morgan's *On Becoming God: Late Medieval Mysticism and the Modern Western Self* (New York: Fordham University Press, 2013).

[7] "A light was given me that I might look upon you / Otherwise it would never have been my fortune. / There is a Threeness about you / You can indeed be God's image." *Mechthild of*

72 REASON AND ITS LIMITS

Lady Knowledge, that I shall not do.
Brides may not tell everything they experience.
...
My privileged experience of God must always be hidden
From you and all creatures except for myself.[8]

Lady Knowledge must remain content merely to praise the image of God she sees in Lady Soul, "my mistress and my queen," rather than being privy to an understanding of the soul's union with God. Mechthild often depicts the Soul in this way—namely, as a bride whose desires are fulfilled by God in ways that she cannot share with Reason, thus emphasizing the apophatic aspect of such union.[9]

Mechthild also takes aim at professors of theology and others trained in argumentative reasoning in a passage in which she expresses worry that her book won't be taken seriously because it's written by a woman outside the formal systems of knowledge.[10] In response God assures her that "the course of the Holy Spirit flows by nature downhill," illuminating and inspiring the lowly, and then takes a bit of a dig at the university set:

One finds many a professor learned in scripture who is actually a fool in my eyes.

And I'll tell you something else:

It is a great honor for me with regard to them, and it very much strengthens Holy Christianity

That the unlearned mouth, aided by my Holy Spirit, teaches the learned tongue.[11]

Magdeburg, The Flowing Light of the Godhead, trans. Frank Tobin (Mahwah: Paulist Press, 1998), p. 81.

[8] *Flowing Light of the Godhead*, p. 82.

[9] See, e.g., the dialogue between the Loving Soul and God in their bridal chamber, where "What happens to her then – [only] she knows – and that is fine with me," *Flowing Light*, p. 62.

[10] For more this topic in Mechthild particularly, see Sara Poor's *Mechthild of Magdeburg and Her Book: Gender and the Making of Textual Authority* (Philadelphia: University of Pennsylvania Press, 2004) and Michelle Voss Roberts's "Retrieving Humility: Rhetoric, Authority, and Divinization in Mechtild of Magdeburg," *Feminist Theology* 18/1 (2009), pp. 50–73.

[11] *Flowing Light of the Godhead*, II.26, p. 97.

TAKING LEAVE OF REASON   73

In short, knowledge of Scripture doesn't necessarily lead to wisdom, whereas Christianity's claim to divine inspiration is made stronger by wisdom being preached by the less erudite.

This skepticism about reason's ability to access divine wisdom (and, in the process, unite human souls with God) not only appears in texts throughout the fourteenth–fifteenth centuries but is amplified in texts that advocate abnegation of the self to the point where no experience of human individuality is left and only God remains. In this tradition, reason's primary role is to demonstrate what it is that the contemplative needs to relinquish, and how clinging to arguments and explanations can impede the process.

Perhaps the most extreme example of this tradition is the early-fourteenth-century *Mirror of Simple Souls*, written by Marguerite Porete, who was burnt at the stake in Paris in 1310 for refusing to recant the views in it judged heretical by a Dominican inquest. Like Mechthild of Magdeburg's *Flowing Light*, Porete's *Mirror* draws on the *fin'amor* tradition and is cast (at least initially) as a dialogue between three noble ladies: Reason, Soul, and Love. Throughout the conversation, which is divided into 136 brief chapters, Lady Love tries to convince Lady Soul to empty herself of everything that is not Love and to herself become Love. As early in chapter 7, Lady Love tells Lady Reason that nothing remains in the individual intellect of the soul annihilated in love;[12] true to character, though, Reason keeps asking questions and demanding answers and explanations. In chapter 21, for instance, Reason asks Love who she is, and receives the following reply: "I am God," says Love, "For Love is God and God is Love, and this Soul is God by the condition of Love. I am God by divine nature and this Soul is God by righteousness of Love. Thus, this precious beloved of mine is taught and guided by me, without herself, for she is transformed into me."[13]

Not surprisingly, Reason doesn't understand what Love is telling her and continues her inquiry, while Love and the Soul become increasingly frustrated with the barrage of questions. As Love comments in Chapter 43,

---

[12] "This gift is given from the most High, into whom this creature is carried by the fertility of understanding, and nothing remains in her own intellect," ch. 7, p. 85, in *Marguerite Porete. The Mirror of Simple Souls*, trans. E. L. Babinsky (Mahwah: Paulist Press, 1993).

[13] *Mirror*, ch. 21, p. 104.

74 REASON AND ITS LIMITS

"Ah Reason, you will always be one-eyed, you and all those who are fed by your doctrine. For, to be sure, one has faulty vision who sees things before her eyes and does not understand them at all. And so it is with you."[14] Reason's one-sided view isn't able to encompass the full scope of Love's vision for the Soul; later, Lady Soul herself complains that Reason's questions have made the book longer than it should be, "because of the answers you need, both for yourself and for those whom you nourish who move along at a snail's pace."[15] Although important dialectically for explaining the overall goal of the Mirror and making initial distinctions (e.g., between Love and the virtues), as the conversation continues, Reason becomes 'that guy'—the one whose constant questioning gets in the way of making any progress—and impedes the Soul's movement towards the goal of emptying herself of all thought and all will to merge in undifferentiated union with Love.

When in chapter 87 Lady Soul begins to realizes that goal, seeing that Love "has no beginning, no end, and no limit" and declaring, "I am nothing except Love," Lady Reason is so overcome by this pronouncement that she perishes.[16] The Soul's response is to rejoice: "Why did it take so long, this death! ... For as long as I had you, Lady Reason, I could not freely receive my inheritance, what was and is mine. But now I can receive it freely, since I have wounded you to death with Love." By the end of the Mirror, Love alone speaks, explaining that Lady Soul now "retains nothing more of herself in nothingness, because God is sufficient of Himself, that is, because He is and she is not. Thus she is stripped of all things because she is without existence, where she was before she was."[17] In this selfless union, in which Soul has lost all individuality and exists in God in the same way she did before she was created, human

---

[14] *Mirror*, ch. 43, p. 122. This seems an explicit reference to the metaphor of Reason and Love as the two eyes of the soul, which we also find in Hadewijch (see Section 3.3).

[15] All quotations in the remainder of this paragraph are to chapter 53 of *Mirror*, p. 131.

[16] "How dare one say this? I dare not listen to it. I am fainting truly, Lady Soul, in hearing you; my heart is failing. I have no more life." All quotes from chapter 87 of *Mirror*, p. 163. The language of inheritance in Lady Soul's reply comes from feudal culture; see Joanne Robinson's *Nobility and Annihilation in Marguerite Porete's Mirror of Simple Souls* (Albany: State University of New York Press, 2001).

[17] *Mirror*, ch. 135, p. 218. One of the reasons Porete is accused of heresy involves her claim that, at this stage of annihilation, the Soul "does not pray, no more than she did before she was." Her explanation that this is because the soul's union with God is so complete that praying to God would be God praying to Godself, as she notes in ch. 136, did not appease her inquisitors.

TAKING LEAVE OF REASON   75

reason has no place. When Love announces in her final soliloquy that "The whole is one to [the Soul] without an explanation [*propter quid*], and she is nothing in such a one,"[18] she is announcing that such a soul has moved beyond any need for even the highest form of knowledge (*scientia*) achievable via reason, for according to the scholastic logical tradition that takes Aristotle's *Posterior Analytics* as its central textbook, demonstrations *propter quid* are what lead to *scientia* in its strictest sense: necessary truths arrived at via demonstrative syllogisms from premises known a priori.

Although Porete's views were condemned along with her, parts of the *Mirror* (with her name removed) were distributed in Latin and vernacular collections and influenced later contemplatives. The *Mirror*'s most famous influence was on Meister Eckhart's views on detachment and self-abnegation.[19] Eckhart, who lived in the Dominican chapterhouse in Paris during parts of Porete's three-year imprisonment and trial, maintains that one of the most important things we must detach from is our reliance on the natural faculty of reason and the knowledge it produces. In making this claim, moreover, Eckhart sometimes contrasts the knowledge that comes through sense perceptions and reason from the sort of knowing that links us most closely with God. As he comments in Sermon 76:

> The soul has something in it, a spark of intelligence, which never goes out...There also exists in our souls a capacity for knowing external things. This is a knowing through the senses and through reason, that is, a knowing through sensible images and through concepts. Such knowing conceals this other knowing from us. How are we Sons of God? By having one being with him.[20]

---

[18] *Mirror*, ch. 135, p. 218.

[19] For further similarities in their thought and other points of Porete's influence, see the relevant essays in *Meister Eckhart and the Beguine Mystics: Hadewijch of Brabant, Mechthild of Magdeburg, and Marguerite Porete*, ed. B. McGinn (New York: Continuum, 1994).

[20] Sermon 76 in *Meister Eckhart: Teacher and Preacher*, ed. B McGinn, trans. McGinn, F. Tobin, and E. Borgstadt (Mahwah, NJ: Paulist Press, 1986), pp. 327–8.

76 REASON AND ITS LIMITS

Here, as in Porete's *Mirror*, we find the idea that the sort of knowledge which human beings acquire through reason can actively impede the most relevant 'inner' sort of wisdom—something that reason can neither grasp itself nor assist in the recognition of. Detachment releases our hold on individuality so that we can draw closer to this shared being and the corresponding surrender of egoistic self: "If I am to know God without means, without images, and without likeness, God actually has to become me, and I have to become God."[21] Reason may be necessary for negotiating the material world, but on this view the unknowable God utterly transcends human rational faculties (as well as being itself).

We also find this attitude towards reason in some English texts, such as the fourteenth-century *Cloud of Unknowing*. Like Porete and Eckhart, the *Cloud* recognizes reason as one of the principal powers of the human soul; it describes it as a power that "helps us distinguish the evil from the good, the bad from the worse, the good from the better, the worse from the worst, and the better from the best."[22] Yet reason and thought cannot assist us in attaining the heights of union with God. Only love can do this: "No matter how sacred, no thought can ever promise to help you in the work of contemplative prayer, because only love—not knowledge—can help us reach God."[23] The *Book of Privy Counseling* (anonymous but likely written by the same author as the *Cloud*) makes the same point, using the Old Testament story of Rachel, who dies giving birth to Benjamin, to emphasize the importance of self-annihilating contemplative love over human rational powers:

Benjamin represents contemplation, and Rachel represents reason. As soon as seekers of God are touched by genuine contemplation, they work to make themselves nothing and God everything, and in this high, noble decision, it's as if their reason dies ... Benjamin is a symbol

---

[21] Sermon 70 in *The Complete Mystical Works of Meister Eckhart*, trans. Maurice Walshe (New York: Crossroads Publishing Co., 2010).

[22] *The Cloud of Unknowing: with the Book of Privy Counselling*, trans. Carmen Acevedo Butcher (Boulder, CO: Shambhala Publications, 2009), ch. 64, p. 144.

[23] *Cloud*, ch. 8, pp. 28–9.

of all contemplatives who experience the ecstasy of love that takes them beyond the powers of the mind.[24]

3.3 Reason as Guide

The idea that reason itself cannot reach all the way to contemplation of God is a common theme in both contemplative and scholastic texts. Thomas Aquinas begins the *Summa theologiae*, for instance, by distinguishing between knowledge gained by the "light of natural reason" and the knowledge gained by the "light of divine revelation,"[25] arguing that human beings cannot reach their ultimate end relying on reason alone. Yet in contrast to the views discussed in Section 3.2, most contemplatives in the thirteenth–fifteenth centuries view reason as an indispensable help towards attaining that end. Reason can guide us towards God, and it can also increase and deepen our love for God (as opposed to impeding it). In fact, reason is often viewed as an essential component of faith, as well as a faculty we have in common with the Incarnate Christ.

The influential early-twelfth-century Hugh of St. Victor, for instance, maintained that reason both can—and should—bear a close and mutually beneficial relationship to theology and contemplation; Richard of St. Victor expands on this idea in his *Twelve Patriarchs*, painstakingly analogizing each of the figures in the biblical story to illustrate the relation between the various faculties of the human soul and various virtues.[26] Reason is personified as Rachel, the beloved wife of Jacob, while Jacob's less-loved wife, Leah, represents affection and the will. This choice underscores the Victorine emphasis on reason as the most important of the soul's rational faculties: while affection results in virtue, reason results in truth.[27] Illumined directly by God, Rachel/reason's role is "to meditate, to contemplate, to distinguish, and to understand."[28]

---

[24] *The Book of Privy Counselling*, ch. 8, p. 193.   [25] *Summa theologiae* Ia 1.1.ad2.
[26] This work, also known as the *Benjamin minor*, is also loosely paraphrased in English in the fourteenth century as *The Pursuit of Wisdom*.
[27] *Richard of St. Victor*, ch. II, p. 54.   [28] *Richard of St. Victor,* ch. IV, p. 57.

78   REASON AND ITS LIMITS

Reason's natural pursuit of wisdom is identified as our proper goal in this life. Yet, just as the matriarch Rachel dies giving birth to her son Benjamin, so reason is ultimately superseded in the highest form of contemplation: "The mind, having been carried away to contemplation [by the light of divinity], experiences how great the failure of human reason is. Let no person suppose that he is able to penetrate to the splendor of that divine light by argumentation; let no person believe that he is able to comprehend it by human reasoning."[29] God's illumination and grace must bridge the gap between human capacities and vision of the divine essence: the intellective union with God that the Victorines portray as our final end is not one in which discursive reason and argumentation can play a part. At the same time, it is reason (rather than the will) that is understood as the highest among natural human faculties on this view, and it is reason (rather than love) that is directly responsible for the work that ultimately gives birth to contemplation of God.

A quite different personification of reason plays a similar role in Alan of Lille's late-twelfth-century allegorical poem *Anticlaudianus*. At the outset of the poem, Nature decides she wants to make an ideal human being but soon realizes that the soul for this human being will need to be created directly by God. It is Reason who then devises a plan for requesting this soul from God: she suggests that Phronesis (practical wisdom or prudence) be the messenger, and she commissions the seven liberal arts to build a chariot in which Phronesis can go to heaven and make Nature's request. Once the chariot is constructed, Reason harnesses the five senses to it as horses, and she begins to drive Phronesis towards God. When they reach the end of the created universe, however, the senses refuse to go farther, and Reason herself falters. Eventually, Phronesis goes ahead with the help of Theology and Faith, with Reason rejoining her for the return journey.

Although Reason's skill in negotiating the material world and in progressing via immaterial truths gained from the material world cannot take us all the way to union with God, Reason is still portrayed as the

---

[29] *Richard of St. Victor,* ch. LXXIV, p. 131. Richard also reiterates the role of self-knowledge in reaching the apex of unitive contemplation: "Do you now see how much the ascent of this mountain is effective, how useful full knowledge of self is?" (ch. LXXVIII, p. 136).

most important of the human rational faculties—without her, there would be no plan, no vehicle for leading Phronesis towards God, and no forward motion for that vehicle. The highest form of contemplation is born from reason, not affection or the will, and practical wisdom is a virtue closely related to reason. In this way, Richard of St. Victor's and Alan of Lille's texts exemplify themes common to many twelfth- and thirteenth-century scholastic texts. Reason allows us to transcend the material world of particulars and to access the realm of immaterial truths and immaterial beings; at the same time (as we saw Aquinas note above), the natural light of reason is not enough in itself to connect us to God in a way that fully satisfies either our intellects or our wills. According to the Victorines and Aquinas, the only thing that can satisfy both perfectly is everlasting contemplation of God's essence—an act which God makes possible via grace and illumination of our intellects.[30]

When Lady Reason appears as the first of the three virtues who helps Christine de Pizan build the City of Ladies, then, Pizan is directly referencing a robust tradition.[31] Although *The City of Ladies* is (like the *Anticlaudianus*) not a contemplative text per se, Pizan's personification of Reason—who is identified as a daughter of God—draws on a number of contemplative and philosophical tropes. In addition to channeling Boethius's Lady Philosophy in both appearance and manner of address, for instance, Reason also carries the mirror of self-knowledge instead of a scepter. (See Figure 3.1.) As Reason tells Christine, "No one can look into this mirror, no matter what kind of creature, without achieving clear self-knowledge.... Thanks to this mirror, the essences, qualities, proportions, and measures of all things are known, nor can anything be done well without it."[32] Reason then tells the stories of a host of women who are celebrated for their knowledge, wisdom, and scientific

---

[30] For further discussion of Aquinas's conception of our final end, see my "Aquinas's Shiny Happy People: Perfect Happiness and the Limits of Human Nature," in *Oxford Studies in the Philosophy of Religion Vol. 6*, ed. J. Kvanvig (Oxford: Oxford University Press, 2015), pp. 269–91.

[31] Reason, Rectitude, and Justice each take on different roles in constructing the city: Reason's primary role is to help Christine clear away the ground and lay the foundations of the city, while Rectitude helps her construct the walls, and Justice helps build the turrets and fortifications.

[32] Christine de Pizan, *The Book of the City of Ladies*, trans. Earl Richards (New York: Persea Books, 1982, rev. 1998), p. 9.

80 REASON AND ITS LIMITS

Figure 3.1 Lady Reason with mirror and laying foundation with Christine, Cité des dames, c.1410–14, Harley MS 4431, f. 290r, British Library.

innovations and discoveries. In this way, she helps Christine lay the foundation of her city, in which women can live safely, and to whose fortress (completed by Rectitude and Justice) the Queen of Reason—the Virgin Mary—is welcomed.

Reason is also frequently portrayed in contemplative texts as helping the will's proper work (namely, desiring the good, whose ultimate manifestation is God). Aquinas's contemporary Bonaventure, for instance, agrees that the knowledge we acquire through rational investigation is distinct from knowledge we gain via doctrine or revelation.[33] Yet Bonaventure is not inclined to give intellect supreme place among our rational faculties. Instead, he identifies the will as the soul's noblest faculty and accordingly stresses the role of the will and love in attaining our ultimate end. (In this, he is joined by a number of thirteenth–fifteenth-century contemplatives and later Franciscans such as, famously, Duns Scotus.) The claim that love is more central than reason in attaining our ultimate end is importantly different, however,

---

[33] See, e.g., his *Commentary on Ecclesiastes* 1.

from the claim of Porete, Eckhart, and Tauler that natural reason *impedes* the love by which we are united to God. In fact, a number of mystics famous for their emphasis on the power and primacy of love— including Hadewijch, Catherine of Siena, and Julian of Norwich—view the faculty of reason as able both to assist and to enhance that love.

Hadewijch, for instance, portrays our ultimate end as the 'fruition of love' in which we can "be God with God"[34]—but she makes it clear that this end is not one we can reach without relying extensively on reason's guidance. As she writes in a letter of advice, "The power of [inner] sight has two eyes: love and reason.... These two are of great mutual help to the other; for reason instructs love, and love enlightens reason. When reason abandons itself to love's wish, and love consents to be forced and held within the bounds of reason, they can accomplish a very great work."[35] Love is a powerful motivating and unifying force, but it needs reason both to hold it in check and to direct it towards its proper end. In another letter, Hadewijch explains that we need wisdom as well as desire to fulfill love's quest: "This is why the bride of whom we read in the *Song of Songs* (3:4) sought her Bridegroom not only with desire but with wisdom; and when she had found him, she was no less anxious to hold him. Every wise soul who has been strongly stirred by love should be likewise."[36] On this view, reason does not damp down but, rather, fans the flames of rightly directed love.

Hadewijch also regularly portrays reason as helping the soul attain its highest end—love's union with the Beloved (God)—in her poems. Employing tropes of *fin'amor* to create a new genre, called *minnemystik* (see also Interlude 4), Hadewijch casts the searching soul as a knight and Reason as a cautionary voice who ultimately holds the key to reaching the culmination of Love.[37] In one poem, Reason seems at first unsympathetic with the soul's quest for Love: when the soul comes crying to Reason for advice after being abandoned by Love, Reason says,

---

[34] *Hadewijch: The Complete Works.* ed. and trans. Mother Columba Hart (Mahwah: Paulist Press, 1980), p. 280.

[35] *Hadewijch*, Letter 18, p. 86.   [36] *Hadewijch,* Letter 10, p. 68.

[37] For more on her use of this genre, and its influence on other contemplatives, see Barbara Newman's *From Virile Woman to Woman Christ: Studies in Medieval Religion and Literature.* (Philadelphia: University of Pennsylvania Press, 1995).

82 REASON AND ITS LIMITS

"Reflect that you are still a human being!," strips the soul of the fine clothing Love had given her, and teaches her to "live the truth." Eventually, however, the soul develops self-knowledge and—armed with this truth—continues her quest for genuine, lasting union with Love. The poem ends with a stanza explaining that perfect love requires the assistance of reason:

> May God grant to all who love
> That they may win the favor of Reason,
> By which they may know
> How fruition of Love is attained.
> In winning the favor of Reason
> Lies for us the whole perfection of Love.[38]

In another poem, Hadewijch describes reason's role as making it clear to the soul where she is falling short in her status as "loved one for the Beloved." This role is both painful and necessary. Reason is described as Love's surgeon (the most skilled of physicians in this period), who cuts as well as heals in guiding us towards our ultimate end:

> Reason herself is Love's surgeoness:
> She can best heal all faults against Love.
> To him who adroitly follows all Reason's moves,
> In all the ways in which she leads him,
> She will speak of new wonders:
> "Behold! Take possession of the highest glory!"[39]

The figure of reason also appears as both vital for and subordinate to the fulfillment of Love in several of Hadewijch's visions. In Vision 9, for instance, Hadewijch sees Reason as a queen attended by three hand-maids: Holy Fear, who keeps track of our progress in the 'life of love'; Discernment, who distinguishes Love's will, kingdom, and pleasure from Reason's; and Wisdom, who allows us to perceive how great

---

[38] Hadewijch, Poem 30: "Love and Reason," p. 215.
[39] Hadewijch, Poem 25: "Reason, Pleasure, and Desire," pp. 198–9.

REASON AS GUIDE   83

Reason's power and works are when Reason lets herself be led by Love.[40] Reason initially dominates Hadewijch by putting her foot on her throat but becomes subject to Hadewijch once she is named, and the vision ends with Hadewijch lost in the embrace of Love. In Vision 12, Hadewijch sees Reason as one of twelve attendants who prepare the loving soul for union with her Beloved (God). Reason's role here is to guide and remind the soul of what God wants.[41] As the bride, clad in a robe "made of her undivided and perfect will," approaches the throne, Hadewijch sees that she herself is that bride and experiences love's fulfillment in union with God. Throughout Hadewijch's works, reason guides us all the way to our highest end: love's ultimate union with the Beloved.

Catherine of Siena also emphasizes the role of reason in attaining the "perfection of [the] unitive state in which souls are carried off by the fire of love." Her *Dialogue*, for instance, describes knowledge and love as an upward spiral: "For love follows upon understanding. The more they know, the more they love, and the more they love, the more they know. Thus each nourishes the other."[42] Artistic representations from this period sometimes portray this dual relationship by having cherubim and seraphim (the highest orders of the angels, associated with wisdom and love and typically portrayed as blue and red) appear around Mary or Christ. (See Figure 3.2, in which Mary, surrounded by cherubim and seraphim, holds the infant Jesus while the Magi pay their respects.) An emphasis on the mutually beneficial relationship between love and knowledge is one of the hallmarks of Catherine's works; in this, she echoes not just Thomas Aquinas's conception of the Beatific Vision but also Dante's early-fourteenth-century *Paradiso*. Catherine's image of the tree of self (see Chapter 2) has rational discernment grafted right into the trunk of charity,[43] and God's favorite expression for human beings in

---

[40] Hadewijch, Vision 9, pp. 285–6.
[41] Hadewijch, Vision 12, p. 295. Wisdom is also present in this vision, "familiar with all the power of every perfect virtue that must be encountered in order to content the Beloved perfectly. Wisdom showed that she also had profound knowledge of each Person of the Trinity in Unity."
[42] *Dialogue*, ch. 85, pp. 157–8.
[43] "For discernment and charity are engrafted together and planted in the soil of that true humility which is born of self-knowledge." *Dialogue*, ch. 9, p. 41.

Figure 3.2 Detail of *Adoration of the Magi*, Andrea Mantegna, mid-fifteenth century, Uffizi Gallery, Florence.

the *Dialogue* is "*la mia creatura che à in sé ragione*," (as when God entreats Catherine to "Open your mind's eye and look within me," for then she will see the "dignity and beauty of my creature who has reason within herself").[44] Love unites us with God on this picture, but it is reason that leads the way.

Reason is also vital for faith for many of these contemplatives. Catherine, for instance, writes that "it is in reason that the light of faith is held, and one cannot lose the one without losing the other."[45] She supports this claim by arguing that the groundwork for faith is created in us as part of the *imago Dei*. We see God when we look into ourselves, and a central part of what we see is reason. As the *Dialogue* immediately continues, in God's voice: "I made the soul after my own image and likeness, giving her memory, understanding, and will." Memory, understanding, and will are all rational capacities, as we saw in Section 3.1, famously linked together in trinitarian form by Augustine—and a standard way by the thirteenth century of explaining the relation between and

---

[44] *Dialogue*, Prologue, p. 26.   [45] *Dialogue*, ch. 51, p. 103.

REASON AS GUIDE 85

use of those faculties.[46] Drawing on this same trio, the late-fourteenth–
early-fifteenth-century English anchorite Julian of Norwich describes
our faith as "a combination of the natural love of the soul, the clear light
of reason, and the steadfast remembrance of God instilled in us when
we were created."[47] Rather than impeding faith, on this view reason is
central to its flourishing. On Aquinas's view, for instance, God's grace
completes rather than destroys human nature, allowing reason a role
even in areas reason can't attain on its own. The realm of faith (and
theology) is one in which reason examines matters that lie beyond its
natural powers via God's grace.[48]

Contemplatives who embrace rather than eschew reason's ongoing
role in the spiritual life also tend to stress the humanity of the incarnate
Christ as a point of connection between us and the Triune God.[49]
Hadewijch, for example, consoles a fellow beguine by linking the hard
work and suffering of Christ's human life with the eternal enjoyment of
Christ's divinity: "With the Humanity of God you must live here on
earth, in the labors and sorrow of exile, while within your soul you love
and rejoice with the omnipotent and eternal Divinity in sweet abandon-
ment. For the truth of both is one single fruition."[50] Catherine of Siena
makes a similar point when she describes a vision of Christ in which he
appeared as a tree reaching to heaven but grounded in humanity:
"I [Christ] showed myself to you under the figure of a tree. You could see
neither its bottom nor its top. But you saw that its root was joined to the
earth—and this was the divine nature joined to the earth of your
humanity."[51] Earlier in the *Dialogue*, Catherine describes the humanity

---

[46] See, e.g., *De trinitate*, Book XV, chs 20–14.

[47] *Showings*, ch. 55, p. 151. Julian is perhaps drawing explicitly on Catherine's *Dialogue* here,
as it was translated into English (as the *Orchard of Sion*).

[48] Not surprisingly, given his conception of our ultimate end, Aquinas's influential account
of faith portrays it as a primarily intellective (rather than volitional) virtue. See, e.g., *Summa
theologiae* IIaIIae 1, particularly 1.1.

[49] This tendency is not universal, though. Eckhart also stresses the role of Christ's humanity
in joining us to God, but in a way that requires us to empty ourselves of any individuality: "So,
since God dwells eternally in the ground of the Father, and I in him, one ground and the same
Christ, as a single bearer of my humanity, then this (humanity) is as much mine as his in one
substance of eternal being, so that the being of both, body and soul, attain perfection in one
Christ, as one God, one Son" (Sermon 70, quoted in McGinn's *Varieties of Vernacular
Mysticism*, pp. 359–60).

[50] *Hadewijch*, Letter 6, p. 59. See also Vision 7.   [51] *Dialogue*, ch. 44, p. 90.

86 REASON AND ITS LIMITS

of Christ—and therefore all human beings—as inextricably mixed with the divinity of God: "When my Son was lifted up on the wood of the most holy cross, he did not cut off his divinity from the lowly earth of your humanity. So though he was raised so high he was not raised off the earth. In fact, his divinity is kneaded into the clay of your humanity like one bread."[52] This homely metaphor of divinity kneaded together with humanity makes a profound theological point; Catherine is consistent in her emphasis on the restoration of all our human faculties through Christ.

Julian of Norwich also stresses the restoration of humanity and human faculties through the Incarnation. Her initial vision is of Christ's head bleeding profusely from the crown of thorns, and the 'dearworthy' blood of Jesus plays a crucial role in her *Showings*; it is his taking on human nature that allows our 'sensuality' (sensory bodies) and all their faculties to be redeemed. Julian's Long Text spends a significant amount of time musing on the Trinity, in which the Second Person (Christ) is consistently linked with knowledge and wisdom. As she writes in chapter 58, "In the Second Person, in knowledge and wisdom, we have our perfection as regards our sensuality, our restoration and our salvation, for he is our Mother, brother, and savior."[53] Rather than advocating the need to annihilate reason, Julian sees not only our rational faculties but also our bodies as important points of connection to the God with whom we unite in our final end.

3.4 Reason as Enhanced by Mystical Union

To this point, I've focused primarily on the role reason plays in helping us attain our ultimate end, for that is the area in which we see most clearly the range of contemplative perspectives on the topic; yet reason

---

[52] *Dialogue*, ch. 26, p. 65.
[53] *Showings*, ch. 58. Julian's late-fourteenth-century depiction of Jesus as mother is part of medieval tradition that can also be found in the works of Bernard of Clairvaux and Marguerite d'Oingt (see, e.g., Marguerite's description of the crucifixion as Christ giving birth to the world in Section 3.2). Caroline Walker Bynum's groundbreaking and exhaustive study of this topic remains a classic: "Jesus as Mother" in *Jesus as Mother: Studies in the Spirituality of the High Middle Ages* (Berkeley: University of California Press, 1982).

REASON AS ENHANCED BY MYSTICAL UNION   87

appears on the 'receiving' end of this equation as well. Mystical union is regularly portrayed in the twelfth–fifteenth centuries (in a wide range of geographic regions, religious orders, and languages) as both resulting in practical and theoretical knowledge and increasing rational abilities in ways that grant their subjects authority to instruct and counsel others, as well as providing insight into God's nature. Julian, for instance, reports being enlightened—rather than awed to apophatic silence—by the mystical experience she recounts in the *Showings* or *Revelations of Divine Love*. She reworks her original 'short' text over the following twenty years, incorporating the continued insights her experience continues to grant her. This 'long' text, which is approximately six times as long as the earlier version, is theologically rich, complex, and highly influential.[54] For contemplatives like Julian, mystical union does not render rational powers moot (or mute), but rather fulfills and enhances them.

The late-thirteenth-century Cistercian nun Gertrude of Helfta, for instance, describes the divine inspiration she receives as allowing her to effortlessly write "of things which I did not know before, as though it were a lesson long since learned by heart."[55] Angela of Foligno, a Franciscan tertiary, also testifies that her experiences of mystical union grant her theological insights she did not previously possess. In fact, Angela explains that when she is present at the 'secret levels' of God, she gains a profound understanding of Scripture:

> Because my soul is often elevated into the secret levels of God and sees the divine secrets, I am able to understand how the Scriptures were written; how they are made easy and difficult; how they seem to say something and contradict it; how some derive no profit from them; how those who do not observe them are damned and Scripture is fulfilled in them; and how others who observe them are saved by them.[56]

---

[54] It is also offered to the reader as the work of an "unlettered" creature whose wisdom comes directly from God. For more on the connection between love, wisdom, and authority, see Section 3.4; for use of humility formulae by women in this period, see Interlude 5.

[55] *Gertrude of Helfta: The Herald of Divine Love*, trans. and ed. Margaret Winkworth (Mahwah: Paulist Press, 1993), ch. 10, p. 110.

[56] *Memorial* IX, p. 214.

88 REASON AND ITS LIMITS

This claim seems hubristic (to say the least), but Angela is quick both to attribute such knowledge to direct contact with God and to explain that the knowledge remains in its purest form only as long as her experience of union lasts. As the experience fades, she says, she loses the ability to put the knowledge into words.[57]

At the same time, Angela also claims that she is united with Christ (whom she also calls 'the God-man') "almost continually" and that he often speaks to her in this state. In that condition, she says, "I see myself as alone with God, totally cleansed, totally sanctified, totally true, totally upright, totally certain, totally celestial in him."[58] Reason is not transcended in this form of union, although it involves mutual 'resting' in each other: "On one occasion, when I was in that state, God told me: 'Daughter of divine wisdom, temple of the beloved, beloved of the beloved, daughter of peace, in you rests the entire Trinity; indeed, the complete truth rests in you, so that you hold me and I hold you.'"[59] This statement echoes the self-abnegating language that we saw from Porete and Eckhart in Subsection 3.2, where we can become God in the sense that we empty ourselves so completely that there is nothing left of us as human individuals, but here it appears more as self-fulfillment than self-annihilation. Later, Angela describes the knowledge she gains from these conversations with God as including both her understanding of and love for the Eucharist: "One of the effects of that state in my soul is to greatly increase my delight and understanding of how God comes into the sacrament of the altar accompanied by his host."[60]

The practical effects of mystical union are underappreciated in most studies of the topic, but in the case of many medieval mystics they are also striking. Julian of Norwich, for instance, becomes so famous a spiritual advisor despite her enclosure in an anchorage that people—most famously Margery Kempe—come from miles away to seek her counsel. A particularly notable example of the practical effects of mystical union can be found in the case of Margaret Ebner, an early-fourteenth-century

---

[57] "When I return to myself after perceiving these divine secrets, I can say some words with security about them, but then I speak entirely from outside the experience, and say words that come nowhere near describing the divine workings that are produced in my soul. My statements about them ruin the reality they represent." *Memorial* IX, p. 214.

[58] *Memorial* IX, p. 215.   [59] Ibid.   [60] Ibid.

REASON AS ENHANCED BY MYSTICAL UNION   89

German Dominican nun,[61] who reports receiving a gift of "divine understanding" that has enhanced her rational powers to the point where she has become the subject of much conversation:

> The next day I was very sick and began to wonder about what was happening to me. I perceived well what it was. It came from my heart and I feared for my senses now and then whenever it was so intense. But I was answered by the presence of God with sweet delight, "I am no robber of the senses, I am the enlightener of the senses." I received a great grace from the inner goodness of God; the light of truth of divine understanding. Also, my mind became more rational than before, so that I had the grace to be able to phrase all my speech better and also to understand better all speech according to the truth. Since then I am often talked about.[62]

Margaret's experience is significant along several dimensions. First, the self-knowledge she demonstrates at the outset allows her to hear God's reassurance. Second, the reassurance that God is an 'enlightener' rather than a 'robber' of the senses (a phrase which also appears later in the *Revelations*) highlights fulfillment of self as opposed to its annihilation.[63]

Most importantly for our purposes, the gift of wisdom Margaret receives is explicitly linked to increased rational abilities. She even offers external support for her claims—the fact that she is now "often talked about." She also explains later that this gift allows her to "understand, read, and write" what she could not before, as well as to tell when someone is either lying or unaware of their true intentions: "And a new understanding of truth was granted me, with which I can often detect

---

[61] Not to be confused with the similarly named Christina Ebner, Margaret Ebner is remembered today primarily for her correspondences with Henry Nördlingen and Johannes Tauler, leaders of the Friends of God movement.

[62] *Margaret Ebner: Major Works*, trans. and ed. Leonard Hindsley (Mahwah: Paulist Press, 1993), p.100.

[63] It's unclear from the text whether Margaret is referring here to the inner or the outer senses—about which see Patricia Dailey's "The Body and Its Senses," in *The Cambridge Companion to Christian Mysticism*, ed. A. Hollywood and P. Dailey (Cambridge: Cambridge University Press, 2012), pp. 264–76—but the restoration of either (or both) is quite different from the total annihilation that Porete counsels.

90 REASON AND ITS LIMITS

when someone speaks untruthfully in my presence....Sometimes I notice that someone intends these things in the heart differently from what comes out of the mouth. Then I respond according to the intention and not to the words."[64] In Ebner's case, as in the others, the beneficial effects of divinely enhanced reason extend beyond the individual to her broader community.

3.5 *Scientia* vs. *Sapientia*

Medieval contemplative conceptions of the relation between reason and our final end are far more complex than often acknowledged. Rather than uniformly counseling us to abandon reason on the path towards selfless union with the Divine, contemplatives in the twelfth–fifteenth centuries advocate taking a variety of attitudes towards reason and report having a variety of unitive experiences with respect to it. (See Chapter 5 for a discussion of such unitive experiences as foretastes of immortality.) At the same time, the need for formal education and technical knowledge (*scientia*) become increasingly portrayed as extraneous to the contemplative life over the course of the thirteenth and fourteenth centuries.

The medieval use of *scientia* as both a general and a specific term reaches back to Augustine, who uses it broadly to refer to human knowledge of the truth and narrowly to refer to knowledge of changing, material realities (in opposition to *sapientia* or wisdom, which refers to knowledge of eternal, unchanging divine truths).[65] By the twelfth century, *scientia* is widely used as a general word for 'knowledge'; it gains new technical significance in the thirteenth century, however, once the Latin translation of Aristotle's *Posterior Analytics* begins to be intensively studied in the universities.[66] As *scientia* becomes increasingly associated with university debates, however, there is a general move away from

---

[64] *Margaret Ebner*, p. 155.   [65] See, e.g., *De Trinitate* XII chs 14–15.
[66] For more about the development of *scientia* in this period, see Robert Pasnau's "Medieval Social Epistemology: *Scientia* for Mere Mortals," *Episteme* 7/1 (2010), pp. 23–41.

SCIENTIA VS. SAPIENTIA   91

incorporating either its technical or general understanding into the contemplative life—part of the well-documented shift in this period towards what's often called 'personal piety.'[67]

In Marguerite Porete's *The Mirror of Simple Souls*, for instance, a crucial component of what we need to renounce is knowledge or scientific understanding: "The whole is one to her without an explanation [*propter quid*], and she is nothing in such a one."[68] The use of the phrase "*propter quid*" here is significant because, according to the Aristotelian medieval logical tradition, demonstrations *propter quid* are what lead to *scientia* in its technical sense—that is, a necessary conclusion reached by means of a demonstrative syllogism whose premises are known a priori. Henry Suso's *Wisdom's Watch upon the Hours* (*Horologium Sapientiae*) also warns against intellectual pride and encourages a simple, humble devotion as the route to marriage with divine Wisdom (understood both as the figure from scriptural wisdom literature and as the second person of the Trinity).[69] Lay disenchantment with *scientia* in the later Middle Ages is widespread: the Latin text of the fourteenth-century English *Cloud of Unknowing* draws an explicit distinction between *scientia* and *sapientia*, contrasting worldly or scientific knowledge with the wisdom that comes from loving God, and Thomas à Kempis's fifteenth-century *De Imitatione Christi*—one of the most popular devotional books of the Middle Ages—stresses virtue and a life of love over academic knowledge. As Kempis remarks, "What good is a brilliant argument about hidden and obscure matters when God does not judge us by our knowledge of such

---

[67] See Herbert Grundmann's groundbreaking 1935 study, translated from the German and published as *Religious Movements in the Middle Ages: The Historical Links between Heresy, the Mendicant Orders, and the Women's Religious Movement in the Twelfth and Thirteenth Century, with the Historical Foundations of German* Mysticism (Notre Dame, IN: University of Notre Dame Press, 1995); Bernard McGinn's *The Flowering of Mysticism: Men and Women in the New Mysticism—1200–1350. Vol. III of The Presence of God: A History of Western Christian Mysticism* (New York: Crossroad Publishing Co., 1998); and Caroline Walker Bynum's *Fragmentation and Redemption: Essays on Gender and the Human Body in Medieval Religion* (New York: Zone Books, 1992).

[68] *Mirror*, ch. 135, p. 218

[69] See Barbara Newman's "Sapientia: the Goddess Incarnate," in *God and the Goddesses: Vision, Poetry, and Belief in the Middle Ages* (Philadelphia: University of Pennsylvania Press, 2003), pp. 190–244, for a detailed discussion of this dual identification, particularly in the works on Henry Suso and Julian of Norwich.

92 REASON AND ITS LIMITS

things?...Why should we bother about clever arguments and subtle reasoning?"[70]

The idea that formal education and *scientia* are extraneous to attaining wisdom is summed up brilliantly in a passage from Book II of Mechthild of Magdeburg's *Flowing Light of the Godhead* (part of which we saw in Subsection 3.2). After she expresses worry about her status as an 'unlearned' woman, God assures Mechthild that all will be well:

> Daughter, many a wise man, because of negligence
> On a big highway, has lost his precious gold
> With which he was hoping to go to a famous school.
> Someone is going to find it.
> By nature I have acted accordingly many a day.
> Wherever I bestowed special favors,
> I always sought out the lowest, most insignificant, and
> most unknown place for them.
>
> ...
>
> It is a great honor for me with regard to them, and it
> very much strengthens Holy Christianity
> That the unlearned mouth, aided by my Holy Spirit,
> teaches the learned tongue.[71]

In short, the path to God is open to anyone who is willing to follow it. In Chapter 4 we'll see the central role that the will and love come to play in finding and following this path.

---

[70] *The Imitation of Christ*, trans. William C. Creasy (Notre Dame, IN: Ave Maria Press, 2017), Book 1, ch. 3, p. 28.
[71] *Flowing Light of the Godhead*, Book II, pp. 97–8.

Interlude Three

When Did Reading Become a Sign of Religious Devotion for Women?

For those (like me) who were taught that women weren't generally allowed to read or write in the Middle Ages, it is striking how frequently medieval women are portrayed in religious art from the thirteenth to fifteenth centuries as holding, reading, and even writing books. (See Figure I3.1, in which St. Humility instructs her sisters are they write; Figure I3.2, in which Mary composes her Magnificat; and Figure I1.2, in which Bridget of Sweden writes her *Revelations*.) These images appear everywhere from Sweden, Germany, and the Low Countries to France, Italy, and beyond, and they appear in all types of media: statuary, stained glass, paintings, altarpieces, carvings, frescoes, illuminated manuscripts, etc. Mary is the woman most often portrayed this way, both because of her status as the mother of Christ—referred to at the outset of John's gospel as the *Logos*, typically translated as 'the Word'—and because

Figure I3.1 Detail of *Saint Humility and Scenes from Her Life*, Pietro Lorenzetti, *c*.1335–40, Uffizi Gallery, Florence.

94   REASON AND ITS LIMITS

Figure I3.2 *Madonna of the Magnificat*, Sandro Botticelli, 1483, Uffizi Gallery, Florence.

of her association with wisdom.[72] (See Figure I3.3, in which Mary has multiple books open in front of her as the Holy Spirit descends, as well as Figures 4.1, 4.2, and 4.4.) Yet Mary is hardly unique in this respect. The iconography of any number of female saints also includes books— St. Barbara, one of the patron saints of the Catholic Church, typically holds the church in one hand and a book in the other, for instance, while Catherine of Alexandria, a patron saint of the Dominican Order

---

[72] See Barbara Newman's "Sapientia: the Goddess Incarnate," in *God and the Goddesses: Vision, Poetry, and Belief in the Middle Ages* (Philadelphia: University of Pennsylvania Press, 2003), pp. 190–244.

WHEN DID READING BECOME A SIGN OF RELIGIOUS   95

Figure I3.3 Annunciation of Mary with reading tree and multiple books, Orsini Castle, Bracciano.

celebrated for having refuted no fewer than fifty pagan philosophers before being stretched on the wheel and finally decapitated, is frequently shown reading a book while standing atop one of the men she has refuted. (See Figure I3.4.) As reading becomes an activity increasingly associated with female piety in the later Middle Ages, women are increasingly represented as holding or reading books as a way of signifying their devotion to God.[73]

---

[73] As Richard Kieckhefer comments in his "Holiness and the Culture of Devotion: Remarks on Some Late Medieval Male Saints": "We know that devotional reading figured prominently in the urban religious culture of the era. Paul Saenger has shown, however, that in the late Middle Ages reading was increasingly associated with inward piety, of a sort that we see most

96 REASON AND ITS LIMITS

Figure I3.4 *St. Catherine of Alexandria*, workshop of Jan Crocq, c.1475–1525, Metropolitan Museum of Art, New York.

The prevalence of such images in public spaces is particularly significant. In contrast to illustrations in manuscripts, which would have viewed by relatively few people (typically of higher social stations), art in churches, cathedrals, and municipal buildings was available to everyone and explicitly meant for the edification of those who saw it.[74] At

---

often in women's vitae. This is not to suggest that pious women read more than men did, or that the content of the books was less important for men than for women. Rather, it may be that the *activity* of reading was in closer accord with the central themes of women's piety than with those of men's, and perhaps for that reason the men's biographers pass over the matter in silence." In *Images of Sainthood in Medieval Europe*, ed. R. Blumenfeld-Kosinski and T. Szell (Ithaca: Cornell University Press, 1991), p. 302.

[74] A visit to surviving cathedrals from thirteenth-fifteenth centuries and museums which contain medieval religious artifacts provides rich illustration of how this worked: the statuary, the figures in stained glass windows, the altarpieces, and the vestments of the priests elaborately

WHEN DID READING BECOME A SIGN OF RELIGIOUS   97

popular sites such as Chartres, St. Denis, Siena, and Canterbury, these images would have been seen by thousands of pilgrims on a yearly basis and also copied and used for instruction back home.[75] The elaborately inlaid marble floor of the duomo at Siena, for instance, contains large panels of each of the seven Sybils (prophetic wise women from each of the 'known' geographic realms who were said to have predicted Christ's coming) with books and/or scrolls; the Libyan Sibyl holds a book in one hand and a scroll in the other. (See Figure I3.5.)

It is not, of course, only religious *women* who are associated with books in this period: religious men are also frequently shown holding, reading, and/or writing books. Indeed, the statuary and stained-glass windows in many Gothic cathedrals depict both men and women holding books, in parallel poses. The cathedral of St. Denis, for instance, contains a series of stained-glass windows portraying famous biblical and historical figures, particularly royalty, with books in their hands, while the cathedral of Chartres also features a similar series of stained-glass windows. At Chartres, in fact, it would have been (and still is) impossible to go through the cathedral's main entrance without passing through ranks of enormous statues of crowned men and women, all of whom hold books or scrolls that herald the coming of Christ (see Figure I3.6). We find men and women holding books in parallel poses in the remaining statuary at the cathedral of Reims from this era as well.[76] (See Figure I3.7.) Using books to symbolize the wisdom passed from God to these people and then shared for the edification of all both reinforces the importance of the written word in religious life and supports the impression that God shares this wisdom with women and men alike.

embroidered with Biblical stories on their backs (the part which would have been facing the congregants during the celebration of the Eucharist) all share a common visual rhetoric meant to instruct their viewers about the do's and don't's of piety.

[75] The extensive decoration of cathedrals with human figures in this period is a distinct departure from the earlier Middles Ages, during which, as Sara Lipton notes in *Dark Mirror: The Medieval Origins of Anti-Jewish Iconography* (New York City: Metropolitan Books, 2014): "for various reasons (including the relative scarcity of surplus wealth; unease about depicting divinity spurred by still powerful memories of antique paganism, the debate over icon worship raging in the Byzantine Empire, and Muslim hostility to divine images; loss of technical expertise; and the ascendancy of nonrepresentational Germanic and Celtic artistic traditions), art was only fitfully and hesitantly enlisted as a way to experience God. This situation changed radically in the high Middle Ages" p. 6.

[76] For detailed discussion of the development and significance of the figures at Chartres and Reims, see Jacqueline Jung's *Eloquent Bodies: Movement, Expression, and the Human Figure in Gothic Sculpture* (New Haven and London: Yale University Press, 2020).

98   REASON AND ITS LIMITS

Figure I3.5 *The Libyan Sibyl*, Guidoccio Cozzarelli, c.1482–3, floor of Siena Duomo.

Not surprisingly, given the predominance of this imagery and its roots in the centrality of Scripture in the Abrahamic faiths, books also play an important role in the visionary literature of many medieval contemplative women. In her *Mirror*, for instance, Marguerite d'Oingt writes that she has taken such care to "write into her heart" the life of Christ that "it sometimes seemed to her that He was present and that he held a closed book in His hand in order to teach from it"—an image that would have been deeply familiar to her readers.[77] In the first chapter of

---

[77] *Marguerite of Oingt*, pp. 41–2.

WHEN DID READING BECOME A SIGN OF RELIGIOUS 99

Figure I3.6 The "Royal Portal," 1150–70, west transept, Chartres Cathedral.

Figure I3.7 Detail of statuary, c.1225–30, north portal, Reims Cathedral.

100   REASON AND ITS LIMITS

the *Mirror*, Marguerite can see and read only the outside of this book, which is "completely covered in white, black, and red letters" with clasps that "had golden letters on them"; as she makes spiritual progress, however, the book opens and she can see inside, finding "a delightful place, so large that the entire world seems small by comparison" illuminated by "a glorious light which divided itself into three parts, like three persons."[78]

The Middle Ages see a dramatic increase in contemplative writing from the mid-thirteenth century onward, and women were involved in every aspect of development. In addition to being "avid collectors, readers, and critics of the vast amount of devotional literature produced in the fourteenth and fifteenth centuries,"[79] women also authored, recorded, and transmitted popular and influential texts throughout this period.[80] The high demand for pocket Bibles, books of hours, and meditative literature for personal devotional use implies that the women who commissioned these works both could and would read them, and the 'sister-books' and convent chronicles generated by and shared between communities of religious women (for example, nuns, beguines, and tertiaries) testify to their active participation in producing such literature.[81] If we look at the women presented to them visually as models of piety, it should come as no surprise that these visionaries would have felt approval for their activities.

---

[78] *Marguerite of Oingt*, pp. 43–4. For more on the significance of these images, see Sergi Sancho Filba's "Colors and Books in Marguerite d'Oingt's Speculum. Images for Meditation and Vision," in *Commitments to Medieval Mysticism within Contemporary Contexts* (Bibliotheca Ephemeridum Theologicarum Lovaniensium, Peeters, 2017), 255–71.

[79] David Bornstein, "Women and Religion in Late Medieval Italy: History and Historiography," in *Women and Religion in Medieval and Renaissance Italy*, ed. D Bornstein and R. Rusconi, trans. Margery Schneider (Chicago: University of Chicago Press, 1996), p. 4.

[80] See Vols 3 through 5 of Bernard McGinn's compendious *The Presence of God: A History of Western Christian Mysticism*: namely, Vol. 3: *The Flowering of Mysticism: Men and Women in the New Mysticism—1200–1350* (New York: Crossroad Publishing Co., 1998); Vol. 4: *The Harvest of Mysticism in Medieval Germany (1300–1500)* (2005); and Vol. 5: *Varieties of Vernacular Mysticism: 1350–1550* (2016).

[81] See Anne Winston-Allen's *Convent Chronicles: Women Writing about Women and Reform in the Late Middle Ages*. (University Park, PA: University of Pennsylvania Press, 2004); for a discussion of women's writing before the thirteenth century, see Diane Watt's *Women, Writing, and Religion in England and Beyond, 650–1100*. Studies in Early Medieval History. (London: Bloomsbury Academic, 2019).

4

Love and the Will

The French contemplative Marguerite Porete (d.1310) begins her *Mirror of Simple Souls* with a cautionary poem:

> You who would read this book,
> If you indeed wish to grasp it,
> Think about what you say,
> For it is very difficult to comprehend.
>> Humility, who is keeper of the treasury of Knowledge
>> And the mother of the other Virtues
>> Must overtake you.
> Theologians and other clerks,
> You will not have the intellect for it,
> No matter how brilliant your abilities,
> If you do not proceed humbly.
> And may Love and Faith, together,
> Cause you to rise above Reason,
> [Since] they are the ladies of the house.
>
> ...
>
> Humble, then, your wisdom
> Which is based on Reason,
> And place all your fidelity
> In those things which are given
> By Love, illuminated through Faith.
> And thus you will understand this book
> Which makes the Soul live by love.[1]

---

[1] *Marguerite Porete. The Mirror of Simple Souls*, trans. E. L. Babinsky (Mahwah: Paulist Press, 1993), p. 79.

102 LOVE AND THE WILL

Porete's warning is aimed at those who rely too much on reason and their own intellectual abilities. As we saw in Chapter 3, reason's proper object is truth, but human beings are not capable of reaching the highest forms of either truth or contemplation on our own—not that this stops most of us from trying. Porete's own position is extreme (see Sections 2.3, 3.2, and 6.2 for more about her views), but in calling us to turn our attention towards the will and love, she gives voice to a central theme in later medieval texts: the power of love and the importance of directing the will towards loving union with God.

If reason's downfall is arrogance, however, then the will's downfall is misdirected love—loving the wrong things, or loving the right things in the wrong way. The primary question in many contemplative texts from the thirteenth to fifteenth centuries thus becomes: 'How can we love the right things in the right way?' In this chapter I begin to address that question in Section 4.1 by laying out medieval views on the general role of the will and love (understood as the will's desire for the good), with particular attention paid to our imaginative and sensory faculties. As I discuss in Section 4.2, meditations on the life of Christ, the most popular devotional literature of the mid-thirteenth through fifteenth centuries, specifically encourage engaging imagination and sense appetite in order to kindle love for God and to develop virtue. As we see in Section 4.3, meditation is also understood as leading directly to contemplation, the highest activity of which the human soul is capable and an activity in which love is placed more highly in later than in earlier medieval thought. In this way, the meditation genre provides a particularly good example of how philosophy (both scholastic and contemplative) impacts moral and spiritual practices in the Middle Ages, for the reasons given for the use of imaginative meditation draw on philosophical theories about human nature.

In Section 4.4 I discuss one of the more interesting and important side effects of the late-medieval emphasis on meditation and love: the space it opens for women's voices to be taken seriously on topics of religious significance. Insofar as meditation is a spiritual exercise aimed at generating affective attitudes and shaping the will's love towards its proper object, it was seen as a form of devotion particularly well suited to women, who were viewed as generally more sensitive to sensory and emotional stimuli—and better at loving—than men. At the same time, the portrayal of contemplation as the highest form of both meditation and cognition means that women were understood as gaining access to philosophical and theological truths as they progressed in meditation. As love becomes increasingly portrayed in the later Middle Ages as the central means to our final end, the widespread popularity of imaginative meditations opens up space for women's claims to knowledge to be accepted *because of* (rather than despite) their association with the body.

4.1 The Will in Context

Throughout the Middle Ages there was general agreement both that human beings are rational animals and that we are created in God's image (*imago Dei*). Insofar as we are animals, human beings are embodied creatures with nutritive and sensory capacities: we can take in nutrition and grow, sense the world around us, move towards things we want, and move away from things we fear. Insofar as we are *rational* animals, we have a set of capacities that separate us from other animals: we can think about the nature of the things we want and fear, make judgments about which ones are 'true' or 'good,' desire things under those abstract descriptions, imagine how things could be different, remember how things used to be, exercise creativity, etc. It is that set of capacities that connects us to immaterial beings and, in particular, to God. To 'image' God is to be a *person* possessing intellect and will. (For more on the medieval conception of 'person,' see Chapter 5.) As Thomas Aquinas writes at the beginning of his *Treatise on Happiness*, "What it means for us to be an image [of God] is that we are intellectual creatures endowed with free choice and capable of controlling our own acts."[2]

---

[2] Preface to *Summa theologiae*, IaIIae. Aquinas motivates his discussion of morality (the entire Second Part of *Summa theologiae*) in terms of our being image-bearers of God: "It remains for us to investigate God's image – namely, human beings – insofar as we are the source of our own acts because we possess free choice and have power over what we do." Thomas Aquinas, *The Treatise on Happiness: Summa theologiae IaIIae 1–21*, trans. Thomas Williams. Hackett Aquinas Series (Indianapolis: Hackett Publishing Co., 2016), p. 1.

104 LOVE AND THE WILL

As we saw in Chapter 3, intellect is aimed at truth, knowledge, and wisdom. The will, in contrast, desires the good *as good* (as opposed to being drawn to it simply because of its scent, appearance, etc.). In the words of the anonymous fourteenth-century *Cloud of Unknowing*, "Will is the power that helps us choose the good that has been selected by reason." The will is also the faculty by which we love—sometimes the wrong things in the wrong way, sometimes the right things in the wrong way, and ideally the right things in the right way. As the *Cloud* continues, the will "also helps us love and desire this good and rest in God, completely confident and joyful."[3] Most things we desire as good are illusory or transient: sourdough starters were all the rage during the early pandemic lockdowns of 2020, for instance, but most people lost interest in making bread after a while and eventually they either threw out their starter or left it to languish in the back of the fridge. The only object which can perfectly and everlastingly fulfill our all desires is the *summum bonum* or Highest Good—namely, God.

Human action is the result of intellect and will working together: intellect presents various options to the will as good, the will chooses one of those options, and its choice moves us to towards action. If I'm deciding what to spend my afternoon doing, for instance, I usually consider various options (e.g., napping, finishing an overdue book review, or having coffee with a friend who's just texted me), and then make judgments about the wisdom of those options (I got plenty of sleep last night, I've been working all morning on the book review without getting anywhere, and I could really use some coffee and time with this friend). My will considers these judgments and chooses one as the best good in this situation (in this case, having coffee with my friend), at which point I'm motivated to text her back with an enthusiastic 'yes, please!', put my shoes on, and head out the door. Without the intellect's judgments, I would have no options to choose from; without the will's desire, I would have no internal motivation to make a choice or do anything about turning that choice into action.[4]

---

[3] *The Cloud of Unknowing: with the Book of Privy Counselling*, trans. Carmen Acevedo Butcher (Boulder, CO: Shambhala Publications, 2009), ch. 64, p. 144.

[4] This is all terrifically simplified, of course—intellect and will work together at various stages throughout this process. Figuring out what shoes to put on, for instance, requires their coordination, as does determining which coffee shop to go to and then how to get there.

THE WILL IN CONTEXT   105

If this were a book on scholastic philosophy, the rest of this chapter would probably address metaphysical intricacies regarding free choice of the will and/or the primacy of intellect vs. will, because these were popular subjects of debate in universities (particularly those at Paris and Oxford) throughout the thirteenth and fourteenth centuries.[5] Contemplative texts from this same period focus primarily on the moral and theological import of the will, however, and so will I. As Johannes Tauler notes in a sermon, "The great clerics and masters of learning dispute over whether knowledge or love is greater or nobler. But we want to speak here about the masters of living [*lebmeistern*]."[6] This focus on living well motivates much of the late medieval contemplative emphasis on love, for there was a common medieval assumption that our ultimate end involves some form of everlasting union with God, and the unitive power of the will—the way it seeks to be one with the object of its desire—is increasingly portrayed as the best and highest way of reaching that end. In the words of the fifteenth-century Marsilio Ficino: "Love unites the mind with divinity much more rapidly, more closely, and more steadfastly than knowledge does, precisely because the power of knowledge consists more in distinction, the power of love in union."[7] As we saw in Section 3.5, the later Middle Ages witnesses a widespread disillusionment with scholastic distinctions, the power of formal argumentation, and the knowledge it yields. As Thomas à Kempis writes in his enormously influential fourteenth-century *De Imitatione Christi*, "When the day of judgment comes we shall not be asked what we have read but what we have done, not how well we have spoken but how well we have lived.... That person is truly great who has great love."[8]

This practical interest leads contemplatives to stress not just the importance of intellect and will but also that of the senses and

---

[5] For an overview of these debates, see Tobias Hoffman's "Intellectualism and voluntarism," in *The Cambridge History of Medieval Philosophy*, ed. R. Pasnau and C. Van Dyke (Cambridge: Cambridge University Press, 2009), pp. 414–27.

[6] Johannes Tauler, V [Sermon] 45, quoted in McGinn, *Harvest*, p. 240.

[7] *Theologia Platonica*, Book XIV.10 (4:316–17), as quoted in McGinn, *Varieties of Vernacular*, 263.

[8] *Imitation of Christ*, trans. William C. Creasy (Notre Dame, IN: Ave Maria Press, 2017), Book 1, ch. 3, pp. 29–30.

106 LOVE AND THE WILL

imagination, since our environment and our reactions to our environment are crucial to our moral and spiritual lives.[9] The scenario sketched above, for instance, required drawing on these capacities in various ways: I used them in remembering that I slept well last night, for instance, and in feeling the sensory 'call' of caffeine and companionship. In the remainder of this section, I look more closely at the general work imagination and sensation play in our moral and spiritual formation before turning to the specific work they are given in the devotional practice of imaginative meditation.

4.1.1 Sensation and sense appetite

Human love is best stirred up by tangible objects, as Augustine famously noted in the fourth century, and as Bonaventure acknowledges in the *Mystical Vine* when Christ says to him, "I became human and visible so that you might see Me and so love Me, since, unseen and invisible in my divinity, I had not been properly loved."[10] The idea that Christ's incarnation occurs at least in part as an effort to connect our flesh-and-blood humanity more closely to God's divinity—both epistemologically and metaphysically—is common in medieval contemplative texts. Catherine of Siena provides an extended metaphor of Christ as bridge between human beings and the divine in her *Dialogue*, for instance, while Julian of Norwich writes in her *Showings* that, "When God knitted Christ's body to ours inside the womb of the maiden, he took on our sensual [i.e. sensory] soul. In taking on our soul, he enclosed us all within himself, joining our earthly nature to our spiritual essence."[11]

---

[9] This is not to imply in any way that sensation and imagination do not play important roles in the epistemological frameworks of thirteenth–fifteenth-century scholastics. They receive relatively less attention than intellect and will, though—a feature which is mirrored in the secondary literature. For some exceptions to this general rule, see chs 1 through 6 in *Emotion and Cognitive Life in Medieval and Early Modern Philosophy*, ed. M Pickavé and L. Shapiro (Oxford: Oxford University Press, 2012).

[10] Bonaventure, *The Works of Bonaventure, Vol. 1: The Journey of the Mind to God, The Triple Way or Love Enkindled, The Tree of Life, The Mystical Vine, On the Perfection of Life, Addressed to Sisters*, trans. J. de Vinck (Mansfield Centre: Martino Publishing, 2016), p. 204.

[11] *The Showings of Julian of Norwich*, trans. Starr, ch. 57, p. 158.

THE WILL IN CONTEXT   107

The question of how best to use our physical faculties to know and love God better is a question of central interest in the twelfth through fifteenth centuries. As we saw in Section 3.1, Richard of St. Victor uses the analogy of Leah and Rachel (the two wives of Jacob, progenitor of the founders of the twelve tribes of Israel) to illustrate the rational faculties of the will and reason, respectively. Leah's and Rachel's children are each given analogical meanings that correspond to their mothers: all seven of Leah's children are virtues, while Rachel's two children (Joseph and Benjamin) stand for practical wisdom and contemplation. Yet, as anyone familiar with the story knows, Rachel and Leah also have handmaids (Bala and Zelpha)—handmaids identified by Richard in his analogy as imagination and *sensualitas*. (The term *sensualitas* defies easy translation into modern English, in part because it possesses both a broad and a narrow sense; in what follows, I'll render it as 'sense appetite' when the more narrow sense is clearly in play, but will use 'sensation' when the word is being used in a more broad sense, and will retain 'sensuality' in quotations of texts which render it this way.)[12]

It is difficult today not be distracted by the chillingly misogynist aspects of this story (so brilliantly captured by Margaret Atwood's *The Handmaid's Tale*), but the idea of imagination and the sensory powers/ sense appetite as indispensable assistants to reason and the will plays a significant part in medieval contemplative discussions from the twelfth century onward.[13] In Richard's words, "without imagination, reason would know nothing; without sensation [*sensualitas*], affection would have sense of nothing."[14] On even the medieval views of cognition that argue for innate ideas and/or divine illumination of universal concepts, human beings are not seen as possessing innate knowledge of particulars, such as which plants are edible or how to tell a dog from a cat. To acquire this sort of knowledge, human beings need to have a variety of sensory experiences of the material world, experiences which are processed first by the appropriate 'apprehensive' faculties (sight, hearing,

---

[12] By the fourteenth century, '*sensualitas*' is regularly rendered in Middle English works as 'sensuality': *Cloud of Unknowing*, Richard Rolle, Julian of Norwich's *Showings*, etc.

[13] See, e.g., Elaine Glanz's "Richard Rolle's Imagery in Meditations on the Passion B: A Reflection of Richard of St. Victor's Benjamin Minor," *Mystics Quarterly* 22/2 (1996), pp. 58–68.

[14] *The Twelve Patriarchs*, ch. V, p. 57.

108 LOVE AND THE WILL

smell, taste, touch, and the 'common sense' that synthesizes the data from the individual senses) and then the 'appetitive' sensory power. Medieval views about this process are extremely complex;[15] for our purposes, it's enough to know that 'sensation' is a term that broadly denotes the work of our sensory capacities, and that those capacities include the 'sense appetite,' whose general purpose is to be drawn on a sensory level towards what's good for us. *The Cloud of Unknowing* describes sensation as "the power that affects and controls our body's perceptions." Its job is to pull us towards physical objects that are good for us and to push us away from things that are bad for us, allowing us to "know and experience all of physical creation, both pleasant and unpleasant."[16] Sense appetite is also frequently divided into the 'irascible' (fight-or-flight, protection-oriented) appetite and the 'concupiscible' (pleasure-seeking, pain-avoiding) appetite. My inclination to hit the person who grabs my arm from behind when I'm walking down a dark street, for instance, comes from my irascible appetite's urge to defend myself from harm; my inclination to smile at babies so they smile back at me comes from my concupiscible appetite's urge to experience pleasant things. Furthermore, as Richard of St. Victor's handmaid analogy implies, our sensory appetite is both responsive to and 'serves' the rational faculties by priming us to react to various stimuli, making us aware of potential dangers and pleasures; reason and will will then work together in determining and choosing the best response. If I know a friend is planning to catch up with me as I walk to the coffee shop, for instance, I might restrain the urge to hit the person who's just grabbed my arm until I see who it is. Or if I'm in a foreign country and unsure of what the social norms are about interacting with other people's children, I might wait to smile and wave at a stranger's baby until I see someone else do so. In both cases, in determining what to do, reason and will must react to the various sensory inputs, such as the rush of adrenaline I feel when my arm is grabbed and the body language of the chubby-cheeked child's mother.

---

[15] For an overview of the issues and positions, see Dag Hasse's "The Soul's Faculties," in *The Cambridge History of Medieval Philosophy* (2009), pp. 305–19. For a classic scholastic discussion of *sensualitas* as a power of the human soul, see Thomas Aquinas's *Summa theologiae* Ia 81.

[16] *Cloud of Unknowing*, ch. 65, p. 147.

THE WILL IN CONTEXT   109

Because the will is also understood as an appetite in medieval discussions—Aquinas, for instance, calls it a "rational appetite for the good"—the sensory power is particularly linked with the will and the development of virtue in the contemplative tradition.[17] Sense appetite is in itself morally neutral in this tradition: although its original function was to help us develop and enact virtue, in the broken world in which we live virtues are difficult to develop in large part precisely because the forbidden kiss is so very appealing, and the delayed flight so very frustrating. As *The Cloud of Unknowing* describes the situation, "Before sin, our sensuality was so obedient to the will—as its servant—that it never led the will down the wrong path."[18] Now, however, we are in the situation where sense appetite goes easily astray, often pulling the will with it: sense appetite "complains when the body lacks what it needs, but it also makes us eat excessively and indulge our other appetites unhealthily." We can no longer simply follow the urges of our sense appetite for our wills to desire what is actually (as opposed to merely apparently) good for us: we need to develop self-control and what we today call will power.

The relationship between our sensory appetite and our rational appetite is thus crucial in the formation and exercise of virtue. Our reactions to the world of sights, smells, and sounds around us can be used to motivate, gauge, and enact moral virtues and spiritual progress—undoubtedly one of the reasons Catherine of Siena offers such a variety of sensory metaphors (often food-related) in her *Dialogue*. As she remarks in chapter 51, "Sensation is a servant, and it has been appointed to serve the soul, so that your body may be your instrument for proving and exercising virtue."[19] My will needs to respond to the impetus provided to it by sensation predictably and appropriately in order to be considered virtuous—indeed, according to many contemplatives, it cannot develop that virtuous inclination in the first place without such sensory inputs.[20]

---

[17] See, e.g., Aquinas's *Treatise on Happiness*, Q 1.2.co.

[18] All quotes in this paragraph are from *Cloud of Unknowing*, ch. 65, p. 147.

[19] *Dialogue*, p. 105. Suzanne Noffke translates *sensualità* as 'sensuality,' which is also how this term is rendered into Middle English in translations of the *Dialogue*.

[20] For more on the relation between virtue and the will and how it changes during this period, see Bonnie Kent's *Virtues of the Will: The Transformation of Ethics in the Late Thirteenth Century* (Washington, D.C.: Catholic University of America Press, 1995).

110 LOVE AND THE WILL

If my sense appetite perceives an adorable baby and is drawn towards giving it enthusiastic cuddles, then my letting someone else who also loves babies snuggle the child instead is an act of generosity that would not be possible without either the initial pull towards the baby or my will's subsequent choice to forego the delight so that someone else can experience it. In the same way, I can only enact the virtue of patience in the face of provoking situations, like a delayed flight or a perennially late friend texting me to say she's finally on the way when I've already been waiting for half an hour: I am not being patient when I am simply waiting at the gate for an on-time departure or hanging out at the coffee shop before my friend is scheduled to arrive.

4.1.2 Imagination

As we saw in Chapter 3, while sense appetite is linked primarily to the will, imagination is linked primarily to the intellect. Imagination's main role is to allow reason to call up images (which can be visual, olfactory, auditory, etc.) which we've stored in our memories: it is "the power that helps us form mental images of anything present or absent."[21] Richard of St. Victor depicts imagination as busily bringing reason whatever information from the senses that it might require: "The imagination (insofar as she is a handmaid) runs between reason and sense. Whatever it imbibes from outside through the senses of the flesh, it represents inwardly for the service of reason.... Even when sense fails, imagination does not cease to provide. For when I am placed in darkness, I see nothing, but if I wish, I can imagine anything."[22] Imagination doesn't require real-time sensory input—you've used it while reading this chapter already to picture a snuggly baby, for instance, and to remember the visceral frustration of a delayed flight.

Once we have those mental images in place, reason and imagination work together to isolate various components, to combine features of experiences in new and interesting ways, and to draw connections

---

[21] *Cloud of Unknowing*, ch. 65, p. 145.   [22] *The Twelve Patriarchs*, ch. V, p. 58.

THE WILL IN CONTEXT 111

between them. Bonaventure uses this relation to explain why he includes a diagram in his *Tree of Life*. "Since imagination aids understanding, I have arranged in the form of an imaginary tree the few items I have collected among many,"[23] he says. In the fourteenth-century English allegorical poem *Piers Plowman*, the character of 'Ymaginatif' plays an important role in helping the central character (significantly named 'Will') negotiate the path between the physical world and God.[24] The ultimate end of imagination is helping the intellect gain knowledge of abstract, universal truths: "Imagination participates centrally in the process by which anything is understood in its fullness."[25] When we've experienced enough different sorts of meowing furry four-footed animals, for instance, and pondered the commonalities and differences between them, we can form the concept 'cat'—a concept that is then modified, corrected, and strengthened by further experiences in the material world and further work by imagination and reason.

Imagination doesn't just aid reason in forming concepts and discovering truths in the world around us, however. It also plays a crucial role in our moral and spiritual formation. If sense appetite can lead us astray with the immediate pull of objects in front of us, imagination can lead us astray not just with images of those same objects later but also with creative and new combinations of images. We might see an appealing but expensive espresso-maker in a store, for instance, and walk away from it, only to find ourselves later imagining it smartening up our kitchen counter while we happily pull espresso shots for friends and family, getting more and better work done because of the excellent quality of the caffeine we're drinking. One click later on their website and we've bought an expensive appliance we don't really need. Fortunately, we can also use imagination to help us resist temptation—perhaps by

---

[23] Bonaventure, *The Soul's Journey into God; The Tree of Life; the Life of St. Francis*, trans. Ewert Cousins (Mahwah: Paulist Press, 1978), p. 120.

[24] As Michelle Karnes notes in *Imagination, Meditation, and Cognition in the Middle Ages* (Chicago: University of Chicago Press, 2011), Ymaginatif helps Will understand how to put his sensory powers to good use: "What most concerns Langland is how to make the transition from natural knowledge, the knowledge that the individual attains through the natural faculties of sense and reason, to what we might call spiritual understanding, that is, understanding created things as they pertain to God" (p. 180).

[25] Karnes, *Imagination, Meditation, and Cognition*, p. 180.

112 LOVE AND THE WILL

calling to mind the plethora of coffee-making devices we already have, or compiling a vivid mental picture of drinking cappuccino in Siena on the trip we're saving up for and could go on sooner if we didn't indulge now in the espresso-maker.

Medieval contemplative texts stress the importance of training the imagination to assist us (as opposed to working against us) in attaining our moral and spiritual goals. As we saw in Chapter 1.3 and Chapter 2.2.3, one of the most commonly recommended methods for training the imagination in this way is engaging in imaginative meditation. We cannot simply 'think' our way to God: we must feel a passionate love for God that motivates the development of virtue in this life and that begins to unite us with the source of love itself. As we'll see in what follows, the genre of meditations on the life of Christ becomes the most popular form of devotional literature in the thirteenth–fifteenth centuries in large part because it focuses on kindling and feeding just this sort of fiery love.

4.2 Meditation and the Will

Human beings are physical creatures, and so our path to God must take the physical world into account; at its most general, the practice of meditation in the Middle Ages involves using the soul's faculties to focus our observations of the external world inward. As Bonaventure writes in *The Mind's Journey into God*, we need to "place our first step in the ascent at the bottom, presenting to ourselves the whole material world as a mirror through which we may pass over to God [who has created it]."[26] Originally an exercise designed for cloistered monks and laid out in the twelfth-century *Ladder of Monks and Twelve Meditations* (written by Guigo II for the Carthusian Order), by the end of the thirteenth century meditation had become a popular spiritual discipline seen as available to anyone. Following Guigo II's lead, meditation was typically portrayed and practiced as the second of four linked exercises: 1) careful focus on passages from Scripture (*lectio divina*); 2) meditation (*meditatio*);

---

[26] Bonaventure, *Mind's Journey into God*, p. 63.

MEDITATION AND THE WILL   113

3) prayer (*oratio*); and 4) contemplation (*contemplatio*).[27] *Lectio divina* fills the senses with the sacred words of Scripture; meditation brings those words to life via imagination's working and kindles the fire of love for God; prayer then connects this love directly to God and works to make the person more receptive to contemplation—which (as we'll see in Section 4.3) culminates in the paradoxically receptive activity of mystical union with God.

An entry point to moral and spiritual transformation, *lectio divina* can be practiced in solitude or communally: in medieval religious communities, it often involved one person reading a scripture passage aloud, slowly and repeatedly, while others listened intently, focusing on the words or phrases that caught their attention.[28] (In religious communities that discouraged causal conversations during meals, someone would often read from Scripture or other holy texts; see Figure 4.1, in which St. Humility is pictured reading to her sisters while they eat.) In meditation, the words absorbed by *lectio divina* are brought to life via imagination's working with the will and the intellect. In the *Ladder for Monks*, for instance, Guigo II describes the difference between *lectio divina* and meditation as the difference between putting food in one's mouth and chewing it: "Reading, so to speak, puts food solid in the mouth; meditation chews and breaks it."[29] Clare of Assisi also uses visual metaphors for this process in her mid-thirteenth-century letters to Agnes of Prague, counseling Agnes first to gaze at Christ (identified as God's *Logos* or

---

[27] For chapter-length discussions of each of these practices, see the following in *The Cambridge Companion to Christian Mysticism*, ed. A Hollywood and P. Beckman (Cambridge, Cambridge University Press, 2012): E. Ann Matter's "*Lectio Divina*" (pp. 147–56), Thomas Bestul's "*Meditatio*/Meditation" (pp. 157–66), Rachel Fulton Brown's "*Oratio*/Prayer" (pp. 167–77), Charlotte Radler's "*Actio et Contemplatio*/Action and Contemplation" (pp. 211–24), as well as Bernard McGinn's "*Unio Mystica*/Mystical Union" (pp. 200–10).

[28] Grace Jantzen captures the connection between *lectio divina* and love when she writes: "The mystical meaning of scripture was not held to be something that could be learned while leaving everything else as it is. It was rather the means whereby one could be soaked in the love of God, so that that divine love could permeate all thought and activity." *Power, Gender, and Christian Mysticism* (Cambridge: Cambridge University Press, 1995), p. 81.

[29] He continues to describe prayer and contemplation with the same metaphor: "Prayer attains its savor/contemplation is itself the sweetness that rejoices and refreshes." Guigo II, *The Ladder of Monks and Twelve Meditations*, trans. Edmund Colledge, OSA, and James Walsh, SJ (Kalamazoo: Cistercian Publications, 1978), pp. 68–9.

Figure 4.1 *Saint Humility and Scenes from Her Life*, Pietro Lorenzetti, c.1335–40, Uffizi Gallery, Florence.

Word) and then to meditate on what she sees, so that she can eventually contemplate God.[30]

To kindle greater devotion to God via love for Christ, books of meditations typically describe events in Christ's life in vivid detail, encouraging their reader/hearer to engage imaginatively in those scenes. As the *Meditations on the Life of Christ* counsels the Franciscan nun to whom it is dedicated, "If you wish to profit from all this, Sister, you must place yourself in the presence of whatever is related as having been said or

---

[30] See, e.g., Clare's second letter to Agnes, in *Francis and Clare: The Complete Works*, trans. R. Armstrong, and I. C. Brady (Mahwah: Paulist Press, 1986), p. 197.

done by the Lord Jesus, as if you were hearing it with your own ears and seeing it with your own eyes, giving it your total mental response: with care, delight, and sorrow, and with all extraneous cares and concerns set aside for the time being."[31] The goal is to engage our affective powers: as we 'watch' Mary snuggle her newborn child, for instance, or 'hear' the Roman soldier's whips hitting Jesus's back, we experience sensations of love, pain, guilt, etc., that are meant to inspire compassion, love, and devotion. This stress on imaginative engagement also has a striking impact on artistic renderings in this period. The Holy Family (Jesus, Mary, and Joseph), for instance, is often represented in 'everyday' situations that would be relatable to their audience, such as a baby Jesus clambering over Joseph and pulling his beard while Mary quietly reads a book. (See Figure 4.2.)

In her late-thirteenth-century *Page of Meditations*, Marguerite d'Oingt evokes a visceral response to Christ's suffering on the cross by

Figure 4.2 *The Holy Family*, attributed to Lux Maurus, *c*.1517–27, Musée de Cluny, Paris.

---

[31] D'Oingt, *Page of Meditations*, p. 4. Here and elsewhere I follow Stallings-Taney's Latin edition, translated as *Meditations on the Life of Christ* by Francis X. Taney, Anne Miller and C. Mary Stallings-Taney (Asheville, NC: Pegasus Press, 2000).

116 LOVE AND THE WILL

comparing it with a mother's suffering in childbirth. Addressing Christ, she writes:

> Are you not my mother and more than mother? The mother who bore me labored at my birth for one day or one night, but you, my sweet and lovely Lord, were in pain for me not just one day, but you were in labor for more than thirty years. Oh, sweet and lovely Lord, how bitterly were you in labor for me all through your life! But when the time approached when you had to give birth, the labor was such that your holy sweat was like drops of blood which poured out of your body onto the ground.... When the hour of birth came, you were placed on the hard bed of the cross where you could not move or turn around or stretch your limbs as someone who suffers much pain should be able to do.... And surely it was no wonder that your veins were broken when you gave birth to the world all in one day.[32]

A Carthusian nun who would have been familiar with Guigo II's *Ladder of Monks* and its emphasis on the linked practices of *lectio-meditation-oratio-contemplatio*, Marguerite here appeals very intentionally to emotion. Given that neither hospitals nor privacy were widely available in medieval Europe, a mother's pain in childbirth would have been intimately familiar to her readers (who ranged from fellow Carthusians—both monks and nuns—to religious and layfolk throughout France).[33] The description of Christ as forced to labor without even being allowed to move around to ease his suffering makes mentally placing oneself at the scene all the more intense, and the idea that Jesus is suffering to give birth to *us* creates a sense of personal connection to the event.

---

[32] *The Writings of Margaret of Oingt, Medieval Prioress and Mystic (d. 1310)*, trans. with an introduction, essay, and notes by Renate Blumenfeld-Kosinski. (Cambridge: D. S. Brewer, 1990), p. 31. Although striking in contemporary contexts, the depiction of Jesus as mother is relatively common in the thirteenth–fifteenth centuries. For a classic study of this, see Caroline Walker Bynum's *Jesus as Mother: Studies in the Spirituality of the High Middle Ages*. (Berkeley: University of California Press, 1984).

[33] For more on Marguerite's use of imagery and readership, see Sergi Sancho Fibra's "Colors and Books in Marguerite d'Oingt's *Speculum*. Images for Meditation and Vision," in *Commitments to Medieval Mysticism within Contemporary Contexts*. Bibliotheca Ephemeridum Theologicarum Lovaniensium (Leuven: Peeters, 2017), 255–71.

MEDITATION AND THE WILL   117

Marguerite's *Meditation* is short and focused entirely on Christ's Passion, but longer and more detailed books of meditations cover a whole range of episodes in the life of both Christ and his mother, Mary. Of these, by far the most widely read and influential example is the late-thirteenth-century *Meditations on the Life of Christ*. Translated into a number of vernaculars, including Nicholas Love's influential English *The Mirror of the Blessed Life of Jesus Christ*, the *Meditations* remained popular well into the sixteenth century; its impact on late medieval culture would be hard to overstate.[34] Building on the knowledge of Scripture the reader would have absorbed via *lectio divina*, the *Meditations*—a combination of vignettes from the gospels, musings on likely events in Christ's life, and paraphrased sermons from Bernard of Clairvaux—instructs its readers to imagine what it would have been like to experience various moments in the life of Mary and Christ with them. To help with this spiritual exercise, the text explicitly suggests ways in which readers can (imaginatively) participate. When discussing Lazarus's resurrection from the dead, for instance, the text advises: "Take care to focus your attention as if you were really there to see and hear what happened here. Feel free to enter into conversation not only with the Lord Jesus and his disciples, but also with that blessed family so devoted to the Lord and so loved by the Lord, namely Lazarus, Martha, and Mary."[35]

Notably, the reader of the *Meditations* is encouraged to imagine having such conversations and to imagine other events in Christ's life, whether or not they are explicitly described in Scripture. (This feature is one of the most important ways in which meditations move beyond *lectio divina*.[36]) In the chapter on the Holy Family's return from their flight to Egypt, for instance, the reader is asked to imagine how difficult the trip must have been for Jesus who, according to tradition, would still have been a small child: "When he came to Egypt, he was such a tiny

---

[34] For the definitive Latin edition, see *Meditationes Vitae Christi*, ed. Mary Stallings-Taney, *Corpus Christianorum Continuatio Mediaevalis* (CCCM 153) (Turnhout: Brepols, 1997).

[35] Ch. 66, on Lazarus being raised from the dead, p. 215.

[36] As Grace Jantzen writes, "Imaginative meditation was to be encouraged, not cramped by the literal or historical sense, because it is by imaginative entry into the mystical sense of scripture that the love and grace of God can be encountered" (*Power, Gender, and Christian Mysticism*, p. 82).

thing that he could be carried. Now, he is just big enough that he cannot be carried very easily and just small enough that he cannot walk very far."[37] We are asked to imagine that some kind soul has given Jesus a small donkey to ride, and that we are walking alongside him. "When he wants to dismount," the text advises, "Take him joyfully in your arms, and hold him a bit." While the Holy Family lives in Egypt, meanwhile, we are encouraged to imagine Mary making ends meet by mending clothes, with Jesus helping her by carrying garments back and forth to their owners.[38] (See Figure 4.3.) Going beyond the recorded events of Scripture in this way was seen as a valuable means of developing a more personal, deeper love for God. Such engagement was also viewed as an important component of developing virtue in both the will and the

Figure 4.3 Detail of *Meditationes vitae Christi*; ms. Ital. 115, Bibliothèque nationale de France.

---

[37] *Meditations*, ch. 13, pp. 50–1.
[38] A wonderfully illustrated manuscript of the *Meditations* (*Meditationes vitae Christi; ms. Ital. 115, Bibliothèque nationale de France*) is available online at https://archivesetmanuscrits.bnf.fr/ark:/12148/cc9195s. For further discussion, see Holly Flora's *The Devout Belief of the Imagination. The Paris Meditationes Vitae Christi and Female Franciscan Spirituality in Trecento Italy. Disciplina Monastica, Vol. 6* (Turnhout: Brepols, 2009).

MEDITATION AND THE WILL   119

intellect: our inclination and our ability to care for ourselves and others increase as our love for God grows. The idea that virtue and love help us make cognitive as well as moral and spiritual progress gains traction in the later thirteenth century and throughout the fourteenth century. As the prologue to the *Meditations* states, the person who meditates frequently "is illuminated by divine virtue in such a way that she both clothes herself with virtue and distinguishes what is false from what is true: so much so that there have been many unlettered and simple persons who have come to know about the great and puzzling truths of God in this way."[39] Later, the *Meditations* paraphrases a sermon of Bernard of Clairvaux to describe how meditating on the life of Christ allows God to illuminate our intellects: "The feelings, which are influenced by the ever-changing passions of a corrupt body, can never be tamed, not to mention cleansed, until the will seeks one goal and moves towards one goal. But Christ enlightens the intellect; Christ cleanses the feelings."[40] This focus of the will enables us to handle the constant barrage of information we get from our senses and their effects on our earthly bodies—effects that impact our intellects as well as our wills, since disordered desires often negatively affect our judgments about the good. (In the life to come, our corrupt earthly bodies will become perfected and incorruptible; for more about embodiment in the afterlife, see Section 6.3.)

The close relationship between intellect and will is also what ties meditation to contemplation. The person who hasn't engaged in extensive meditation on the fully human (yet fully divine) Second Person of

---

[39] Prologue to the *Meditations*, 3. As I discuss in Section 3.4, the progression from imaginative meditation to knowledge of divine truths is seen as applying to women as well as men: the *Meditations* is itself addressed to a woman and uses female pronouns throughout for the human being. This has led to speculation that the author of the *Meditations* might have been a woman (see Sarah McNamer's "The Origins of the Meditationes Vitae Christi" in *Speculum* 84 (2009), pp. 905–55), but most scholars today agree that its author was likely a Franciscan friar writing to a sister in the same Order. See, e.g., Michelle Karnes's "Exercising the Imagination: The *Meditationes vitae Christi* and *Stimulus amoris*" in *Imagination, Meditation, and Cognition*; Dávid Falvay and Peter Tóth's "New Light on the Date and Authorship of the *Meditationes vitae Christi*" in *Devotional Culture in Late Medieval England and Europe: Diverse Imaginations of Christ's Life*, eds. Stephen Kelly and Ryan Perry (Turnhout: Brepols, 2015), pp. 17–104; Isa Ragusa's "L'autore della Meditationes vitae Christi sedondo il codice ms Ital. 115 della Biblioteque Nationale di Parigi", in *Arte medievale*, 11 (1997), 145–50.

[40] *Meditations*, ch. 51, p. 175.

120   LOVE AND THE WILL

the Trinity won't be capable of focusing their attention on contemplation of the higher truths of the Trinity itself. We embodied creatures need to begin by using images of the world around us to inspire our attention and love and to work up to higher levels of contemplation. This is, in fact, the ultimate purpose of meditation—to "propel your fervor towards higher aspirations." As the *Meditations* continues: "It is fitting that you arrive at greater heights by traveling this route. Along the way, your affection may be inflamed enough for you to warm your whole self in it."[41]

This progression from imaginative meditation to knowledge of divine truths is an important part of the shift from the exercise of meditation to that of contemplation.[42] The message of the *Meditations* is that anyone who practices this discipline sincerely and consistently—whether ordained clergy or layperson, male or female—can gain access to the higher truths of God via contemplation. In Trinitarian fashion, contemplation was often divided into three levels or stages, with meditation frequently portrayed as the initial stage.[43] "Do not ever believe that you can elevate yourself mentally to the sublimities of God," the Meditations warns, "Unless you devote yourself long and diligently to this [meditation on the life of Christ]."[44] As we see in Section 4.3, the final stage of contemplation transcends anything we are capable of attaining on our own; it requires God's grace (frequently depicted as a 'gift of love'), for which we can merely make ourselves receptive with "mighty effort and burning longing."[45] God's goodness transcends "our greatest imagination," writes Julian of Norwich, as well as all thought and comprehension. When we are truly united with God, "All we can do is contemplate him and rejoice. We allow ourselves to be filled with the overwhelming

---

[41] *Meditations*, ch. 107, p. 330.

[42] As Michelle Karnes notes, "The most important cognitive task assigned to medieval imagination was the discovery of truth" (*Imagination, Meditation, and Cognition*, p. 4).

[43] As Mari Hughes-Edwards notes, in this period "contemplation united many restorative, spiritual activities together and cannot be understood as a signifier for one alone." Mari Hughes-Edwards, *Reading Medieval Anchoritism: Ideology and Spiritual Practices* (Cardiff: University of Wales Press, 2012), p. 83.

[44] *Meditations*, ch. 50, p. 172. The *Meditations* identifies itself as involving a third, 'imperfect' form of contemplation focused on the humanity of Christ, while the other two stages of contemplation (focused respectively on the heavenly court and—ultimately—on God's essence) remain inaccessible to us without extensive meditation.

[45] Richard of St. Victor, *Twelve Patriarchs*, ch. LXXIII, p. 131.

desire for one-ing with our Beloved, to listen deeply for his call. We delight in his goodness and revel in his love."[46]

4.3 Contemplation and Love

"You see then," the *Meditations* says, "to what an exalted height meditation on the life of Christ leads. Like a sturdy platform, it lifts one to greater heights of contemplation."[47] In this section I address those 'greater heights,' which virtually every contemplative tradition (whether ancient, medieval, or contemporary, monotheistic, polytheistic, or pantheistic) identifies as unmediated contact with the Divine. As anyone who has loved knows, it is one thing to love someone from afar and quite a different thing to enter into the most intimate union possible with that person. This holds particularly true when the person you're entering into union with is the ultimate source of everything in the universe, including love. Medieval contemplatives are agreed that meditating on Christ's life and attempting to mirror Christ's love for God and neighbor constitute important preparation for contemplative union, and that attaining this final unitive stage of contemplation depends entirely on God's grace. They disagree, however, with respect to the best means of preparing ourselves, with different views dividing according to the fault lines separating conceptions of our final end which we have seen already in Chapters 1–3. The main point of disagreement is whether we should continue to practice imaginative meditation, or whether we should seek to transcend meditation and attachment to the material world altogether.

As we saw in Section 4.2, the spiritual practices of *lectio divina*, meditation, prayer, and contemplation are understood as intrinsically linked. Meditation employs sense appetite and imagination to engage with the words of Scripture, while the primary focus of contemplative prayer (as opposed to petitionary prayer or prayers of confession) is preparing ourselves for union with God. As Julian of Norwich puts it, "The whole

---

[46] *Showings*, ch. 43, pp. 107–8.   [47] *Meditations*, Prologue, p. 3.

122 LOVE AND THE WILL

purpose for praying is to be made one with the vision and contemplation of the One we long for."[48] One of the central ways in which prayer prepares us for that vision and contemplation is by seeking to further conform our wills with God's. When we are feeling distant from God, Julian counsels, we need to pray "to be made soft and supple, aligned with the divine will, for the Divine does not align himself to our will." As she goes on to observe: "No amount of prayer will make God conform to us: God is eternally shaped like love."

The best model human beings have for how to align our wills with God's is, of course, the one human being who is also God: Christ. The practice of imitating Christ thus becomes closely linked to prayer and contemplation in this period, both as a means of preparing ourselves for union with God and as a result of such union. In her third letter to Agnes of Prague, for instance, Clare of Assisi encourages her spiritual sister to place mind, soul, and heart in God so that she can be transformed via contemplation into an image of God:

> Place your mind before the mirror of eternity!
> Place your soul in the brilliance of glory!
> Place your heart in the figure of the divine substance!
> And transform your whole being into the image of the Godhead Itself
> through contemplation![49]

Catherine of Siena also begins her *Dialogue* with an emphasis on the unitive power of prayer and imitation. "There is no way [one] can so savor and be enlightened by this truth," she observes, "As in continual humble prayer, grounded in the knowledge of herself and of God. For by such prayer the soul is united with God, following in the footsteps of Christ crucified, and through desire and affection and the union of love he makes of her another himself."[50] Catherine's description of God making 'another himself' of her (which appears a number of times throughout the *Dialogue*) references both the result of imitating Christ and the Aristotelian idea that the true friend of virtue is 'another self.'

---

[48] All quotes from Julian in this paragraph are from *Showings*, ch. 43, p. 107.
[49] *Francis and Clare: the Complete Writings*, p. 200.
[50] Prologue to *The Dialogue*, trans. Suzanne Noffke, OP (Mahwah: Paulist Press, 1980), p. 25.

CONTEMPLATION AND LOVE   123

Catherine's description of such prayer as grounded in "the knowledge of herself and of God" also demonstrates the way in which moving forward via prayer and contemplation requires self-knowledge. As we saw in Chapter 1, medieval contemplatives view introspection as essential for moral and spiritual growth. The recommendation of *The Book of Privy Counselling* to "gnaw on the naked blind feeling of our own being," for instance, is reinforced in the book's description of practices vital for reaching higher stages of contemplation: "There's nothing else I can do and no other exercise my mind or body can practice that brings me so close to God and so far from this world, as does this naked little awareness of my blind being, offered to God."[51] In fact, the text goes on to identify this self-knowledge as necessary for contemplation: "The foundation of your contemplation is located in the clear vision and blind awareness of your very essence."[52] The unifying power of love is also key here: the more we love God, the more we become like God and the more likely we are to reach the higher stages of contemplation that, in Bonaventure's words, lift us above everything "sensible, imaginable, and intelligible."[53]

Medieval contemplatives disagree, however, about whether, once we begin to reach those higher stages, we should also continue the practice of meditation, with its use of the senses, imagination, and natural reason. The *Meditations* advises its readers to continue meditating even after progressing to the 'greater heights' of contemplation of God's essence, for instance, lest we start to attribute our spiritual growth to ourselves rather than to God's grace and thus lose our humility: "Those who strive for greater contemplation ought never to give up on this kind of meditation, wherever or whenever it occurs."[54] In Marguerite Porete's *Mirror of Simple Souls*, in contrast, imitation of Christ and even the practice of virtue occupies only the first three of the seven stages towards our final end; stages four through six focus on aligning one's will with God so completely that we fall into an 'abyss' of humility such that, when God

---

[51] *Book of Privy Counselling*, ch. 3, p. 179, from *Cloud of Unknowing*.
[52] *Book of Privy Counselling*, ch. 4, p. 181.   [53] *The Threefold Way* 1.15–17.
[54] *Meditations*, ch. 107, pp. 330–1. The text goes on to assure the reader that Bernard of Clairvaux (whose sermons make up a substantial portion of the *Meditations* and is, thus, the most relevant authority figure to hand) never abandoned the practice of meditation but returned to it regularly as part of his spiritual practices.

124   LOVE AND THE WILL

looks at us, the only thing God sees is, in fact, God, while the seventh stage is entirely ineffable and attained only after death.[55] The thought that we must leave meditation behind as we progress spiritually is especially prominent in apophatic texts that stress self-forgetting and the unknowability of God. *The Cloud of Unknowing*, for instance, explicitly advises leaving meditation behind in order to lift one's heart with love into the "darkness" of the highest stage of contemplation, which is described in carefully paradoxical terms as "a blind gazing at the naked being of God alone."[56] Meditation is important only for the intermediate stages of spiritual progress, according to the *Cloud*. While "without countless sweet meditations on these very subjects—our agony, our shame, Christ's Passion, God's kindness, God's unfailing goodness, and God's worth—the contemplative person won't advance," continuing in this practice after one has become proficient at them becomes counterproductive: "The man or woman experienced in these meditations must quit them. Put them down and hold them far under the cloud of forgetting, if you want to penetrate the cloud of unknowing between you and God."[57] According to this tradition, only the 'humble stirring of love' can unite us with the Divine.

Although it gains a certain popularity in the fourteenth century, the idea that we must leave meditation behind as we mature spiritually never becomes the dominant view. Instead, contemplatives often counsel returning to meditation in order to stay grounded, echoing the juxtaposition of humility and dignity we saw in Chapter 2 (and will see again in Chapter 5). Meditation provides the foundation from which we can rise up to the heights of contemplation; we continue to need that foundation in this life, and so the contemplative regularly returns to humble meditation. In the final chapter of *The Twelve Patriarchs*, Richard of St. Victor uses the analogy of Rachel's children (Joseph and Benjamin) embracing in Egypt after many years of separation to illustrate this process. "What does it mean that Benjamin descends into Egypt except that

---

[55] For further discussion of these issues that also place Porete's views in the context of earlier beguines such as Hadewijch and Mechthild of Magdeburg, see Juan Marin's "Annihilation and Deification in Beguine Theology and Marguerite Porete's *Mirror of Simple Souls*," *Harvard Theological Review* 103/1 (2010), pp. 89–102.

[56] *Cloud of Unknowing*, p. 28.   [57] *Cloud of Unknowing*, p. 24.

the mind's consideration is called back from contemplation of eternal things to contemplation of temporal things?" Richard asks rhetorically, before continuing: "And what does it mean that Joseph and Benjamin come together and join in kisses except that meditation and contemplation often run to meet each other with the witness of reason? For...just as the grace of contemplation is understood by Benjamin, so the grace of meditation is understood by Joseph."[58] For Richard, the touching scene of fraternal reunion in Genesis demonstrates how human reason and divine revelation come together rather than separate in the final stages of spiritual progress. As he concludes, "In the death of Rachel, contemplation ascends above reason; in the entry of Benjamin into Egypt, contemplation descends to the imagination; in the affectionate kissing of Benjamin and Joseph, human reason gives applause to divine showing."[59]

The continued practices of meditation, prayer, and contemplation are also seen as having a Trinitarian structure which echoes the Augustinian trinity of the soul as being created in God's image with understanding, memory, and will. According to Hadewijch, "God gave us his Nature in the soul, with three powers whereby to love his Three Persons: with enlightened reason, the Father; with the memory, the wise Son of God; and with the high flaming will, the Holy Spirit."[60] As we've seen, meditation, prayer, and contemplation involve all three of these powers in important ways. The identification of the Three Persons as one God also provides a model in which fulfillment of one power is naturally linked to the fulfillment of the others. As Julian of Norwich writes, "Truth sees God. Wisdom contemplates God. When these two things come together, a third gift arises: the wondrous delight in God, which is love." Made in this image, the human soul does best when it does "what it was made to do: see God, contemplate God, and love God."[61]

---

[58] *Twelve Patriarchs*, ch. LXXXVII, p. 146.

[59] *Twelve Patriarchs*, ch. LXXXVII, p. 147. It's worth noting that the fourteenth-century Middle English 'translation' of this text (*The Pursuit of Wisdom*, which is more a paraphrase of what the anonymous author takes to be its central points), does not include this return to imaginative meditation and human reason but, rather, ends with meditation and prayer finally leading to "the mind being ravished above itself" in contemplation.

[60] *Hadewijch: The Complete Works*, Letter 22, ed. and trans. Mother Columba Hart, OSB (Mahwah: Paulist Press, 1980), p. 97.

[61] *Showings*, ch. 44, p. 109.

126 LOVE AND THE WILL

On this model, a claim to great love is often simultaneously a claim to great knowledge. As we will see in Section 4.4, the importance of love for attaining the highest form of contemplation and love's integral connection with wisdom have the unexpected effect of legitimizing medieval women's claims to such wisdom, creating space in which they not only speak with confidence about their experiences of the Divine but what they have to say is heard—by other women, laypeople, university masters, and the highest echelons of the Catholic Church.[62]

4.4 Clear Eyes, Full Hearts: Women's Bodies and the Reception of Truth

The portrayal of women in medieval medical texts and popular culture as less physically and emotionally stable than men was used to justify all sorts of structural injustices throughout the Middle Ages, including the exclusion of women from the priesthood and the university system.[63] At the same time, women were believed to be physically and emotionally more sensitive, better at forming imaginative impressions, and—quite simply—better at loving than their male counterparts.[64] The emergence of meditation as a spiritual discipline that uses sensory and imaginative powers to fire up the will's love for Christ thus made it a natural fit for women's devotional lives. As mentioned in Section 4.2, the *Meditations* is addressed to a Franciscan-affiliated woman; affective representations of not just Christ's but also Mary's childhood are widespread through the fifteenth century, for Mary was understood to be a model of both humble love and profound wisdom. The identification of Mary with

---

[62] Catherine of Siena, for instance, was not yet 30 years old when she was sent to Avignon in 1376 to intercede with Pope Gregory XI to end the 'papal exile' (and the pope's war with Florence); later, the pope cites her counsel as one of the reasons he returns to Rome.

[63] See Prudence Allen's *The Concept of Woman* (Grand Rapids: Wm. B. Eerdmans Publishing Co., 2006) for a detailed history of these arguments—and medieval responses to them.

[64] For more on women's superior claim to loving, see Barbara Newman's "La mystique courtoise: Thirteenth Century Beguines and the Art of Love," in *From Virile Woman to Woman Christ: Studies in Medieval Religion and Literature.* (Philadelphia: University of Pennsylvania Press, 1995), pp. 137–67, as well as her ch. 4, "Love Divine, All Loves Excelling," in *God and the Goddesses: Vision, Poetry, and Belief in the Middle Ages* (Philadelphia: University of Pennsylvania Press, 2003), pp. 137–89.

CLEAR EYES, FULL HEARTS   127

wisdom is so strong that she is sometimes pictured holding a book even at the crucifixion, as in Figure 4.4. (See Interlude Three for more on reading as a devotional act particularly associated with women in the later Middle Ages.) As love becomes seen as increasingly central not just in meditation but also in contemplation, women gain epistemic authority by speaking about what Love—that is, God—has taught them.

A striking example of this can be found in the late-thirteenth-century Marguerite d'Oingt's *Page of Meditations*. A rare instance of a Carthusian nun whose writings survive, Marguerite (whose works were widely read and well respected in both her own time and in following centuries) appears at first glance to be highly apologetic about her authorship:

> I began to think about and to contemplate the sweetness and goodness which is in Him, and the great good He had done me and all of humanity [via his Incarnation]. I was so full of these thoughts that I lost my appetite and my sleep.... I thought that the hearts of men and women are so flighty that they can hardly ever remain in one place, and because of that I fixed in writing the thoughts that God had ordered into my heart so that I would not lose them when I removed them from my heart, and so that I could think them over little by little whenever God would give me His grace. And for that reason, I ask all those who read this text not to think badly [of me] because I had the presumption to write this, since you must believe that I have no sense or learning with which I would know how to take these things from my heart,[65] nor could I write this down without any other model than the grace of God which is working within me.[66]

To read this passage as it would have originally been understood, however, we need to note three things. First Marguerite, who is proficient in several languages, obviously does not lack either 'sense or learning'; in fact, she writes these words in Latin—the language of scholarship and the church—and in the meditations genre discussed in Section 4.2.

---

[65] Alternately translated as "I have in myself neither the understanding nor the clerical office by which I would know how to draw out these things from my heart," as rendered by Charles Stang in "Writing," in *The Cambridge Companion to Christian Mysticism*, p. 263.

[66] *The Writings of Margaret of Oingt, Medieval Prioress and Mystic (d. 1310)*, p. 26.

128　LOVE AND THE WILL

Figure 4.4 Detail of *Memorial Tablet of Hendrik van Rijn*, Johan Maelwael, c.1363, Rijksmuseum, Amsterdam.

(For more on medieval women's use of humility topoi, see Interlude Five.) Second, the Carthusian order, which took strict vows of silence and solitude, had as one of its central spiritual metaphors the image of God inscribing words directly into the human heart, and portrayed the act of writing and transcribing as an important spiritual discipline.[67] Thus, Marguerite's claim that God ordered these thoughts "into her heart" and that she is in turn transcribing those thoughts directly from her heart is extremely significant. Third, Marguerite attributes her ability to compose this text to nothing less than the model of God's own grace moving within her, giving both the origin and the means of her writing a divine source. Although she initially frames the composition of this text in terms of an aid to her own future meditation, she assumes a wider readership in asking for kindness from "all those who read this text." Taken as a whole, then, this statement actually positions what Marguerite is about to say as an important contribution to the teachings of her religious order—and it is a contribution she attributes entirely to love: "Who gave me the audacity to speak of such marvelous things if not you who are the true God and my brother and who showed us the greatest love? Oh beautiful sweet Lord, how great was that love!"[68]

In a later letter, Marguerite describes how, after being caught up in mystical contemplation, she has the experience "written in her heart in such a way that she could think of nothing else." In fact, she explains that if she had not "put these things into writing in the same way that our Lord had put them into her heart," she would have died or gone mad.[69] The words God has given her must be shared: writing about her revelations thus becomes for Marguerite "a discipline with which she can negotiate the overpowering presence of the divine not merely by relieving the pressure of that presence but also by responding to it creatively."[70] The fourteenth-century Margaret Ebner reports a similar experience in her *Revelations*: "I am compelled to write by the will and

---

[67] As Bennett Gilbert writes, "Transcription, filling the monk's mind with truthful words, was the first step in a [Carthusian's] spiritual reflection", in "Early Carthusian Script and Silence," *Cistercian Studies Quarterly* 49/3 (2014), pp. 367–97, p. 372. See also Stephanie Paulsell's "Writing and Mystical Experience in Marguerite d'Oingt and Virginia Woolf," *Comparative Literature* 44/3 (1991), pp. 249–67.

[68] *The Writings of Margaret of Oingt*, p. 27.   [69] D'Oingt, *Letters*, pp. 64–5.

[70] Stang, "Writing," *The Cambridge Companion to Christian Mysticism*, p. 263.

130 LOVE AND THE WILL

the command of God."[71] In fact, she claims that she kept trying to drag her feet: "I have actually delayed a long time because I could never write it down." Yet, when she finally aligns her will with God's and writes about her experiences, she finds that her "delight in His holy works of love was made stronger." Both women justify their writing by appeal to God's will and presence; their descriptions of being overwhelmed by love to the point where they must write down and share their experiences is a common one among medieval mystics—particularly women.

The common belief that women loved more and better than their male counterparts actually stemmed from negative conceptions of women rooted in Aristotelian and Galenic biology, according to which the paradigm of human physiology is male and the highest achievement of the human race is intellective. Because women do not produce the 'active seed' from which other humans are generated, in women the instantiation of human nature was viewed as incomplete and/or 'misbegotten' (*mas occasionatus*).[72] Female bodies were also thought to be composed of colder and more watery matter than male bodies; this physical constitution was seen as making women, with their softer bodies, more impressionable to sensory stimuli and passions and thus less able to exercise self-control and detachment.[73] At the same time, women were viewed as having the same general makeup as men, both mentally and physically, and the active and enthusiastic participation of women

---

[71] All quotes from Ebner in this paragraph are from *Revelations*, in *Margaret Ebner: Major Works*, trans. and ed. Leonard Hindsley (Mahwah: Paulist Press, 1993), p. 132.

[72] Thomas Aquinas's discussion of the nature of women and women's bodies in *Summa theologiae* Ia 92 presents a standard account of this view. Galenic biology saw women as also producing seed necessary for generation, but of a lesser sort; on this view, female reproductive systems were essentially an inverted version of male, and thus there was always the possibility of changing from one sex to another. This conception of the biological differences between men and women leads to a fascination with hermaphrodites and spontaneous sex changes throughout the Middle Ages.

[73] On the other side of this spectrum were the 'natural laborers,' whose bodies were too tough to take in sense impressions well and who thus weren't naturally suited for intellective labor or ruling. Somehow, the pale, softer-but-still-just-firm-enough bodies of upper-class men ended up having the right constitution for taking on all the most important intellectual, political, and spiritual responsibilities. Amazingly, the received 'wisdom' about these sorts of physiological differences and their effects continues to ground arguments for natural subjection today.

CLEAR EYES, FULL HEARTS   131

in virtually every aspect of medieval religious life from the thirteenth to the early fifteenth centuries is one of the most striking features of this period. Forms of religious expression and practices of piety vary over time and across geographical regions, of course, but the virtual explosion of beguine communities through Western Europe in the thirteenth century means that vast numbers of women were suddenly devoted to the religious life. (For more on the beguines, see Interlude Two.)

Furthermore, many of these women could both read and write—some because they came from noble families and had been educated to manage (or, in a pinch, rule) large households (or, in a pinch, city-states and countries), and some because their fellow beguines taught them. As I discuss in Interlude Three, the activity of reading was widely associated with holiness and religious devotion for women in the thirteenth–fifteenth centuries, and so women in this period are often depicted holding and/or reading books.[74] (See Figure 4.5.) Small wonder, then, that women make the most of the thin edge of the wedge constituted by this broad cultural focus on love. Hadewijch, Mechthild of Magdeburg, Mechthild of Hackeborn, Gertrude of Helfta, and Marguerite of Porete, for instance, all incorporate elements from secular love songs and poetry into their religious texts, in addition to drawing extensively on the *Song of Songs* commentary tradition popularized by Bernard of Clairvaux. (See Interlude Four for more on the resulting genre of '*minnemystik*' or '*mystique cortoise*.') Women contemplatives speak with confidence and authority throughout the thirteenth and fourteenth centuries about love, the self, and God; they both share their own experiences and advise those less experienced about the trials and delights yet to come.[75] Aware that their claim to love is their authority, they use it wisely.[76]

---

[74] As Richard Kieckhefer notes, "We know that certain women saints were enthusiastic readers, and we know that devotional reading figured prominently in the urban religious culture of the era." "Holiness and the Culture of Devotion," in *Images of Sainthood in Medieval Europe*, ed. R. Blumenfeld-Kosinski and T. Szell (Ithaca: Cornell University Press, 1991), p. 302.

[75] The claim that they speak with authority and confidence might seem belied by their frequent use of self-denigrating language and humility topoi; see Interlude Five for an argument that some women contemplatives actually use this rhetoric to establish authorial authority.

[76] As Barbara Newman writes, "It was an artful knowing, not mere desire, that made them into those dangerously subtle creatures, *beguines clergesses*" ("*La mystique courtoise*", p. 137).

Figure 4.5 Detail of *Virgin of the Rose Garden*, Master of the Saint Lucy Legend, c.1475–80, Detroit Institute of Arts Museum.

The influence of women-authored texts throughout this period testifies to the fact that women were taken seriously as contemplatives, whose insights into God (understood to be the only true source of knowledge and truth) made them authoritative sources on moral and theological matters. Furthermore, as Chapter 5 demonstrates, these texts impact medieval conceptions not only of knowledge and love but also of what it is to be a human person.

Interlude Four

Where Does the Erotic Imagery
of Medieval Mystics Come from?

Anyone who delves into late medieval contemplative literature expecting to encounter only sober advice for pious living is in for a spicy surprise. In Book II of Mechthild of Magdeburg's *Flowing Light of the Godhead*, for instance, Lady Soul goes to meet her 'Fairest of lovers' in a secret room and finds a bed prepared. "Take off your clothes," the Lord tells her. "What will happen to me then?" asks Lady Soul. The following exchange is heated:

> "Lady Soul, you are so utterly formed to my nature
> That not the slightest thing can be between you
> and me.[77]
> …
> And so you must cast off from you
> Both fear and shame and all external virtues.
> Rather, those alone that you carry within yourself
> Shall you foster forever.
> These are your noble longing
> And your boundless desire.
> These I shall fulfill forever
> With my limitless lavishness."
> "Lord, now I am a naked soul
> And you in yourself are a well-adorned God.
> Our shared lot is eternal life without death."
> Then a blessed stillness
> That both desire comes over them.
> He surrenders himself to her,

---

[77] See also Hadewijch: "If two things are to become one, nothing may be between them except the glue wherewith they are united together. That bond of glue is Love, whereby God and the blessed soul are united in oneness." *Hadewijch*, Letter 16, p. 80.

134 LOVE AND THE WILL

> And she surrenders herself to him.
> What happens to her then – she knows.
> And that is fine with me.
> But this cannot last long.
> When two lovers met secretly,
> They must often part from one another inseparably.[78]

Mechthild's depiction of the secret love-making of Lady Soul and her Lord conjures up images of knights and ladies, castles, quests, and—of course—passion. Whether referred to as 'courtly love' (a label now controversial in academic circles because it was applied retroactively to the tradition, rather than being how the originators of the tradition described themselves) or *fin'amor*, love reigns supreme in the Middle Ages. And this love is not a quiet affection—it is a scorching fire that overwhelms all else and drives men and women to sacrifice everything for its sake. The medieval sagas of both Tristan and Iseult and Lancelot and Guinevere, for instance, contain sections in which their love-frustrated heroes go mad and live like animals in the forest for a time. Elaine, 'the Fair Maid of Astolat,' not only pines for Lancelot but eventually dies from her unrequited love, while Merlin becomes so enamored of Nimue that he allows her to imprison him in an oak tree, even knowing in advance what his fate will be.

Love's supremacy—both the fall of the wise and mighty to its power and its tendency to upend priorities—is a common subject in secular poetry, stories, and art of the thirteenth century and beyond.[79] The great philosopher Aristotle (whose works had been translated into Latin at the outset of the thirteenth century and become the subject of great controversy) joins Merlin, for instance, in being made a fool by love in

---

[78] *Flowing Light of the Godhead*, Book I, p. 62.

[79] One of the most famous secular examples of this genre is the *Roman de la Rose*. The epic poem, begun in the early thirteenth century by Guillaume de Lorris, was completed by Jean de Meun in the later 1200s. (For more on its history, see the introduction to *The Romance of the Rose*, trans. C. Dahlberg (Princeton: Princeton University Press, 1971).) In the early fifteenth century, Christine de Pizan makes a stir with her objections to de Meun's highly negative portrayal of the nature of women in a lively correspondence with three members of the French court. The fame Christine garners via this 'Querelle de la Rose' is what establishes her as an author and grounds the success of her subsequent *City of Ladies*—a book-length defense of the nature and actions of women.

another medieval tale. While tutoring Alexander the Great, the story goes, Aristotle becomes frustrated by Alexander's passion for his wife distracting him from study and scolds him for not being stronger-minded. In response, Alexander's wife, Phyllis (whose name simply means "Love"), decides to teach Aristotle a lesson. In a short period of time, she causes Aristotle to burn so hotly for her that when she says the price of her affections is that he allow her to put a saddle and bridle on him and ride him around like a pony, he readily agrees. Alexander is in on the plot, and husband and wife get a good laugh at seeing the preeminent philosopher brought so low by love. (See Figure I4.1, in which Aristotle tutors Alexander on the left panel and then is being ridden by Phyllis in the next panel while Alexander watches from atop the castle.) This story often appears as a panel in portrayals of 'Attack on the Castle of Love,' a popular subject on ivory caskets and the backs of mirrors. (See Figure I4.2, in which the winged figure of Love shoots arrows at the knights while ladies throw down flowers.)

This interest in love and sex is highly relatable, but it still might seem surprising to find religious figures dedicated to a life of chastity enthusiastically discussing burning with passion. Yet medieval mystics and

Figure I4.1 Detail of side panel, "Attack on the Castle of Love," ivory casket, c.1300–25, Musée de Cluny, Paris.

Figure I4.2 Mirror-case with "Attack on the Castle of Love," Paris workshop, c.1320–40, Museo Nazionale del Bargello, Florence.

contemplatives frequently use these tropes to express their experiences and to encourage others towards moral and spiritual progress. As we've seen throughout this book, the contemplative project is at heart both practical and universal: its ultimate goal is not theoretical knowledge but lived experience that culminates in actual union with God, and this goal is recommended for any and all who are willing to work towards it. Contemplative texts are thus meant to be accessible and engaging—and what better way to engage a wide audience than to link your subject matter to topics in which they're already interested? When God tells Mechthild's Soul to get naked, we're hooked.

Furthermore, in part because their texts are often meant for regular laypeople as well as the higher-ups of ecclesiastical, university, and governmental institutions, a number of contemplatives in the thirteenth–fifteenth centuries write in the emerging vernaculars of their local regions rather than in Latin, which is increasingly the language of the elite. The use of the vernacular encourages an emphasis on emotion and love, for "the major literary genres available in these languages were various kinds of love poetry and romantic stories: the vocabulary

WHERE DOES THE EROTIC IMAGERY 137

provided by such genres was therefore a vocabulary of *feelings*."[80] Hadewijch, for instance, called "the most important exponent of love mysticism and one of the loftiest figures in the Western mystical tradition," uses this vocabulary to portray the soul's search for God as a knight's quest for his Beloved.[81] (See Section 3.3 for examples.) Her poetry is a masterpiece of genre-flipping: she takes the tropes popularized by French troubadours and trouvères (such as the twelfth-century Chrétien de Troyes[82]) and exemplified in the *minnesang* (literally, 'love song') of her own region and recasts them as the soul's longing for God. In the process, the masculine knight becomes the feminine-gendered soul, and the noble lady for whom the knight pines becomes God.[83] Hadewijch is hardly alone in this respect: Mechthild of Hackeborn joins Mechthild of Magdeburg in drawing on elements of *fin'amor*, while Marguerite Porete frames her entire *Mirror of Simple Souls* in terms of the nobility of love's quest, describing the soul who has reached the fourth stage of the journey towards God as "so impenetrable, noble, and delicate that she cannot suffer any kind of touch except the touch of the pure delight of love, by which she is singularly joyful and charmed."[84] Catherine of Siena, in turn, is often portrayed exchanging hearts with God, as medieval lovers would do as a pledge of devotion. (See Figure I4.3.)

Finally, the ultimate goal of the contemplative life is an ineffable experience—it cannot be described in literal, prosaic terms. In this way, it resembles transcendent moments of sexual union, which also can be expressed only in metaphor. The way in which medieval Christian mystics and contemplatives frequently use metaphors of sexual intercourse (a physical experience they chose to forswear for God's sake) to express

---

[80] Caroline Walker Bynum, "The Female Body and Religious Practice," in *Fragmentation and Redemption: Essays on Gender and the Human Body in Medieval Religion* (New York: Zone Books, 1992), p. 196.

[81] Preface by Paul Mommaers, SJ, in *Hadewijch: The Complete Works*, xiii.

[82] See *The Complete Romances of Chrétien de Troyes*, trans. David Staines (Bloomington: Indiana University Press, 1990).

[83] See Barbara Newman's "*La mystique coutoise*: Thirteenth-Century Beguines and the Art of Love," in *From Virile Woman to WomanChrist: Studies in Medieval Religion and Literature* (Philadelphia: University of Pennsylvania Press, 1995).

[84] *Mirror of Simple Souls*, ch. 118, p. 190. For more on Porete's use of this tradition, see Joanne Robinson's *Nobility and Annihilation in Marguerite Porete's Mirror of Simple Souls* (Albany: State University of New York Press, 2001).

138 LOVE AND THE WILL

Figure. I4.3 *St. Catherine of Siena Exchanging Hearts with Christ*, Guidoccio Cozzarelli, late fifteenth century, Pinacoteca Nazionale di Siena.

how love for and experience of God overwhelms them is strikingly similar to the way in which medieval Islamic mystics and contemplatives use metaphors of drunkenness (a physical experience they chose to forswear for Allah's sake) to express how love for and experience of Allah overwhelms them.[85] Mystics in both these traditions use the ecstatic qualities and appeal of sex and drink to heighten both understanding of and appreciation for the ultimate experience of God.

---

[85] See, for instance, *The Wine of Love and Life: Ibn al-Farid's al-Khamriyah and al-Qaysari's Quest for Meaning*, ed. and trans. Th. Emil Homerin (Middle East Documentation Center on behalf of the Center for Middle Eastern Studies, University of Chicago, 2005). Both Islamic and Christian contemplatives draw on Scripture, particularly the Song of Songs (a sexually explicit love poem which was understood by medieval Christians as an allegory for Christ's relation to his bride, understood simultaneously as the entirety of the Church and as each individual Christian) in their use of these metaphors.

5

Persons

The previous three chapters of this book have focused on medieval contemplative theories about the roles self-knowledge, reason, and the will play in our moral and spiritual lives. In this chapter I take a step back to look more closely at views about who "we" are in the first place, for how best to answer to that question is a topic of much discussion in the thirteenth through fifteenth centuries, and one that has important implications for expectations about immortality and the afterlife (the topic of Chapter 6). The prevailing assumption throughout this period is that "we" (that is, those most involved in asking and answering these questions) are both human beings and persons. As we've seen, human beings were understood to be rational animals, composites of physical body and immaterial soul, who live simultaneously in the world of rocks and trees and in the world of universal concepts and abstract truths. As animals, we do things like eat, grow, reproduce, and have sense perception; as intellective beings, we do things like think, hope, believe, and love. Also, as intellective beings, we are persons.

What precisely it means to be a person is the subject of lively and wide-ranging debates from antiquity onward: by the end of the twelfth century, the Latin term '*persona*' has separate but overlapping uses in a number of different fields, including grammar, logic, law, politics, and theology.[1] In Section 5.1 I describe these uses, arguing that together they yield a general understanding of 'person' in which individuality, dignity, and rationality are key. In Section 5.2 I turn to the way in which the concept of persons as rational individuals who possess intrinsic dignity appears in a wide range of contemplative texts, including those

---

[1] For book-length discussions of the development of the concept of person, see *Persons: a History*, ed. A. LoLordo, Oxford Philosophical Concepts Series (Oxford: Oxford University Press, 2019) and Theo Kobusch's *Die Entdeckung der Person: Metaphysik der Freiheit und modernes Menschenbild* (Darmstadt: Wissenschaftliche Buchgesellschaft, 1997).

140 PERSONS

by Hadewijch, Meister Eckhart, Catherine of Siena, and Julian of Norwich. In Section 5.3 I discuss how this concept combines with the contemplative use of first- and second-person perspectives, personification, and introspection to yield a rich (and perhaps surprisingly familiar) understanding of what it means to be a person—an understanding that forms a vital part of who medieval thinkers believe we are, both in our own right and in connection to God, whose Trinity was held to be composed of three distinct persons. I conclude the chapter with a brief overview of how these discussions impact early modern and modern discussions of persons in ways that have been largely overlooked— particularly John Locke's famous seventeenth-century definition and the development of personalism in the nineteenth century and beyond.

5.1 Putting 'Person' in Perspective

We can divide the contexts in which the term '*persona*' appears into three general categories: logical/grammatical, legal/political, and metaphysical/theological.[2] In this section I address the use of the term in each of these contexts, explaining what it contributes to the general understanding of 'person' that contemplatives and scholastics inherit in the thirteenth century and onward. In logical and grammatical discussions, for instance, the word 'person' is used to indicate a distinct individual, in contrast both to universal concepts (like 'justice') and to qualities common to a number of different objects (like a color or a shape). In the realm of law and politics, by contrast, the term 'person' is used primarily to distinguish *who's* from *what's* (e.g., one's neighbor from one's neighbor's field) for the purposes of determining rights, duties, and penalties. In metaphysical and theological discussions, the term appears most often in Christian debates about the nature of God, for God is held to be three persons in one being, and Christ to be one person with both a human nature and a divine nature. As we'll see, the general understanding of 'person' that emerges from these complex and overlapping discussions is one which stresses individuality, dignity, and rationality.

---

[2] For more detail on these histories, see chs 1–3 of LoLordo, ed., *Persons: a History*.

5.1.1 Grammatical and logical context

Medieval logical and grammatical discussions use '*persona*' both to distinguish constructions with a subject from those without one and to contrast individuals with classes, species, groups, and universals. In suppositional theory, for instance, which focuses on the semantic roles of terms in sentences (including what we now refer to as reference and meaning), 'personal' supposition applies when there is an individual subject for a grammatical sentence, such as "Hildegard wrote to the bishop," in contrast with impersonal supposition, such as "It is true that Hildegard was an abbess."[3] What is most crucial to the concept of person in both grammatical and logical contexts is individuality. In fact, the term '*persona*,' as denoting an individual, is so commonly contrasted with the term '*populus*,' as denoting a particular group of persons, that in the emerging English vernacular the plural of 'person' eventually becomes 'people' rather than 'persons' (a term increasingly reserved for technical discussions, particularly in theological contexts, as we see in Subsection 5.1.3). The use of '*persona*' throughout these discussions yields a grammatical and logical notion of 'person' in which individuality is the most relevant quality.

Another important feature that 'person' connotes in these contexts, however, is incommunicability, which entails a certain sort of uniqueness and non-repeatability. Universals such as 'human being' or 'green,' for instance, are inherently communicable in that they can exist (or, to use more technical language, 'be instantiated') in any number of objects. So, for instance, both my mother and my sister are human beings, as are the middle-school students my sister teaches: they all instantiate the universal 'human being' at the very same time. Universals can be instantiated in objects over time as well: the leaves on the trees outside my window right now are green, and so were the leaves on the same trees

---

[3] The classic work on supposition theory is L. M. deRijk's *Logica Modernorum—A Contribution to the History of Early Terminist Logic*, which was published in two parts: *On the Twelfth Century Theories of Fallacy* (1962) and the two-volume *The Origin and Development of the Theory of Supposition* (1967) by Van Gorcum and Co. For more recent perspectives that take later developments and also grammatical texts into account, see *Medieval Supposition Theory Revisited*, ed. E. P. Bos (Leiden: Brill Publishing, 2013).

142 PERSONS

last year (before they turned colors and fell in autumn). 'Greenness' is something many objects can instantiate both at a time and over time—like 'humanness,' it is a 'communicable' property that can be shared by many things. A person, by contrast, is a unique individual who is intrinsically non-communicable and cannot be shared or held in common between objects.[4] If a person were cloned, for instance, the result would be two separate persons, not two instantiations of the 'same' person.

The incommunicability of persons becomes important in the Middle Ages primarily for its logical significance in discussions of the Trinity, particularly attempts to explicate and defend the claim that God is three persons in one being.[5] The incommunicability and inherent individuality of persons also play an important role in philosophical and theological discussions of the nature of the rational soul and human cognition. During the Averroistic controversies in the thirteenth century, for instance, the possibility that there is one universal 'agent intellect' for all human beings (somewhat like a computer mainframe we all use when cognizing) is often criticized sharply for not maintaining the individuality and non-fungibility necessary to maintain our status as individuals with distinct moral and spiritual accountability.[6]

5.1.2 Legal and political context

Medieval legal and political theory is heavily indebted to Roman law, which was structured around the relation between persons (*personae*),

---

[4] For further discussion of the importance of the property of incommunicability for persons, especially as it applies in theological contexts, see John Crosby's "The Incommunicability of Human Persons," *The Thomist* 57/3 (1993), pp. 403–42.

[5] Maintaining the distinction between the three persons of the Trinity is crucial in Christological debates throughout the Middle Ages. For detailed discussion of the logic as well as the theology of these debates, see Tim Pawl's *In Defense of Conciliar Christology*, Oxford Studies in Analytic Theology (Oxford: Oxford University Press, 2016).

[6] The Averroistic position has the virtue of explanatory simplicity, in that it explains how everyone's concepts of universals like 'dog' and 'justice' share the same referents—namely, there is only one intellect producing those concepts, to which everyone has access. At the same time, the theory of the Unity of the Intellect raises a number of vexed questions for the possibility of post-mortem existence, because it's not clear what persistence conditions would suffice to individuate non-embodied beings with just one 'thinking center.' For the range of positions taken on these issues, see Richard Dales's *The Problem of the Rational Soul in the Thirteenth Century* (Leiden: Brill, 1995).

PUTTING 'PERSON' IN PERSPECTIVE   143

things (*res*), and events or transactions (*actiones*). In this context, the term *persona* connotes different sorts of roles available to individual agents, such as spouse, property owner, or defendant.[7] This use carries over into medieval legal theory, in part because of the Herculean efforts of the mid-twelfth-century Benedictine monk Gratian to preserve and systematize all the legal codes he had access to as a professor of law at the University of Bologna, many of which have Roman origins. In his massive *Decretum*, also referred to as the *Decretum Gratiani*, Gratian not only records but also synthesizes and resolves apparent disagreements between the roughly 3,800 texts he has compiled, using an early version of the disputed question genre (in which a teacher or 'master' examines apparently opposing views on a particular question and then 'settles the question' by providing a resolution that draws on recognized authorities, such as Augustine, Boethius, Cicero, and Gregory of Nyssa).[8]

The *Decretum* and subsequent *Decretals*—papal pronouncements about legal issues that need to be addressed after the *Decretum* is published— become the main source for canon law in the later Middle Ages and form part of Catholic canon law straight through to the early twentieth century.[9] The *Decretum's* understanding of 'person' as an individual subject who has certain inherent rights, capacities, and duties thus forms the standard for civil and religious legal debates.

Given the extensive overlap between legal, scholastic, and religious systems in this period, it should come as little surprise that theologians and philosophers as well as canon lawyers were familiar with the *Decretals*, drawing from them as necessary, and frequently using the term '*persona*' as a synonym for 'human being' (*homo*) in discussions with legal overtones.[10] The term '*persona*' also features in medieval accounts of just war theory, particularly in contexts in which 'who's' are

---

[7] This use of the term draws on the way in which the Greek word *prosopon* (from which the Latin word '*persona*' is derived) refers not just to the masks used in drama but also to the various roles those masks signify.

[8] For an overview of Gratian's compilation of the *Decretum* and the history of the *Decretals*, see Brian Tiereny's *Medieval Poor Law: A Sketch of Cannonical Theory and Its Application in England* (Berkeley: University of California Press, 1959), pp. 7–10.

[9] The *Decretals* forms the first part of the Roman Catholic *Corpus Iuris Canonici* until 1917, at which point the *Corpus* is replaced by the *Codex Iuris Canonici*—itself still heavily indebted to medieval and Roman sources.

[10] See, for instance, Aquinas's discussion of marriage in *Summa contra gentiles* 3.125.

144 PERSONS

distinguished from 'what's,' subjects with moral standing from things (*res*). Discussions of right conduct in war (*jus in bello*), for instance, employ the concept of person in detailing appropriate rules of conduct towards the enemy, whether combatants, noncombatants, or prisoners of war. (What rights do prisoners of war retain, for instance, simply by virtue of being a person?)

The concept of 'person' is also used in delineating a group of human beings who merit special protection under the law: *miserabiles personae* (literally, persons owed mercy or pity). One of the main considerations in generating this category was preserving the inherent dignity of the person by ensuring that all persons had access to fair legal representation: "The term *miserabiles personae* was used, in the *Decretum* and thereafter, to designate precisely a category of persons recommended to judicial benevolence, whom the clergy would represent in cases where this was normally forbidden."[11] If you were a member of a class or group often in need and deserving of aid but also often unable to find or afford just legal representation, the label of '*miserabiles persona*' entitled you to representation by an assigned clergy member. Originally this label applies only to widows, children (particularly orphans), and the poor—categories specifically recommended for aid in Scripture. By the mid-thirteenth century, however, the scope of the term had expanded to include lepers, merchants, and pilgrims as well, on the grounds that the people falling into these categories also often lacked access to fair legal representation.[12] Merchants and pilgrims, for instance, were physically removed via travel from their local communities of support (familial, religious, legal, or otherwise), while lepers (a category that included not only those who had actually contracted leprosy but also others with long-term and potentially contagious conditions, particularly skin diseases) were socially and physically isolated.

---

[11] Janet Coleman, 'Property and Poverty,' in *The Cambridge History of Medieval Political Thought c.350–c.1450*, ed. J. H. Burns (Cambridge: Cambridge University Press, 1988.), p. 627.

[12] For further discussion of this category and the complications involved in determining to whom it applied, see Robert Shaffern's *Law and Justice from Antiquity to Enlightenment* (Lanham, ML: Rowman & Littlefield Publishers, 2009), pp. 131–3. See also Michael Cusato's "Poverty," in *The Cambridge History of Medieval Philosophy*, eds. R. Pasnau and C. Van Dyke (Cambridge: Cambridge University Press, 2009), pp. 577–92.

Figure 5.1 *Dittico del Beato Andrea Gallerani*, verso, detail showing four mendicant pilgrims, Dietisalvi di Speme, *c*.1270, Pinacoteca Nazionale di Siena.

Given the growth of trade routes and the prevalence of pilgrimage, not to mention the increase in widows and orphans as a result of the Crusades and more localized warfare, the number of people who fall into the category of *miserabiles personae* becomes rather substantial in the later Middle Ages; saints and holy people are often depicted in this period interacting with these groups, performing acts like giving alms, preaching, and healing. (See Figure 5.1.) It is Francis of Assisi's experiences with lepers (qua *miserabiles personae*), for instance, that convince him that all human beings are equal in the eyes of God—that is, that "every person without exception was seen to be graced with the same inestimable worth and dignity given by God."[13] The idea that the 'least

---

[13] Cusato, "Poverty," p. 587.

146 PERSONS

of these' deserves to be treated with the same respect and compassion as princes and popes becomes increasingly mainstream in the age of the mendicant Dominican and Franciscan Orders, which are established in the early thirteenth century and are devoted to preaching, teaching, and ministering to everyone, not just the rich and powerful.

The concept of dignity is also increasingly associated with persons from the thirteenth century onwards. Understood as conferred in large part because of the connection of human beings with God via our creation in the image of God (*imago Dei*) and the Incarnation (see Subsection 3.3), dignity becomes one of the central features seen as distinguishing persons (*personae*) from things (*res*). Thus, the radical fourteenth-century Franciscan Ubertino da Casale argues that treating a pauper as lacking in dignity or worth is equivalent to treating God that way; the poor possess a positive right to better treatment. In his influential *Arbor vitae crucifixae Iesu* (*Tree of Life of the Crucified Jesus*), Casale writes that those without material resources have "a right to be sustained in dignity" and denounces "stripping the poor Crucified One [Christ] in the persons of the poor."[14] Persons have intrinsic worth, and all human beings are persons.

5.1.3 Theological context

Although all human beings were considered persons, no one in this period would have supposed that human beings were the *only* persons. Indeed, theological discussions of persons from the thirteenth to fifteenth centuries tend to focus more on God's nature than on our own— particularly on how the term '*persona*' applies to the mysteries of the Triune God (who is professed to be three persons in one God) and the Incarnate Christ (who is professed to be one person with two natures).[15]

---

[14] *Arbor vitae crucifixae Iesu* I.1. See Campion Murray, OFM, "Poverty in *The Tree of the Crucified Life of Jesus* by Ubertino da Casale," in *Poverty and Devotion in Mendicant Cultures 1200–1450*, ed. C. Mews and A. Welch (London: Routledge, 2016), pp. 45–60.

[15] Nestorianism is the objectionable view in the neighborhood, where Christ's human and divine natures are viewed as separate persons. For a detailed philosophical discussion of the concept of 'person' as it relates to the Incarnation, see Pawl, *In Defense of Conciliar Christology*.

PUTTING 'PERSON' IN PERSPECTIVE 147

Theological discussions of the nature of persons date back to the earliest attempts to hammer out the doctrine of the Trinity, but it is Boethius's sixth-century definition of a person as 'an individual substance with a rational nature' that becomes accepted as standard in the theology faculties at Paris and Oxford by the thirteenth century and is cited by all the major scholastics, including Aquinas and Bonaventure.[16] Taking each part of *'individual substance with a rational nature'* in turn, we see that the definition begins by emphasizing the same features of 'person'—namely, individuality and incommunicability—that take central place in logical and grammatical discussion. In theological contexts, the individuality and incommunicability of persons become particularly important in spelling out how the Three Persons of the Trinity remain distinct despite their being one God. As we see in in Section 5.2 (and also Section 6.3), the resulting idea of 'personal distinction within unity' provides medieval contemplatives with a model for communicating the experience of mystical union with God.

The description of persons as individual *substances* indicates that persons have independent existence. Medieval thinkers inherited the substance/accident distinction of ancient philosophy, according to which accidents (like color and shape) have dependent existence—that is, they can't exist without inhering in a substance (like a book or a person). Substances have independent existence in that, although they depend on things like book presses and parents to come into existence, their existence once created is independent—the book or the person continues to exist whether that book press or those parents continue to exist or not. In the case of the Trinity, the claim that persons are individual substances means that, while God the Creator, God the Savior, and God the Holy Spirit are one God, the 'being' (*esse*) of each Person of the Trinity is independent from the being of the other two Persons: the Savior is not dependent for existence on the Creator, nor the Spirit on the Savior, nor the Creator on the Spirit, etc.

---

[16] See Scott Williams's "Persons in Patristic and Medieval Christian Theology," in LoLordo, ed., *Persons: a History*, pp. 52–86, for further discussion of the development of this definition and the various controversies it involves.

148 PERSONS

In the case of human beings, this aspect of the definition of person raises questions about whether it's the composite of matter and form/body and soul or the rational soul that is the person—that is, whether the soul is one *part* of the substance that is the human being or a substance in its own right. On the one hand, possessing the capacity for independent subsistence is one of the primary characteristics of a substance, and the rational soul was widely believed to subsist in separation from matter between death and the general resurrection. On the other hand, the doctrine of the bodily resurrection was taken to entail that body and soul together make up the human being, and the view that the soul is the human being or the person was associated with gnostic heresies. (See Section 6.1 for fuller discussion of the issues these views raise about human immortality and the afterlife.)

Questions about the status of the rational soul occupy a great deal of attention throughout the thirteenth century; the general consensus that emerges, however, is that the soul is by nature only *part* of the human person and, thus, cannot be a person in its own right.[17] As Bonaventure writes in his discussion of the bodily assumption of the Virgin Mary to heaven, "[Mary's] blessedness would not have been complete unless she were there [in heaven] as a person. The soul is not a person, but the soul joined to the body is a person. Thus, it is clear that she is there in soul and in body."[18] Thomas Aquinas agrees, writing that, in the case of human beings, 'person' signifies "this flesh, these bones, and this soul," and stating definitively that "neither the name nor the definition of 'person' belongs to the rational soul."[19] As Aquinas explains in his *Disputed Questions on Power*, "the separated soul is *part* of [something with] a rational nature, namely, a human being, but it is not the *whole* rational human nature, and therefore it is not a person."[20] In the case of human

---

[17] See Dales, *Problem of the Rational Soul*, for a comprehensive discussion of the issues and which figures took which position on them.

[18] Bonaventure, *Assumption of the Blessed Virgin Mary* I.2.9.

[19] Aquinas, *Summa theologiae* Ia 29.4.co and 29.1.ad5 respectively. The rest of ad5 reads as follows: "the soul is *part* of the human species; for this reason, since it is still by nature unitable [to a body] even when it is separated, it cannot be the sort of individual substance which is called a 'hypostasis' or 'first substance' any more than a hand or any other part of a human being can." (Translation mine.)

[20] Aquinas, *Summa theologiae* 9.2.ad14.

PUTTING 'PERSON' IN PERSPECTIVE   149

beings, it is the substance composed of body and soul, not the soul alone, that qualifies as a person.

Human beings are unusual in being physical substances that qualify as persons, for the other beings generally considered to fit this definition in the Middle Ages are immaterial beings such as demons, intelligences, seraphim, cherubim, and God. The reason human beings fall into this category while other animals are excluded is that, according to common consensus, human beings are *rational* animals.[21] Rationality specifically and rational capacities generally (see Chapters 2 and 3) are understood throughout this period as distinguishing human beings from everything else in the terrestrial realm: rational beings are self-aware and capable of reflecting on their thoughts, desires, and feelings, while non-rational beings not only don't but can't participate in such activities.

This distinction between rational and non-rational beings was also understood as dividing those entities who are capable of consciously working towards their final end and attaining happiness (in the sense of *eudaimonia* or *beatitudo*) from those who merely move as they are naturally inclined (as a stone falls when dropped or a plant grows towards the light).[22] Although today we tend to associate 'rationality' with only intellective abilities, in this period it was viewed as involving volitional abilities as well. Thus, Boethius's inclusion of 'rational nature' in his definition of person encompasses not just the ability to think but also all the aspects involved in having control over one's own actions—intellect and free choice of the will first and foremost, but also memory, imagination, understanding, and creativity. (See Section 4.1 for a detailed discussion of how imagination fits into this picture.) Boethius's definition of persons as individual substances with a rational nature thus entails that persons are uniquely capable of love and knowledge in their richest and most meaningful forms. Love in its purest form is the desire for and union with the highest good; knowledge in its deepest form is possession

---

[21] For more on medieval views about animals, particularly as these views develop in the thirteenth century, see Nigel Harris's *The Thirteenth-Century Animal Turn: Medieval and Twenty-First-Century Perspectives* (Cham: Palgrave Macmillan, 2020); and Ian Wei's *Thinking about Animals in Thirteenth-Century Paris: Theologians on the Boundary Between Humans and Animals* (Cambridge: Cambridge University Press, 2020).

[22] See, e.g., Aquinas's *Treatise on Happiness* (ST IaIIae 1–5) for further discussion, as well as his all-too-often-overlooked discussion of happiness in *Summa contra gentiles*, chs 25–63.

150 PERSONS

of eternal and unchanging truth. God is understood both as the Highest Good and as Truth itself, and so union with God is the final end (that is, happiness) for all persons.

The category of 'person' in theological contexts picks out all and only those beings capable of true happiness. On this framework, we can call other creatures happy to the extent to which they fulfill their natural ends (think of Bob Ross painting his 'happy little trees'), but only persons are capable of consciously working towards, experiencing, and appreciating happiness qua the fulfillment of their natures (via loving and knowing God). Of course, the fact that persons possess free will means that they can—and often do—choose things that work against this volitional and intellective union. (The fall of Lucifer is a classic example of this.) Yet all rational beings can participate in this union, and the stakes involved in attaining or not attaining it are the highest possible. As we've seen in Chapter 3 and Chapter 4, there is a lively debate in the thirteenth–fifteenth centuries about whether happiness consists primarily in the activity of the intellect or of the will, with Dominicans (like Thomas Aquinas) tending to stress the centrality of intellect in the activity of perfect happiness, and Franciscans (like John Duns Scotus) tending to stress the centrality of the will and love. This disagreement over the nature of perfect happiness is hardly restricted to disputed questions generated by university masters, however—as we've seen already (and will see in more detail in Sections 5.2 and 5.3 as well as Chapter 6), contemplatives take different positions on this question as well.

5.2 Individuality, Dignity, and Rationality in Contemplative Texts

Medieval logical/grammatical, legal/political, and theological understandings of what it is to be a person stress the importance of individuality, dignity, and rationality (in the broad sense that involves both intellection and volition). In this section, I explore the role these three concepts play in contemplative discussions about who we are and what

INDIVIDUALITY, DIGNITY, AND RATIONALITY 151

our final end is; as we'll see, these discussions both echo the importance of these features and offer further insight into how they relate to our moral and spiritual lives.

Before I turn to this exploration, however, a historical note about the languages in which these discussions occur is in order. Prior to the thirteenth century, both contemplative and scholastic texts in the Rome-based Christian tradition are written in Latin, the language spoken as well as written throughout the majority of Europe. Starting in the late thirteenth century, however, contemplative texts also appear in the developing vernaculars, while the language of the church and of the universities remains Latin.[23]

The rise of contemplative texts in the vernacular has two consequences that prove important for our purposes. First, vernacular texts represent a wider range of voices than texts written in Latin. From the thirteenth century onward, Latin increasingly becomes the language of the elite: it is the tongue of authority used by ecclesiastical hierarchs, university masters, magistrates of all ranks, royalty, etc. The regional vernaculars that develop across France, Italy, Germany, England, and the Low Countries by contrast, become the language of everyday life. As religious movements spearheaded and promulgated by laypeople sweep through Europe in the fourteenth and fifteenth centuries, we find contemplative literature written in the vernacular by people from all walks of life—a great deal of it written by women.[24] The beguine Hadewijch, for instance, who writes in early Middle Dutch, appears to have come from a wealthy Flemish family and to have been quite well educated—as noblewomen often were in this period, given that they would be

---

[23] Both contemplative and scholastic texts tend to focus on topics in which our status as persons is less relevant than our unique status as intellective beings who are also material substances, such as the development of virtue and how human beings will experience the afterlife. For this reason, the Latin word for human being (*homo*) is used more often than the word for person in these conversations; the term 'person' tends to appear in discussions with legal and political overtones. This is often obscured in modern English translations of these texts, however, which often render the terms for 'man' or 'human being' as 'person', to capture the original, gender-neutral sense of those terms or to be more inclusive.

[24] For a sense of the full range of voices involved in vernacular conversations and more on the history of the development of these conversations, see Bernard McGinn's *Varieties of Vernacular Mysticism: 1350–1550*, Vol. 5 of *The Presence of God: A History of Western Christian Mysticism.* (New York: Crossroad Publishing Co., 2016.)

responsible for running households the size of small towns (if not entire city-states or countries) when they were married. (See Figure 5.2, which depicts Arithmetic personified as a noblewoman taking care of financial affairs in a counting house.) Catherine of Siena, on the other hand, is the twenty-fourth child of a cloth dyer in the emerging Sienese lower middle class, who dictated her *Dialogue* (and almost 400 letters) in her native Tuscan dialect because she hadn't been taught to write. Between these two extremes we find a range of other contemplatives who express their insights in vernacular: Angela of Foligno, a wealthy widow who dictates her *Memorial* in her Umbrian dialect to a Franciscan friar who records her words in Latin; Marguerite Porete, whose controversial *Mirror of Simple Souls* appears in Old French as well as Latin (and who apparently also translated part of the Bible from Latin into the vernacular when this was still expressly forbidden by the pope); Mechthild of Magdeburg, a beguine who writes her *Flowing Light of the Godhead* in Middle Low German; Margaret Ebner, a Dominican nun who composes her *Revelations* and letters in Middle High German; and Julian of

Figure 5.2 Detail of tapestry of Arithmetic, Flanders workshop, *c.*1520, Musée de Cluny, Paris.

INDIVIDUALITY, DIGNITY, AND RATIONALITY 153

Norwich, an anchorite whose *Showings* or *Revelations of Divine Love* is written in Middle English.

Second, the rise of the vernacular is associated with the development of what is often called 'personal piety.'[25] This religious sensibility focuses on forming a meaningful emotional attachment to God, particularly Christ, the incarnate Second Person of the Trinity; it also emphasizes humility and self-reflection, and its devotional literature is widely read by an increasingly literate population.[26] (For more on the importance of humility and the recommended role of emotion in the moral and spiritual life, see Chapters 2 and 4.) Arising partly in response to persistent gnostic heresies, the forms this affective piety took were strongly influenced by the popularity of the songs, stories, and poems about *fin'amor* or 'courtly love.' (See Interlude Four.) An emphasis on a personal, affective connection to God was hardly the exclusive purview of women—any number of male contemplatives during this period also exemplify strongly affective piety, including Bernard of Clairvaux, Francis of Assisi, Jan van Ruusbroec, Richard Rolle, and Thomas à Kempis—but at the same time this form of embodied and creative piety was particularly well suited to women as they were perceived at this time (see Section 4.5). The dramatic increase in affective devotional literature written by and for women across Europe in this period testifies to the extent to which it spoke to them; the development of this 'vernacular piety' thus cuts across gender lines as well as social hierarchies.

---

[25] For an extended discussion of this connection, see Barbara Newman's "Love Divine, All Loves Excelling," in her *God and the Goddesses: Vision, Poetry, and Belief in the Middle Ages* (Philadelphia: University of Pennsylvania Press, 2003), pp. 138–89. For an argument that personal piety was alive and well long before the thirteenth century, however, see Lauren Mancia's *Emotional Monasticism: Affective piety in the eleventh-century monastery of John of Fécamp* (Manchester: Manchester University Press, 2019).

[26] The popular devotional *Meditations on the Life of Christ* (*Meditationes vitae Christi*), for instance, is translated from its original Latin into a number of vernaculars and disseminated widely. This speaks to the "expanded audience for devotional texts of all kinds" that Thomas Bestul notes characterizes the later Middle Ages, and which is "occasioned by the increase in literacy, particularly among laypersons of the aristocratic and bourgeois classes, and the growth of opportunities for private leisure and devotion" ("*Meditatio*/Meditation," in *The Cambridge Companion to Christian Mysticism*, ed. A. Hollywood and P. Dailey (Cambridge: Cambridge University Press, 2012), p. 163).

154 PERSONS

5.2.1 Individuality and agency

A crucial feature of affective devotional piety is an awareness of the self as a unique individual. Although the collective nature of sin and guilt (particularly as it relates to original sin and its consequences) also features in medieval theological discussions, it is the status of the person as a morally responsible individual that forms the backbone of discussions of vices and virtues, punishments and rewards. The status of the person *qua individual* also proves significant for contemplative discussions of mystical union with God, because this union both happens on a deeply personal (in the sense of individual) level and also frequently involves experiences which blur—and perhaps erase—the boundaries separating individual human beings from God.

Contemplative views about our relation to God in both mystical union and the afterlife differ widely, as I discuss in detail in Chapter 6. Contemplatives in apophatic-leaning mystical traditions, for instance, often speak of our final goal as a self-abnegation so complete that any sense of individual experience disappears. The question of whether this self-annihilation involves ontological as well as phenomenological and epistemological erasure is subject to debate; among medieval Christian contemplatives, Marguerite Porete appears to go the furthest towards advocating this possibility. In her *Mirror of Simple Souls*, for instance, Porete describes the goal of the spiritual life as one in which the human person so fully merges with God that "nothing is, except He who is, who sees Himself in such being." When the soul has so emptied herself that all that remains "is properly His own, and His own proper self," then it is as though the soul is not merely "without existence" but was never created as a separate being in the first place, existing simply as in idea in God's mind, "where she was before she was created."[27]

Meister Eckhart also maintains that the closest union with God requires relinquishing our individual personhood to become one with the Second Person and, thus, God; to do this, we must cease to think of

---

[27] *Mirror of Simple Souls*, trans. E. L. Babinsky (Mahwah: Paulist Press, 1993), ch. 118, p. 194, and ch. 135, p. 218.

INDIVIDUALITY, DIGNITY, AND RATIONALITY   155

(or experience) ourselves as persons with distinct intellects and wills.[28] In explaining how emptying one's self allows God to enter, Eckhart appeals to the distinction between individual human beings and common human nature—a move that draws on the logical/grammatical contrast between the individual member of a species and the species nature itself. When God took on human nature and "united it with his own Person," Eckhart writes, Christ assumed "bare human nature"—not the specific created nature of any existing human being. Eckhart's advice to us is to mimic this action to whatever extent possible by emptying ourselves of whatever is particular in us: "The eternal Word did not put on a [particular] human being, so go out of whatever is a human being in you...and take yourself just as bare human nature, and then you will be the same to the eternal Word as human nature is to him. For between your human nature and his there is no difference: it is one, for it is in Christ what it is in you."[29] Johannes Tauler, Eckhart's student and fellow Dominican, agrees that union with God requires complete self-abnegation. Rather than portraying love in positive terms as a rushing torrent or burning fire, as was popular in his day,[30] Tauler writes that the highest form of love "is nothing else than a loss of self" in which "there is no affirmation." Rather than being something we possess or experience, love is "a privation."[31]

Other medieval contemplatives (such as Hadewijch and Angela of Foligno) use both the language of self-loss *and* of continued personal distinction in their descriptions of mystical union. Angela of Foligno, for example, reports that she regularly experiences two different sorts of mystical union: in the first, she loses her self completely and is unable to remember "anything about anything human, or the God-man [Christ],

---

[28] See, e.g., Sermon 70 in *Complete Mystical Works of Eckhart*, trans. Maurice O'C. Walshe (New York: Crossroad Publishing Co., 2010).

[29] Sermon 92, *Complete Mystical Works of Eckhart*, p. 450.

[30] Richard Rolle's most famous work, for instance, is titled simply *The Fire of Love*. Hadewijch also uses the language of burning flame for mystical union with God, as well as that of rushing water. See, e.g., Letter 16, where she writes that "love enkindles faith; works with faith must precede love; then love will set them on fire" (p. 81), and Letter 6, in which she describes Love as "bursting her dikes" and overwhelming the lover like a flood (p. 63).

[31] Sermon for the Twenty-Second Sunday after Trinity (V 76), as quoted in B. McGinn, *The Harvest of Mysticism in Medieval Germany (1300–1500)*, Vol. 4 of *The Presence of God: A History of Western Christian Mysticism* (New York: Crossroad Publishing Co., 2005), p. 274.

156   PERSONS

or anything which has a form" in this state, while seeing and understanding "all and nothing"; in the second, she experiences direct union with Christ while retaining a sense of self. After looking at the cross (as encouraged by the *Meditations on the Life of Christ*), for instance, she "saw and felt that Christ was within me, embracing my soul with the very arm with which he was crucified," at which point she explains that she now understands "how we will see that through [Christ] our flesh is made one with God."[32] Individual subjectivity remains intact in this second sort of union, while it disappears entirely in the first, which she sometimes describes as a 'blazing darkness.'

Finally, other contemplatives (including Marguerite d'Oingt, Mechthild of Magdeburg, Richard Rolle, and Jan van Ruusbroec) employ a 'personal distinction within unity' model in their depictions of mystical union. Marguerite d'Oingt, a thirteenth-century Carthusian nun (and author of some of the earliest extant texts written in Franco-Provençal), for instance, describes the beatified as completely immersed in God but nevertheless retaining distinct, individual existence: "The saints will be within their Creator as the fish within the sea: they will drink as much as they want, without getting tired and without diminishing the amount of water."[33] Mechthild in turn writes of the "special intimacy with separation" as well as the "complete fulfillment" involved in union with God in her *Flowing Light of the Godhead*, and in his *Fire of Love* the influential fourteenth-century English mystic Richard Rolle describes affective embodied experiences of mystical union that not only do not extinguish but actually enhance his sense of self, such as 'glowing' or heat in the chest, a taste of unimaginable sweetness, and the sound of celestial music.[34]

Hadewijch writes of how God and the Beloved "penetrate each other in such a way that neither of the two distinguishes himself from the other," but immediately goes on to comment that although "one sweet divine nature flows through both and they are both one thing through

---

[32] Ch. 6, 4th Supplemental Step, from the *Memorial*, in *Angela of Foligno: Complete Works*, trans. Paul Lachance, OFM (Mahwah: Paulist Press, 1993), p. 175.

[33] Ch. 2, para. 19, in *The Writings of Margaret of Oingt, Medieval Prioress and Mystic (d. 1310)*, trans. with an introduction, essay, and notes by Renate Blumenfeld-Kosinski (Cambridge: D. S. Brewer, 1990), p. 44.

[34] Book II, *Flowing Light of the Godhead*, pp. 70–1.

INDIVIDUALITY, DIGNITY, AND RATIONALITY 157

each other, at the same time they remain two different selves—yes, and remain so forever."[35] Jan van Ruusbroec, who is influenced by Hadewijch, also describes our final end as a "blissful unity... in which there is nothing but God and the spirit united with God without intermediary,"[36] while likewise agreeing that this unity does not involve an actual merging of the individual self with God. Ruusbroec in fact takes pains to be clear that we retain our human individuality in union with God: "I just said that we are one with God, something to which Scripture bears witness. I now wish to say that we must forever remain different from God, which is also taught us by Scripture."[37] In describing the highest experience of mystical union, he writes that, although we "feel ourselves to be one with God, for by means of our transformation in God we feel ourselves to be swallowed up in the groundless abyss of our eternal blessedness, in which we can never discover any difference between ourselves and God," we are not annihilated into God, for in that case "we would cease to be creatures."[38] On this view, mystical union joins human and divine persons directly in a way that simultaneously retains their individuality.

The concept of individuality and its experience in union with God plays a key role in medieval contemplative thought—whether as something to be lost or something that is retained. As we'll see in Subsections 5.2.2 and 5.2.3, this feature of personhood is also linked to the dignity and the broad sense of rationality central to the concept of 'person' in this period.

5.2.2 Dignity

The importance of dignity in discussions of the human person in the Italian Renaissance is well known, and so it comes as little surprise that the concept features prominently in the writings of fifteenth-century

---

[35] *Hadewijch*, Letter 9, p. 66.
[36] *John Ruusbroec: The Spiritual Espousals and Other Works*, ed. and trans. John A. Wiseman. (Mahwah: Paulist Press, 1985), Book II, Part 4, p. 119.
[37] *Ruusbroec: Spiritual Espousals*, p. 174. This is the opening of a section in *The Sparkling Stone* bluntly titled "Our Union with God is Not an Identification: Four Ways of Experiencing This Union."
[38] *Ruusbroec: Spiritual Espousals*, p. 176.

158   PERSONS

mystics such as Marsilio Ficino and Giovanni Pico della Mirandola.[39] Ficino—deeply involved in the translation from Greek of Plato's dialogues, the works of Plotinus, and other Platonists—stresses the role of dignity in human activities, not just as it manifests in intellection but as it appears "in every aspect of human creativity."[40] Pico della Mirandola shares Ficino's emphasis on the importance of dignity for understanding human nature and our place in the cosmos; in fact, his *Oratio* becomes known as the *Oration on the Dignity of Man*. What has frequently been ignored in these works, however, in favor of looking for Platonism's impact on Renaissance thought, is the extent to which these scholars' (and their contemporaries') understanding of dignity is both contiguous with and indebted to that of the contemplative traditions which preceded them.

In theological discussions, as we saw in Section 5.1, persons are understood as individual substances with intellects and wills, deserving of respect and possessing intrinsic dignity. In medieval civil law and political theory, all human beings are considered persons, *who's* rather than *what's*, and as such possess certain rights and responsibilities that set us off from the other animals and plants, as well as from non-animate objects; these rights and responsibilities ground which actions are permissible and impermissible both by and towards us. Over the course of the Middle Ages, dignity is a quality that becomes consistently attributed to all human beings simply insofar as they are human, as opposed to only those few fortunate enough to be born into the nobility. As the English Augustine Alexander Nequam writes in his early-thirteenth-century *Commentary on Proverbs*, for instance, "In meditating on humanity, the meditator considers the dignity of human nature as well as its fragility."[41]

---

[39] See, for instance, Paul Oskar Kristeller's "The Dignity of Man," in *Renaissance Concepts of Man and Other Essays* (New York: Harper & Row, 1972), pp. 1–21, as well as any number of his other works on Ficino and Pico della Mirandola, and Charles Trinkaus's two-volume *'In Our Image and Likeness': Humanity and Divinity in Italian Humanist Thought* (Chicago: University of Chicago Press, 1970).

[40] McGinn, *Varieties of Vernacular Mysticism*, p. 257; for a helpful overview of Ficino and Pica della Mirandola's Platonic-influenced mysticism, see pp. 252–84.

[41] Nequam's unpublished manuscript in Oxford, Jesus College, MS. 94, fol. 57r, as reported by Thomas H. Bestul in *The Cambridge Companion to Christian Mysticism*, p. 161.

INDIVIDUALITY, DIGNITY, AND RATIONALITY   159

One might suppose that the contemplative emphasis on humility would preclude dignity's also being given a positive role in our moral and spiritual lives, but dignity features prominently in the work of a number of contemplatives—often as humility's complement. (See Subsection 2.2.2.) Richard of St. Victor, for instance, writes in *The Mystical Ark* that

> "at one time, [the wisdom of God] lifts the soul to a high place and at other times presses it down to a low place and abandons it to itself…so it first begins to kindle the soul of the contemplative with longing for flying and at the same time to instruct it perfectly for full flight. Here, first of all, the soul recovers its ancient dignity and claims for itself the inborn honor of its own freedom."[42]

Hadewijch also stresses the need for the restoration and recovery of the intrinsic dignity we possess by creation, but which has been marred by sin: "With his whole heart and his whole soul, and with all his strength, and in each and every circumstance, Christ was ready to perfect what was wanting on our part. And thus he uplifted us and drew us up by his divine power and his human justice to our first dignity, and to our liberty, in which we were created and loved."[43] The dignity conferred on us by association with Christ also sets an imposing standard which we must strive to live up to. As Hadewijch writes in a letter to a fellow beguine, "Oh, you have much to do if you are to live the Divinity and the Humanity and come to full growth, according to the measure of the dignity in which you are loved and destined by God!"[44] Paradoxically, it is only when we become fully humble that we attain true dignity.

In Mechthild of Magdeburg's *Flowing Light of the Godhead*, we see the interplay between dignity and humility when the Bride of Christ comes to Him with four bridesmaids, the first of whom is love, "clothed in chasteness and crowned with dignity," and the second of whom is humility, "clothed with lowliness and crowned with eminence."[45] In *The Herald of Divine Love*, Gertrude of Helfta also muses on the paradoxical nature

---

[42] *Richard of St. Victor: The Twelve Patriarchs, The Mystical Ark, Book Three of the Trinity*, trans. Grover Zinn (Mahwah: Paulist Press, 1979), p. 192.
[43] *Hadewijch*, Letter 6, p. 63.   [44] *Hadewijch*, Letter 18, p. 85.
[45] *Flowing Light of the Godhead*, p. 63.

160 PERSONS

of human persons: "Oh, the dignity of this minutest speck of dust that has been lifted up out of the mud and taken as a setting for the noblest gem of heaven! Oh, the excellence of this tiny flower which has been drawn up out of the mire by the sun's rays, so that it might shine with the sun's light!"[46]

The relation between dignity and humility also forms an important theme in Catherine of Siena's *Dialogue*, a work which would have been known to both Ficino and Pico della Mirandola. Although, as we saw in Section 2.2.2, Catherine sees that the tree of self must be rooted in humility in order to bear fruit, Truth also counsels her to opens her mind's eye and look within God, where she will see "the dignity and beauty (*la dignità e bellezza*)" of the human person.[47] As God tells her, "Because of the union I effected between my Godhead and human nature, your excellence and dignity is greater than that of the angels.... I, God, became human, and humanity became God through the union of my divine nature with your human nature."[48] Throughout the *Dialogue*, the humility that grounds us in God is linked with the recognition of our intrinsic dignity as formed in God's image—a recognition that grants Catherine the ability to "stand with confidence in God's presence" to intercede for the world,[49] for it is in the "dignity of our existence" that we taste the immeasurable goodness and uncreated love of God.[50]

Although not a contemplative per se, the fifteenth-century Christine de Pizan also appeals to the dignity inherent in the human person in her *City of Ladies*. When the personifications of Reason, Rectitude, and Justice appear to her in order to help construct a fortress that can stand against attacks on woman's character, Lady Reason holds a 'mirror of self-knowledge' in place of a scepter and describes it as having "such great dignity" that it is appropriately surrounded by rich and precious gems. When we gain knowledge of ourselves via this mirror, we see not only our humble status as specks of dust but also our intrinsic worth. In the words of Lady Reason, "Thanks to this mirror, the essences, qualities, proportions, and measures of all things can be known, nor can

---

[46] *Gertrude of Helfta: The Herald of Divine Love*, trans. and ed. Margaret Winkworth (Mahwah: Paulist Press, 1993), p. 108.

[47] Prologue to the *Dialogue*, p. 25.   [48] *Dialogue*, p. 205, slightly modified translation.

[49] *Dialogue*, ch. 13, p. 49.   [50] *Dialogue*, ch. 51, p. 104.

INDIVIDUALITY, DIGNITY, AND RATIONALITY   161

anything be done well without it."[51] (Catherine of Siena also associates the metaphor of the mirror of self-knowledge with dignity: "in the gentle mirror of God she sees her own dignity: that through no merit of hers but by his creation she is the image of God."[52])

5.2.3 Rationality

Dignity might be a feature of personhood that we share with God, but for medieval contemplatives the most important point of similarity between human persons and God is rationality, in its broadest sense. As we saw in Subsection 5.1.3, medieval conceptions of 'rational nature' go beyond mere reasoning abilities to include such things as intellection, volition, understanding, memory, love, and imagination. All and only persons were understood in this period to be capable of representing different potential courses of action to themselves, judging between those options, choosing which to enact, and reflecting on the results. In the case of human persons, the ability to choose consciously in accordance with or against God's will separates us from all other material creatures (who were viewed as lacking second-order reflective capacities) at the same time that it connects us to the other sorts of beings (God and the whole host of immaterial creatures, such as angels and demons) who are responsible for their actions and, thus, blame- or praiseworthy. Because contemplative texts are written in a variety of genres, many of which focus on first-person experience and the development of our rational capacities, they provide an important complement to the analytic, impersonal discussions of the nature of rationality that we find in scholastic texts.[53]

One of the primary purposes of contemplative literature in this period is to provide spiritual counsel—a task that often involves explaining

---

[51] *The Book of the City of Ladies*, trans. Earl Richards (New York: Persea Books, 1982, rev. 1998), p. 9.

[52] *Dialogue*, ch. 13, p. 48.

[53] It's worth noting in this respect that Bonaventure and Meister Eckhart, both of whom wrote popular (and thus surviving) mystical/contemplative treatises in addition to their scholastic works, present a valuable opportunity to examine how modalities of expression affect the content of what is expressed.

162 PERSONS

what the author sees as the ideal relation between the various aspects of the self. Some contemplatives, for instance, advise working towards the simultaneous fulfillment of the components of the person qua rational substance, as when Hadewijch writes in a letter to a fellow beguine, "It is truly fitting that everyone contemplate God's grace and goodness with wisdom and prudence: for God has given us our beautiful faculty of reason, which instructs us in all our ways and enlightens us in all works. If man would follow reason, he would never be deceived."[54] If we use reason to help us better contemplate God's goodness and love, Hadewijch maintains, we will grow in virtue and wisdom as well as love.

Other contemplatives stress the importance of the human will's complete alignment with God's will via the uniting act of love and downplay the work of other parts of human nature—particularly the faculty of reason. (For more on contemplative attitudes towards reason in this period, see Chapter 3.) Marguerite Porete, for instance, casts her *Mirror of Simple Souls* as a lively dialogue between Love, Reason, and the Soul to better portray the proper relation between the different components of human nature. Throughout the conversation, the characteristics and limitations of Reason serve as an important foil to the Soul's growing understanding of the expansive possibilities of Love. Indeed, as the personification of Love tells Reason in chapter 21, "I am God by divine nature, and this Soul is God by righteousness of Love." The proper use of reason is to help the soul progress to the point where it glimpses this truth, at which point the soul is meant to focus on abnegating herself, with the help of the love that unites them. As Love says, "Thus, this precious beloved of mine is taught and guided by me [Love], without herself, for she is transformed into me."[55]

Meister Eckhart also repeatedly counsels detaching from the external world and our own individuality as a way of moving beyond our attachment to self and becoming one with God. What is important about our rational nature for Eckhart is not the uniqueness of our thoughts and experiences (or even our individual personalities) but simply its likeness to God's nature. As we saw in Subsection 5.2.1, this connection comes most centrally from our possessing the same human nature that the

---

[54] *Hadewijch*, Letter 14, p. 77.   [55] *Mirror of Simple Souls*, p. 104.

INDIVIDUALITY, DIGNITY, AND RATIONALITY   163

Second Person of the Trinity assumes in the Incarnation, not in our particular expressions of that rational nature. Focusing too much on using our individual rational powers to learn about the physical world around us—what Eckhart describes as "knowing through sensible images and through concepts"—can distract from or even actively obscure our access to the other, far more important, way of knowing. We are one with God not through our knowledge of the world but by our "having one being" with God.[56] Johannes Tauler also counsels that we must leave the unique expression of our rational capacities behind to become one with God through love. To expand on a passage quoted in Subsection 5.2.1, "This love is nothing else than a loss of self, there is no affirmation.... In it there is ignorance and unknowing; it is far above understanding, above all essence and modes of being."[57]

As we saw in Section 3.5, the idea that our ultimate goal as human persons involves moving beyond reason and knowledge via love becomes an increasingly common theme from the late thirteenth to the fourteenth century, even among contemplatives who don't counsel self-abnegation. This increasing distrust of 'book learning' or *scientia* reflects growing frustration with the elitism of the universities and the specialized discussions they churned out.[58] What contemplatives sought was something deeper than mere 'head' knowledge—they wanted nothing less than a personal connection with and experience of God; the massive rise in lay religious movements in this period testifies to this being a widely shared desire.[59] By the outset of the fifteenth century, frustration with scholastic discussions of highly specialized topics had become widespread enough that Jean Gerson, a master at the University of Paris himself, gave two lectures titled "Against the Vain Curiosity of Students," and Thomas à Kempis's fifteenth-century *De Imitatione Christi*—which counsels readers to follow the model of Christ's life, and stresses virtue

---

[56] Sermon 76 in *Meister Eckhart: Teacher and Preacher*, ed. B McGinn, trans. B. McGinn, F. Tobin, and E. Borgstadt (Mahwah, NJ: Paulist Press, 1986), pp. 327–8.

[57] Sermon for the Twenty-Second Sunday after Trinity (V 76), trans. McGinn, in *The Harvest of Mysticism*, from Vetter's *Die Predigten Taulers*.

[58] For more about the history of *scientia* in this period, see Robert Pasnau's "Medieval Social Epistemology: *Scientia* for Mere Mortals," *Episteme* 7/1 (2010), pp. 23–41.

[59] For more about these movements, see McGinn, *The Harvest of Mysticism in Medieval Germany*.

164 PERSONS

and a life of love over academic knowledge—is one of the most popular devotional books of the later Middle Ages. As à Kempis writes, "Many people, even after hearing scripture read so often, lack a deep longing for it, for they do not have the spirit of Christ. Anyone who wishes to understand Christ's words and to savor them fully should strive to become like him in every way." After all, he continues, "What good does it do to debate about the Trinity, if by a lack of humility you are displeasing to the Trinity?"[60]

Even this cautioning against the value of specialized theoretical expertise, however, retains the idea that we must make the most of our rational capacities in order to reach our final end—it just warns against prioritizing knowledge over love. A number of contemplatives known for their emphasis on the unifying power of love, such as Hadewijch, Catherine of Siena, and Julian of Norwich, highlight the importance of knowledge as well. Their understanding of what it means for human beings to have a 'rational nature' involves all the ways in which we image God, not just our wills.

Catherine's *Dialogue* (which is cast as an intimate conversation between Catherine and God), for instance, characterizes the relationship between knowledge and love as an upward spiral. Calling her 'my dearest daughter,' God tells Catherine about how the unitive state "in which souls are carried off by the fire of my charity" perfects those souls so that they may reach "the eternal vision of me in which they see and taste me in truth." This process of perfection involves the interplay of intellect and will, infused by God's grace: "In that charity, they receive supernatural light, and in that light they love me. For love follows upon understanding. The more they know, the more they love, and the more they love, the more they know."[61] God's grace allows our souls to love God even more intensely as our intellects are illuminated: the ideal relation between the various components of a rational nature on this view is not competitive but symbiotic. Rather than subordinating intellect to will (or vice versa), we are encouraged to see each as supporting and

---

[60] Thomas à Kempis, *The Imitation of Christ*, trans. William C. Creasy (Notre Dame, IN: Ave Maria Press, 2017), ch. 1, p. 25.
[61] *Dialogue*, p. 85.

PERSONAL PERSPECTIVES, PERSONIFICATION   165

uplifting the other in the process of moral and spiritual development that culminates in the eternal vision of God. The ultimate model for this process, of course, is the incarnate Christ who is both identified with Wisdom and exemplifies perfect love.[62]

As we've seen, the concepts of individuality, dignity, and rationality run throughout medieval contemplative discussions of who we are (and what our ultimate end is). These discussions are further enhanced by the contemplative use of personal perspective, personification of abstract concepts, and an emphasis on introspection that involves a narrative sense of self. In Section 5.3 I address each of these techniques in turn, showing how they encourage the development of a rich inner life. The resulting understanding of what it means to be a person might feel rather familiar, for (as I discuss in Section 5.4) it has influenced contemporary conceptions of the person in ways that have often gone unacknowledged.

5.3 Personal Perspectives, Personification, and Introspection

Contemplative literature, meant to inspire and instruct, lends itself to dynamic expression: in the vast corpus of contemplative texts produced during the thirteenth to fifteenth centuries we find advice, expressions of inner joys and pains, admonishments for wandering souls (from beguines to bishops), and reports of insights gained via mystical experiences—all written with the aim of encouraging their audiences towards moral and spiritual growth. To express this encouragement, medieval contemplatives tend to avoid the impersonal constructions of the scholastic disputed questions, which use formulae such as 'in response, it should be said that' both for organizational purposes and to stress the truth of what is being said over the person who happens to be sharing that truth. Instead, contemplatives use all three 'personal perspectives' (the first-personal 'I/we,' the second-personal 'you,' and the

---

[62] See Barbara Newman's "Sapientia: the Goddess Incarnate," in *God and the Goddesses* (pp. 190–244) for a detailed discussion of this identification.

166 PERSONS

third personal 's/he/they') to connect to and engage their audiences.
To make discussions of abstract and weighty matters more lively and
accessible, they also regularly personify virtues, vices, and various components of human nature; this method is used to help us gain deeper
insight into our own spiritual journeys, via allegories like Richard of
St. Victor's *The Twelve Patriarchs* (see Chapter 4), *Piers Plowman* and
The Pearl, and fifteenth-century devotional texts set in the Garden of
Contemplation and inspired by the secular French *Roman de la Rose*.[63]
In addition, contemplatives throughout the Middle Ages rely on and
counsel others towards rigorous introspection and self-improvement:
an essential part of this project is the development of a robustly narra-
tive sense of self.

The use of first-, second-, and third-personal vs. impersonal grammatical constructions may at first seem disconnected from the project of
moral and spiritual growth, but a closer look reveals the importance of
number and person for expressing different sorts of sentiments and better communicating various aspects of the contemplative life. Medieval
contemplatives often use the first-person singular perspective when
reporting mystical experiences and in offering spiritual advice based on
their own journeys; there is an intimacy and a humility involved in linking particular experiences and suggestions to a particular person rather
than conveying them as impersonal truths, at the same time that this
evokes authority. (First-person plural constructions appear more often
in professions of common belief and when the text is written for particularly close-knit communities.) The first person is also used to give
voice to personified qualities, as in Porete's *Mirror*, in which Love, Soul,
and Reason all speak for themselves. This allows for vigorous disagreement between aspects of a unified self, while also depicting the 'how' of
spiritual progress through the resolutions of these disagreements.

---

[63] As Gabriela Badea notes in "Allegories of Selfhood in Medieval Devotional Literature"
(Doctoral Thesis, Columbia University, 2018), "The literary setting of the Roman de la Rose
came to be associated with a devotional representation of the self in the later Middle Ages." The
popularity of this trend is reflected in the fact that Catherine of Siena's *Dialogue* is titled *The
Orchard of Syon* when it is translated into English at the turn of the fifteenth century. For more
on the history of this translation, see Sister Mary Denise's "The Orchard of Syon: an
Introduction," *Traditio* 14 (1958), pp. 269–93.

PERSONAL PERSPECTIVES, PERSONIFICATION   167

Not surprisingly, correspondence by and between contemplatives often employs the second-personal perspective. From Francis and Clare of Assisi to Hadewijch to Margaret Ebner to Catherine of Siena, we find medieval religious figures drawing on the epistles of the New Testament and using letters to provide vital sources of encouragement and support—as well as warning and critique—to individuals and communities large and small. The second-personal perspective frequently appears in sermons and books of counsel as well: contexts in which the audience is being addressed simultaneously as a group and as individual people, meant to take what they hear to heart and apply it to their own lives. The use of the second person is also common in dialogues and poetry in which God (or personified quality) is talking directly to the subject, or in which the subject is speaking directly to God. The effect has an engaging directness. When Angela of Foligno reports shrieking, "Love yet unknown, why do you leave me?!" repeatedly as her vision of God fades at Assisi, she illustrates the personal nature of that mystical experience (and reminds her audience of times when they've also felt abandoned by love). When Hadewijch exclaims, "Oh, you have much to do if you are to live the Divinity and the Humanity and come to full growth!" the reader can't hide behind a comforting veil of anonymity. There is a zing of immediate connection formed by use of the second person—it both assumes and creates a relationship between speaker and audience; it is the difference between my giving a lecture on Aristotle's virtue ethics in which I say, "Generosity can be expressed in a variety of ways depending on one's individual mean," and one in which I say directly to a student, "Tony, do remember when you lent your pen to Xinyi last week? Aristotle thinks that whether that act was generous or not depends on why you did that, and how you felt when you did." Medieval contemplatives are committed to the lifelong process of changing for the better, and they're invested in helping you—yes, *you*, whenever and wherever you may be—to do the same.

The third-personal perspective also appears in contemplative texts. Because the third person is distanced both from the self who authors a text and that text's audience, however, contemplatives tend to use it less often than the first or second person. When they do use the third person, it is often to report general states of affairs or facts, as when

168 PERSONS

Hadewijch and Angela of Foligno report visions in which they are given explanations about what is happening around them or insight into the differences between virtues and vices, etc. Sometimes the choice of the third person is meant to demonstrate humility and modesty, as when mystics like Marguerite d'Oingt and Mechthild of Hackeborn share mystical experiences in the third person, although it is clear from context and the rest of the text that the experiences they report are their own. (See Interlude Five for more on the relation between this and medieval methods for establishing authority as an author.) Other times, the third person is chosen as a way of introducing the speaker, as in Julian of Norwich's *A Vision Showed to a Devout Woman*, which begins by linking what follows to a particular person, time, and place: "Here is a vision, showed by the goodness of God to a devout woman. And her name is Julian, who is a recluse at Norwich, and is still alive in the year of our Lord 1413. In this vision are very many comforting and greatly stirring words for all those who desire to be Christ's lovers."[64] Finally, the third person is also used by those writing the vitae ('lives' or personal histories) of mystics and contemplatives: this genre, which is meant to underscore the sanctity and devotion of holy men and women, and to offer models of piety for their readers, talks *about* its subjects and thus lacks the sense of connection and urgency generated by the use of the first and second person.[65]

The technique of imagining abstract concepts (such as the seven liberal arts, virtues, and vices) and different components of the human soul as persons with their own characters and motivations also plays an important role in many contemplative texts—and the same is true in art from this period as well. (See Figure 5.3, which shows some of the qualities needed for good government in *The Allegory of Good and Bad*

---

[64] "A Vision Showed to a Devout Woman," in *The Writings of Julian of Norwich: A Vision Showed to a Devout Woman and A Revelation of Love*, ed. N. Watson and J. Jenkins. (University Park, PA: Pennsylvania State University Press, 2006), p. 63.

[65] For examples of how complicated it becomes to tease apart the actual histories, attitudes, and actions of the subjects of these vitae from what is written about them, see the essays in Catherine Mooney's edited collection *Gendered Voices: Medieval Saints and Their Interpreters* (Philadelphia: University of Pennsylvania Press, 1999), as well as those in Caroline Walker Bynum's *Fragmentation and Redemption: Essays on Gender and the Human Body in Medieval Religion* (New York: Zone Books, 1991).

Figure 5.3 Detail of *Allegory of Good Government* from *The Allegory of Good and Bad Government*, Ambrogio Lorenzetti, 1338–9, Palazzo Pubblico, Siena.

Government, including personifications of Magnanimity, Temperance, Fortitude, and the three theological virtues; see also Figures 2.2, 3.1, 5.2, and I5.1.) Unlike the dialogues of the earlier Plato and Augustine (and the later Berkeley and Hume), which are framed as conversations between two or more human beings, the dialogues of Mechthild of Magdeburg, Marguerite Porete, Catherine of Siena, and others tend to take place between various facets of the inner self, or between the self and God. This enables the author to draw out the nature of certain inner conflicts and to encourage personal growth by modeling solutions and ways forward. In Porete's *Mirror of Simple Souls*, for instance, Reason consistently asks for explanations (which do not satisfy her), while Love seeks to lead the Soul towards union with God, and the Soul wonders what she should do. Towards the end of the *Mirror*, these tensions have been resolved by the Soul's recognition of her identity as Love, and it is only the Annihilated Soul who speaks, having become One with this Love.

The personification of various aspects of the self in these dialogues is often humorous as well as instructive. In chapter 2 of the first book of

170 PERSONS

Mechthild's *Flowing Light of the Godhead*, for instance, Soul leaves the body, sees "one complete God in three Persons and knows three Persons in one God undivided," experiences bliss—and then is sent back down to earthly life, where she has a decidedly prosaic squabble with her body:

> Then the body speaks: "Well, woman, just where have you been? You come back so love-struck, lovely and vibrant, free and witty. Your carrying on has cost me my appetite, sense of smell, color, and all my strength."
>
> She says: "Shut up, murderer! Quit your bellyaching. I'll always be on my guard with you around. That my enemy has been wounded – what do we care about that? It makes me glad."[66]

These sorts of imaginative conversations allow their authors to articulate complex theologies and experiences in vivid and relatable ways, 'showing' rather than 'telling' how the various aspects of the human person relate to each other.

The use of inner dialogue also reflects the enormous importance of introspection and self-knowledge for thirteenth–fifteenth-century mystical and contemplative thought. A precondition for spiritual growth and mystical union, introspection is also portrayed as the best means for gaining knowledge about both self and the divine. (See Chapter 2 for fuller discussion.) Even contemplatives with vastly different conceptions of the final end of human beings (such as Meister Eckhart and Julian of Norwich) enjoin their readers to regularly look inward—not just at the beginning of their spiritual journeys but at various intervals along the way. In Catherine of Siena's *Dialogue*, Truth itself proclaims, "Here is the way, if you would come to perfect knowledge and enjoyment of me, eternal Life: Never leave the knowledge of yourself."[67]

The narrative sense of self that this sort of introspection both requires and develops is vital to the contemplative project. As Hadewijch makes clear in a letter to a fellow beguine, this introspection not only involves

---

[66] *Flowing Light of the Godhead*, Ch. 2, Bk I, p. 41. The Soul's indifference to Body's suffering is reminiscent of Soul's rejoicing in Porete's *Mirror* at the death of Reason, and is meant to show us what the proper attitude to such things should be.

[67] *Dialogue*, p. 29.

LOOKING FORWARD: LOCKE AND PERSONALISM 171

an examination of one's current states ("in all your conduct, in your attraction or aversion, in your behavior, in love, in hate, in fidelity, in mistrust, and in all things that befall you") but also involves projecting oneself forward into the future and learning from one's past: "You must examine yourselves as to how you can endure everything disagreeable that happens to you, and how you can bear the loss of what gives you pleasure."[68] Contemplative texts throughout this period stress the existence of the self as a unified and reflective consciousness that persists through (and, in fact, can be both improved by and corroded by) changes over time. As I discuss in Section 5.4, many of these underlying medieval assumptions about who we are carry forward into what we think about the self today.

5.4 Looking Forward: Locke and Personalism

As we saw in Section 5.1, the overlapping contexts in which the term 'person' is employed in medieval discussions—legal, political, grammatical, logical, and theological—give rise to an understanding of the term which emphasizes unique individuality, intrinsic dignity, and rationality (in a broad sense). In the thirteenth–fifteenth centuries, an emphasis on these features combines with the use of first- and second- person perspectives, personification and inner dialogue, and an emphasis on introspection to create a much richer understanding of who we are as persons than the accepted scholastic definition, 'individual substance with a rational nature,' might imply. Furthermore, although largely neglected by scholars of medieval philosophy (who concentrate on texts produced by masters of theology at the universities at Oxford and Paris), the complex conception of the self that emerges from medieval contemplative texts is both important in its own time and prefigures John Locke's classic seventeenth-century definition of the person, as well as influencing the nineteenth–twentieth-century theory of personalism.

Contemporary philosophical discussions of persons often go back only as far as John Locke's 1689 *Essay Concerning Human Understanding,*

---

[68] *Hadewijch*, Letter 14, p. 77.

172 PERSONS

in which Locke characterizes the person as a "thinking intelligent Being, that has reason and reflection, and can consider it self as it self, the same thinking thing in different times and places; which it does by that consciousness, which is inseparable from thinking, and as it seems to me essential to it."[69] There are obvious differences between Locke's definition and medieval understandings—most significantly, the fact that Locke distinguishes between the human being and the human person, which medieval treatments of the term do not, and the use of the word 'consciousness,' which is not yet in play in medieval discussions.[70] At the same time there is a great deal of (indeed, for scholars of philosophy in the early modern period and later perhaps a startling amount of) overlap between Locke's definition and medieval contemplative conceptions of what it means to be a person. Central to both are intelligence and rationality; central to both are the idea of the self as reflexive and introspective. Locke and medieval contemplatives also agree that this capacity for self-reflection connects our present with our past and future selves. The stress on the continuity of a narrative sense of self, as opposed to physical continuity, forms another important point of connection. (See Chapter 6 for discussion of how this plays out in medieval discussions of death, immortality, and the afterlife.)

Another influential modern theory of persons—personalism—also resonates deeply with thirteenth–fifteenth-century contemplative conceptions of who we are. Usually understood as taking root in the nineteenth century and flowering in the early twentieth century, personalism sees the line drawn between persons and non-persons as carving nature at its joints: only persons have an awareness of themselves as subjects and agents, only persons are free, and only persons are morally

---

[69] John Locke, *Essay Concerning Human Understanding*, ed. Peter Nidditch (Oxford: Oxford University Press, 1975), 2.27.9, p. 335. For discussion of this definition and later developments of the term in Western philosophy, see chs 5–8 of LoLordo, ed., *Persons: A History*.

[70] The concepts of human person and human being are inextricably intertwined in the Middle Ages; they become separable only after a mechanistic worldview starts to crowd out the teleological notion of substantial form, and 'human being' starts to connote something different from what 'person' connotes—an animal body with a soul, as opposed to subject of consciousness. For more on the decline of teleology and substantial forms, see Robert Pasnau's *Metaphysical Themes 1274–1671* (Oxford: Oxford University Press, 2011) and *After Certainty* (Oxford: Oxford University Press, 2017).

LOOKING FORWARD: LOCKE AND PERSONALISM   173

responsible for their actions.[71] Like medieval contemplative discussions which emphasize the importance of individuality, dignity, and rationality both in relation to self and in relation to God, personalism stresses the "moral and religious dimensions which are part and parcel of the person's nature as a conscious, intelligent, free, willing subject in relation with God and others."[72]

Finally, both the medieval contemplative tradition and personalism see creativity and emotionality as intimately connected with rationality. The meditations genre is meant to encourage and evoke certain affective modes (see Section 4.2), and one of the main tools of contemplation is introspection, whose language is intimately personal, stressing individual accountability and experience. Attempts to convey the results of such self-reflection give rise to a variety of forms of creative expression in the thirteenth–fifteenth centuries, including but not limited to poetry, dialogues, and visionary literature. Furthermore, the aim of these forms of creative expression is typically communal edification in addition to personal improvement—the inherently practical bent of contemplative philosophy keeps it grounded in the reality of our individual experiences, which include our connectedness to the world around us. Personalism shares this grounded vision of who we are: "As free, thinking subjects, persons also exercise creativity through their thought, imagination, and action, a creativity which affects both the surrounding world and the person [herself]."[73] Personalism often acknowledges its debt to medieval scholastics such as Thomas Aquinas; it seems to me past time for it to rediscover its connection to the contemplative movement as well.[74]

---

[71] Three of the major works which define and develop this theory are Borden Parker Browne's *Personalism* (Boston: Houghton Mifflin Co., 1908), Martin Buber's 1923 *Ich and Du (I and Thou)*, trans. Ronald Gregor Smith (Edinburgh: T&T Clark, 1987, 2nd ed.), and Albert Cornelius Knudson's *The Philosophy of Personalism* (New York: Abingdon Press, 1927).

[72] https://plato.stanford.edu/entries/personalism/.

[73] Ibid.

[74] For personalist acknowledgments of its scholastic forbears, see, e.g., Étienne Gilson's "Le personnalisme chrétien," in *L'esprit de la philosophie médiévale* (Paris: Librairie philosophique J. Vrin, 1932), ch. 10, pp. 195–215; and Karol Wojtyla's "Thomistic Personalism," in *Person and Community: Selected Essays (Catholic Thought from Lublin*: Vol. 4), ed. Andrew Woznicki (New York: Peter Lang, 1993), pp. 165–75.

174 PERSONS

Interlude Five

Why Do Medieval Women Talk like They Hate Themselves?

The way medieval women talk about themselves can strike the modern reader as rather horrifying. Clare of Assisi, for instance, refers to herself as an "unworthy servant" and a "useless handmaid," while Marguerite d'Oingt describes herself as a "small worm," and Julian of Norwich tells her readers not to think of her as a teacher on the grounds that she is "a woman, lewd [uneducated], feeble, and frail."[75] This has contributed to the impression that women authors from this period weren't intellectually sophisticated and didn't consciously engage in philosophical and theological debates, as well as bolstering perceptions of the Middle Ages as a period in which a healthy sense of self-worth was discouraged by the Catholic Church and women in particular suffered from external and internalized misogyny. It has also led to something like despair among feminist scholars, leading one to ask, "Can anything be reclaimed from the self-denigrating rhetoric of medieval women in the Christian tradition?"[76] Yet though even the most brilliant women in this period faced significant obstacles to being heard—especially insofar as they were barred from holding prominent positions in ecclesiastical and university hierarchies—there are at least two good reasons not to read medieval women's self-effacing claims at face value. First, many of these self-descriptors appear as part of formulaic 'humility topoi,' a common trope in texts written by both women and men in this period, and one that women in particular use to demonstrate their familiarity with literary niceties and to forestall objections to their exercising philosophical and theological authority. Second, the virtue of humility gains special importance in the Middle Ages as the necessary counterpoint to pride, the deadliest of sins. (See Figure I5.1, in which the personification of

---

[75] *Francis and Clare: The Complete Works*, trans. R. J. Armstrong and I. C. Brady (Mahwah: Paulist Press, 1986), p. 195; *The Writings of Margaret of Oingt, Medieval Prioress and Mystic (d. 1310)*, p. 27; Short Text, section 6, my rendering into modern English from the text in *The Writings of Julian of Norwich*, p. 75.

[76] Michelle Voss Roberts, "Retrieving Humility: Rhetoric, Authority, and Divinization in Mechthild of Magdeburg," *Feminist Theology* 18/1 (2009), pp. 50–73, p. 50.

Figure I5.1 Personified figures of Humility and Pride from illumination of *La Somme le Roi*, workshop of Honoré, c.1280.

humility stands on the left and a figure representing pride literally takes a fall.) The more women emphasize (and even exaggerate) their humble stations, the more strength they give to their claims to be mouthpieces of God—the only universally recognized authority in their world.

Humility topoi ("I, of course, know little, and yet…," "You must excuse me for the errors I am sure to make," etc.) appear in all sorts of contexts across all sorts of traditions, but the emphasis on self-examination and moral and spiritual development in contemplative texts entails that they are especially likely to feature there. Such formulae can take different forms depending on the context; in the medieval Christian tradition, humility formulae tend to include professions of unworthiness, of low value relative to others as well as God, and of an inability to express properly what should be said due to lack of knowledge and/or education. Thus Anselm of Canterbury (author of the famous 'Ontological Argument' for God's existence) calls himself "a trivial and inconsiderable fellow" and "a man of very little knowledge," despite the fact that he is the head of the Church in England at the time, and Bonaventure (Aquinas's

176   PERSONS

renowned contemporary) states that he feels "unworthy and unequal to the task" of writing the life of St. Francis when he is the Minister General of the entire Franciscan Order.[77] Medieval humility formulae also frequently contain pleas for divine illumination and/or note that anything of value in the following work should be attributed entirely to God's grace. Importantly, they also often set out the text's motivation and larger purpose and provide a justification for why the project is being tackled by this particular author.[78]

In the case of medieval women, understanding the conventions of the humility topos helps us to see how women often use these conventions to establish authorial authority. Clare of Assisi, for instance, refers to herself as "Clare, an unworthy servant of Christ and a useless handmaid of His handmaids in the monastery of San Damiano of Assisi" as part of a greeting in in her fourth letter to Agnes of Prague. Clare's mention of herself as an unworthy servant directly follows Christ's instruction to his disciples: "So you also, when you have done everything you were told to do, should say, 'We are unworthy servants; we have only done our duty'" (Luke 17:10). Yet Clare is also echoing the founder of her Order and personal mentor, Francis, who refers to himself as "brother Francis, a useless man and unworthy creature of the Lord God" in a letter written to his entire Order (and with which Clare, as head of the Second Order of the Franciscans, would have been familiar).[79] In using these descriptions for herself, Clare is simultaneously modeling humility to Agnes and demonstrating her familiarity with and connection to the head of her Order.

Similarly, when the Carthusian prioress Marguerite d'Oingt calls herself a "small worm," it is again instructive to look at the broader context in which she writes these words. First, she has just identified God (in the form of the Second Person of the Trinity) as her own brother: "Sweet dear Lord, you are my brother; but it is very presumptious

---

[77] *Anselm: The Complete Treatises*, trans. Thomas Williams (Indianapolis: Hackett Publishing Co., 2022); *Bonaventure: The Soul's Journey into God; The Tree of Life; the Life of St. Francis*, trans. Ewert Cousins (Mahwah: Paulist Press, 1978), pp. 182–3.

[78] For further discussion of this, see my "Lewd, Feeble, and Frail: Humility Formulae, Medieval Women, and Authority," in *Oxford Studies in Medieval Philosophy* Vol. 10 (Oxford: Oxford University Press, 2022), forthcoming.

[79] *Francis and Clare*, "A Letter to the Entire Order," p. 60.

WHY DO MEDIEVAL WOMEN TALK LIKE THEY HATE   177

[*sic*] of me to say this, since I am a small worm and you are so great and worthy that all learned people who ever were and who will ever be do not know how to describe you or to think about you."[80] Second, Marguerite is writing these words in Latin, the language of scholarship—the fact that she explicitly mentions the inability of 'learned people' to comprehend the mystery of the Incarnation is no accident. Third, in the very next sentence, Marguerite makes it clear that the source of her words is not human but divine: "Oh beautiful sweet Lord Jesus Christ, who gave me the audacity to speak of such marvellous [*sic*] things if not you who are the true God and my brother and who showed us the greatest love?" Taken in context, Marguerite's apparent self-denigration actually highlights the fact that she is claiming wisdom that comes directly from God.

Julian of Norwich also uses the same strategy, as do any number of other contemplatives in this period, downplaying her education and literary abilities in order to emphasize that the source of what she has to say is the highest authority possible. What immediately follows her self-effacing comment about being "a woman, lewd [uneducated], feeble, and frail," for instance, is a confident assertion that highlights her work's emphasis on God's love: "But I know well that what I say I have received from the showing of him who is sovereign teacher. Indeed, charity stirs me to tell you it." Finally, she responds explicitly to worries about a woman's writing about such important theological matters by appealing to Augustine's theory of divine illumination:

But because I am a woman, should I therefore believe that I should not tell you the goodness of God, since I saw in that same time that it is his will that it be known? And that [it is God's will] you shall well see in what follows, if it be well and truly understood. Then shall you soon forget me who is a wretch, and do so that I not interfere with your learning, and behold Jesus who is the teacher of all.[81]

---

[80] *The Writings of Margaret of Oingt*, p. 27.
[81] *The Writings of Julian of Norwich*, p. 75.

178 PERSONS

Julian's calling herself a wretch functions in this context primarily to draw attention to the fact that *all* human beings are wretches in comparison to God; drawing on the Augustinian theology that informs her work, Julian reminds her readers that the only real teacher is God, from whom all authority comes.

In short, far from expressing self-loathing and internalized misogyny, medieval women's use of humility formulae and apparent self-denigration more often indicate self-conscious engagement with the theological and philosophical debates of their day, as well as establishing the source of the authority for their claims as God. Although this may not satisfy modern readers who would rather see women claim authority in their own right, it is vital to understand that no one writing contemplative literature in the Middle Ages would make this move—the confidence which university masters settling disputed questions appear to display is a function of the genre more than a function of men's and women's differing self-assessments in this period.[82]

---

[82] An earlier version of this piece was published as an APA (American Philosophical Association) blog post at https://blog.apaonline.org/2021/05/19/lewd-feeble-and-frail-subverting-sexist-tropes-to-gain-authority. For a much more developed discussion, see my "Lewd, Feeble, and Frail: Humility Formulae, Medieval Women, and Authority."

6

Immortality and the Afterlife

For medieval contemplatives, the debates laid out in Chapters 2–5 about who we are and how we should live are not just theoretically interesting—they revolve around pressing questions whose answers have potentially eternal consequences. In this final chapter I turn to views about the culmination of the contemplative life in the afterlife. As we'll see, discussions of immortality and the afterlife also speak volumes about a host of other important philosophical issues, including views about God, embodiment, happiness, love, and what it means to be human.

One of my goals in this chapter is to offer a more holistic framework of medieval perspectives on immortality and the afterlife than is currently available, which I hope will prove useful for future discussions. The scholastic (that is, university-based) and contemplative traditions of the thirteenth–fifteenth centuries share a common interest in our ultimate end, but they differ widely with respect to methodology and focus, and most contemporary philosophical discussions of medieval views on the afterlife engage only scholastic sources. These formal disputations tend to concentrate on the nature of the rational soul and its prospects for surviving the death of the body, the state of the rational soul while separated from the body, and/or puzzles surrounding the identity of the resurrected body. They address the question of what we might expect immortality and the afterlife to be *like* only tangentially, in discussions of the bodily resurrection, the nature of perfect happiness (which we can attain only in the life to come), and scriptural passages such as the story of the rich man and Lazarus that were taken to refer to or provide insight into the afterlife.[1] Scholastic discussions tend to be theoretical as

---

[1] As I discuss in "I See Dead People: Disembodied Souls and Aquinas's 'Two-Person' Problem," in *Oxford Studies in Medieval Philosophy* Vol. 2, pp. 25–45, this story in particular was understood as describing real events, not as a parable or metaphor.

180 IMMORTALITY AND THE AFTERLIFE

opposed to experiential, often displaying a lively curiosity about questions such as how long our hair will be and how old we will look in heaven.[2] Contemplative and mystical works, by contrast, are interested more in the phenomenology of immortality—what we can expect to experience in the life to come, and to what extent mystical union in this life might provide a foretaste of those experiences. The result is a less systematic approach to the topic that contains a wealth of first-person reports of union with God.

I begin this chapter by sketching in Section 6.1 the Platonist and Aristotelian theories of the rational soul and its relation to human nature that set the general metaphysical parameters for medieval discussions of immortality and the afterlife. Because contemplative accounts of this topic have received so much less philosophical attention than their scholastic counterparts, I concentrate in Sections 6.2 and 6.3 on contemplative expectations for our experience of immortality, looking first (in Section 6.2) at accounts that describe transcending the soul's experiences of individuality to merge with God in selfless union, and then (in Section 6.3) at accounts that portray everlasting union with God in affective and embodied terms. In Section 6.4, I argue that the extremes of the views discussed in the previous sections can be taken as ideological endpoints of what I call an 'experiential continuum of immortality.' Appreciating the full range of this continuum—which extends well beyond the endpoints typically found in scholastic accounts of immortality—allows us not just to better understand contemplative motivations, advice, and views, but also to better situate different scholastic positions with respect to each other, as I demonstrate in Section 6.4 via a brief comparison of Robert Grosseteste's and Thomas Aquinas's views. As a whole, the chapter provides the final case study of the philosophical methodology I laid out in Chapter 1 and have been employing in each subsequent chapter: including contemplative perspectives about immortality and the afterlife *corrects* mistakenly narrow impressions of

---

[2] Standard answers to these two questions are "As long as God deems appropriate" and "33." There are far more scholastic texts dealing with our embodied resurrected state than most people realize. For a book-length history of this tradition (and its predecessors), see Caroline Walker Bynum's *The Resurrection of the Body in Western Christianity, 200–1336* (New York: Columbia University Press, 1995).

THE METAPHYSICS OF IMMORTALITY   181

what medieval figures thought about the topic, and it *complements* existing scholarship by expanding the range of both the views under discussion and the voices offering those views.

6.1 The Metaphysics of Immortality

Questions of the 'how' and 'what' of immortality in the Middle Ages tend to revolve around the relation of rational soul to human body.[3] It was generally assumed that non-rational animals did not survive their death, whereas intellective, immaterial beings such as angels were immortal, since their lack of connection to matter meant that they were in no danger of corruption.[4] The case of human beings was complicated by the fact that we are both animals whose bodies suffer corruption and rational beings capable of intellective cognition. Our ability to transcend matter via intellection indicates that our existence itself might transcend our death; for Augustine and later adherents of (increasingly complex) illuminationist theories, the soul's ability to grasp eternal, unchanging truths indicates that, like other intellective beings (such as angels and the celestial spheres), human souls exist forever once they are created by God.[5] Aristotelians disagreed about the mechanics of human cognition, but they agreed that the soul's ability to grasp immaterial truths demonstrates that the soul itself was the sort of being whose existence (*esse*)

---

[3] For a book-length discussion of the status of the rational soul at this time, see Richard C. Dales's *The Problem of the Rational Soul in the Thirteenth Century* (Leiden: Brill, 1995). Anton Pegis's *St. Thomas and the Problem of the Soul in the Thirteenth Century* (Toronto: Pontifical Institute of Mediaeval Studies, 1934) is a classic treatment of the topic with special attention on Thomas Aquinas.

[4] The question of celestial intelligences—the incorruptible 'heavenly bodies'—was trickier. See, e.g., Steven Marrone's "From Gundisalvus to Bonaventure: Intellect and Intelligences in the Late Twelfth and Early Thirteenth Centuries," in *Intellect et imagination dans la philosophie médiévale*, ed. M. C. Pacheco and J. F. Meirinhos (Brepols: Turnhout, 2006), II: pp. 1071–81; and Richard C. Dales's "The De-Animation of the Heavens in the Middle Ages," *Journal of the History of Ideas* 41/4 (1980), pp. 531–50.

[5] See Steven Marrone's two-volume *The Light of thy Countenance: Science and Knowledge of God in the Thirteenth Century* (Leiden: Brill, 2001) for a comprehensive (if idiosyncratic) study of the development and decline of theories of illumination.

182   IMMORTALITY AND THE AFTERLIFE

transcends matter and thus *could* continue to exist in separation from the matter of which it was the form.[6]

At the same time, the fact that we die at all—unlike other intellective beings—raises worries about our persistence. These worries are compounded by the Christian doctrine of the resurrection of the body: philosophical arguments for the immortality of the soul stretch back before Plato, but the Christian insistence that the soul would not only continue to exist after death but would also be rejoined to a numerically identical and incorruptible version of our earthly body puts serious constraints on medieval accounts of our post-mortem possibilities.[7]

To vastly oversimplify matters in ways that will be helpful for what follows, two main camps of explanation form in response to these issues: one is indebted more to the Platonic tradition, the other to the Aristotelian tradition. The main problem for medieval Platonists—who tended to understand the soul as a *substance in its own right*—lies not in accounting for the survival of our souls but in providing any motivation at all for the soul's continued connection to a material body in the afterlife. The main problem for Aristotelians, in contrast, lies in explaining how the rational soul—understood in hylomorphic terms as *the substantial form of a material body*—could, first, survive the death of that body and, second, survive it in a way that grounds our continued identity even when joined to the body again at the final resurrection.

If the soul is understood primarily as a substance in its own right, accounting for the soul's persistence at the death of the human body poses no real problem. Substances are exactly the sorts of things that have independent existence, and both the soul's immateriality and its intellective nature put it in the same category as incorruptible and immortal substances such as the angels. This view also avoids worries about the continued identity of the human person through death and resurrection, since the person is identified with the soul that persists through these changes. The main problem for Platonic traditions arises from the doctrine of the bodily resurrection and its implication that the

---

[6] See, e.g., Pegis, *St. Thomas and the Problem of the Soul*; and Dale, *The Problem of the Rational Soul*.

[7] The moment of body being reunited with soul was said to happen at the Final or Last Judgment.

THE METAPHYSICS OF IMMORTALITY   183

unity of soul and body is somehow essential for our continued survival in the afterlife. The doctrine states that our bodies will be raised incorruptible and that we will continue forever as physical and not merely spiritual beings—but why bother with bodies if we survive just in virtue of our soul's survival? Bodies seem at the very least to be an unnecessary addition and (as the *Phaedo* famously argues) might even endanger our quest to reach our final end. If the soul is a substance in its own right, it's unclear how soul and body together would make up a human being that is a genuine unity, or what role our bodies would play in our continued existence in the afterlife.

If the soul is understood primarily as the substantial form of the body, on the other hand, explaining the unity of the human being doesn't pose a serious problem. On this view, popular among Aristotelian-influenced figures (most notably, Thomas Aquinas), human beings are composites of matter and form. The rational soul functions as the substantial form that structures matter and makes the human being the thing that it is, but there is only one substance on the table, so to speak: the human being.[8] This view also provides philosophical motivation for the doctrine of the bodily resurrection, since the body is an essential component of the human being and needs to be present for *you* to be present in the afterlife. The importance of the body raises issues of persistence and identity for this view, however. For one thing, how can a substantial form continue to exist in separation from the matter/body of which it is the form?[9] For another, even if we grant that the rational soul survives the death of the body (in virtue of its intellective nature), this account faces further puzzles about personal identity through death and the bodily resurrection. Either the human being ceases to exist at the death of the body, in which case it's difficult to explain how the human being

---

[8] This doctrine is typically referred to as the unicity of substantial form. For secondary sources that defend this position, see Van Steenberghen's *Thomas Aquinas and Radical Aristotelianism* (Washington, D.C.: Catholic University Press, 1980) and Van Dyke's "Not Properly a Person: the Rational Soul and 'Thomistic Substance Dualism,'" *Faith and Philosophy* 26/2 (2009) pp. 186–204.

[9] This has been a heated subject of debate since Aristotle's *De Anima* 3.5 suggested that, if any part of the soul persisted through the death of the organism of which it was the substantial form, it would be the intellective part. In the Islamic tradition, this claim famously inspired the doctrine of the Unity of the Intellect.

184 IMMORTALITY AND THE AFTERLIFE

who is resurrected can be numerically the same as the one who dies, or the human being persists in virtue of the persistence of the rational soul, in which case this view picks up the problems associated with Platonism that are mentioned above.[10]

For our purposes, we can grant that the soul survives the death of the body and that there is a coherent story to tell about both the unity and the continued identity of the resurrected human being. The primary reason to sketch these views and highlight these puzzles is to provide the general framework—complete with internal and external tensions— within which medieval figures in the Rome-based Christian tradition speculate about the phenomenology of immortality.

6.2 Transcending Matter, Becoming God

The majority of extant medieval contemplative literature originates from outside the university system and remains largely overlooked by contemporary philosophers. Yet this literature provides a wealth of views about the ultimate goal of life and our experience of it. As we've seen in Sections 1.2, 2.3.1, 3.2, and 5.2.1, some figures (such as Marguerite Porete, Meister Eckhart, and Johannes Tauler) portray our final end as a 'surrender of self'—an apophatic loss of individual experience as the soul empties itself to 'become God'—whereas, as we've seen in Sections 1.3, 2.3.2, 3.3, and 5.2.1, other figures (such as Hadewijch, Angela of Foligno, Jan van Ruusbroec, and Julian of Norwich) describe our final end in terms of a 'personal distinction within unity' that fulfills rather than annihilates the self. In this section, I address self-abnegating conceptions of our final end; in Section 6.3, I turn to self-preserving accounts.

---

[10] This problem has received particular attention in Aquinas's treatment of it, leading people to divide responses between 'survivalists,' who argue that the soul's survival is sufficient for the survival of the human being without being numerically identical to the human being, and 'corruptionists,' who maintain that the human being ceases to exist at death. For examples of survivalist readings of Aquinas, see Jeff Brower's *Aquinas's Ontology of the Material World: Change, Hylomorphism, and Material Objects* (Oxford: Oxford University Press, 2014) and Eleonore Stump's *Aquinas* (New York: Routledge, 2003). For examples of corruptionists, see Patrick Toner's "St. Thomas Aquinas on the Problem of Too Many Thinkers," *The Modern Schoolman* 89 (2012), 209–22, and my "I See Dead People: Disembodied Souls and Aquinas's 'Two-Person' Problem," *Oxford Studies in Medieval Philosophy* Vol. 2, ed. R. Pasnau (Oxford: Oxford University Press, 2014), pp. 25–45.

As discussed in Section 1.2, apophaticism is the view that human language and thought cannot capture Divine Truth in any deep or meaningful way; apophatic mysticism applies this belief to unmediated experiences of the Divine.[11] The fourteenth-century Franciscan tertiary Angela of Foligno, for instance, reports that, "when I return to myself after perceiving these divine secrets...and speak entirely from outside the experience, I say words that come nowhere near describing the divine workings that are produced in my soul. My statements about them ruin the reality they represent."[12] If we characterize mystical experiences generally as inherently *phenomenological* ("concerning individual felt experience in addition to systems of knowledge or belief"[13]) and *transcendent* ("involving an encounter—whether direct or mediated, transformatively powerful or paradoxically everyday—with God"), as I think we should, then we can think of the apophatic tradition as further characterizing the content of those experiences as inherently inexpressible. This characterization might make apophatic texts seem like a nonstarter for medieval views of immortality, but in fact they frequently contain detailed instructions for attaining the ineffable union that those who have experienced a taste of can talk *around* if not *about*.

A central theme in apophatic mysticism is that reaching our final end requires moving through various stages of self-abnegation. Medieval apophatic mysticism's roots in Platonism and Neoplatonism mean that its proponents often use the language of 'ascent' or 'grades' or 'stages' to characterize the contemplative life's progression. In her *Mirror of Simple Souls*, for instance, Marguerite Porete describes seven distinct stages that culminate in radical self-annihilation. In the final stage, the Loving Soul loses herself in God to the point where "He is, and she is not," for "He is sufficient of Himself," while she is "nothing in such a One."[14] According to Porete, in this state (available only to the 'noble soul') it as

---

[11] For a detailed treatment of this topic with particular attention paid to Meister Eckhart's views, see Denys Turner's *The Darkness of God: Negativity in Christian Mysticism* (Cambridge: Cambridge University Press, 1995).

[12] Angela of Foligno, *Memorial* IX, p. 214.

[13] Both quotes in this paragraph are from Nicholas Watson's Introduction to *The Cambridge Companion to Medieval English Mysticism*, ed. S. Fanous and V. Gillespie (Cambridge: Cambridge University Press, 2011), p. 1.

[14] *Marguerite Porete. The Mirror of Simple Souls*, trans. E. L. Babinsky (Mahwah: Paulist Press, 1993), p. 218.

186 IMMORTALITY AND THE AFTERLIFE

if God had never created the Soul in the first place: "the Soul is stripped of all things because she is without existence, where she was before she was created." The annihilated soul has no sense of individuality or self; it transcends the experience of physicality altogether. (As Barbara Newman notes in her discussion of Porete's theory, "In this dissolution of the ego no room remains for the body: even the physical humanity of Christ is no longer cherished by the free soul."[15])

The idea that our final end involves literally 'self-less' union with God is not unique to Porete, although she is one of this theory's most radical defenders. Meister Eckhart also repeatedly counsels his disciples to strive for detachment, not just from worldly goods but also from any sort of attachment to the self. This process is portrayed as both ongoing and essential: "You should know that there was never any man in this life who forsook himself so much that he could not still find more in himself to forsake.... But as much as you go out in forsaking all things, by so much, neither less nor more, does God go in."[16] Emptying oneself allows God to fill the void and, thus, facilitates mystical union. Reaching our ultimate end involves more than just detachment, however: it involves self-annihilation. "After detachment is complete," Eckhart says, "There is still one work that remains proper and his own, and that is annihilation of self."[17]

Eckhart and Porete both motivate the work of self-abnegation by appeal to our final end. For Porete, our final end is Love, for Love is God, and Love is the only thing that remains in the annihilated soul.[18] For Eckhart, our final end is found in the "hidden darkness of the eternal divinity." This darkness "is unknown, and it was never known, and it

---

[15] Barbara Newman, *God and the Goddesses: Vision, Poetry, and Belief in the Middle Ages* (Philadelphia: University of Pennsylvania Press, 2003), p. 203. For further discussion of Porete's views, see also Amy Hollywood's *The Soul as Virgin Wife: Mechthild of Magdeburg, Marguerite of Porete, and Meister Eckhart* (Notre Dame, IN: University of Notre Dame Press, 1995) and Joanne Robinson's *Nobility and Annihilation in Marguerite Porete's Mirror of Simple Souls* (Albany: State University of New York Press, 2001).

[16] *Meister Eckhart*, Counsel 4, p. 250. [17] *Meister Eckhart*, Counsel 23, p. 280.

[18] "I am God, says Love, for Love is God and God is Love, and this Soul is God by the condition of Love. I am God by divine nature and this Soul is God by the righteousness of Love. Thus, this precious beloved of mine... is transformed into me." *Mirror of Simple Souls*, ch. 21, p. 104. (The original French title of the treatise is *Le Mirouer des simples âmes anieéanties et qui seulement demeurent en vouloir et désir d'amour.*)

TRANSCENDING MATTER, BECOMING GOD   187

will never be known. God remains there within himself, unknown."[19] God is not only beyond knowledge for Eckhart—God is beyond being itself. The belief that one has achieved any sort of knowledge or understanding of the divine is itself an indication that one has further to go on the path to genuine union with God.

What proceeds from this total self-abnegation is a state in which the human being's will is subsumed in God's. In this state, no sense or experience of individuality remains in which the person could take pride, or for which she could claim responsibility: "Perfect humility proceeds from annihilation of self."[20] In the words of Eckhart's follower and fellow Dominican, the fourteenth-century Johannes Tauler, "Our Lord says: 'One thing is necessary.' What is this one thing that is necessary? The one thing is that you know your own nothingness—that is what is yours, what you are, and who are you from yourself."[21] This call to nothingness also features in the climax of the *Sister Catherine* treatise, written by an anonymous follower of Eckhart in the fourteenth century. After experiencing a mystic death, Sister Catherine rises and announces to her former confessor, "Rejoice with me, I am become God!" Catherine is not here claiming divinity for herself with this startling announcement; rather, the claim is meant to indicate that Catherine's self-annihilation is complete; God is there because Catherine is not.[22]

Whether or not the self-annihilation advocated in these passages is ontological, epistemological, or 'merely' phenomenological is impossible to determine from the texts themselves, which so frequently appeal to the inadequacy of words to express the realities involved. For our purposes here, this question is also moot: our focus is medieval apophatic views about the experience of immortality and the afterlife, and what we've seen makes it clear that according to this tradition, the experience

---

[19] As quoted in McGinn, *Harvest of Mysticism in Medieval Germany* (vol. 4 of *The Presence of God: A History of Western Christian Mysticism* (New York: Crossroad, 2005), p. 142.

[20] *Meister Eckhart*, p. 286.

[21] Tauler, V [i.e., Sermon] 45, *Die Predigten Taulers*, ed. Ferdinand Vetter (Berlin: Wiedmann, 1910; photomechanical reprint 1968), trans. Bernard McGinn.

[22] *The "Sister Catherine" Treatise*, trans. Elvira Borgstädt, in *Meister Eckhart: Teacher and Preacher*, ed. B. McGinn, trans. McGinn, F. Tobin, and E. Borgstadt (Mahwah, NJ: Paulist Press, 1986), p. 358. For a book-length treatment of this topic that focuses particularly on Meister Eckhart, see Ben Morgan's *On Becoming God: Late Medieval Mysticism and the Modern Western Self* (New York: Fordham University Press, 2013).

188 IMMORTALITY AND THE AFTERLIFE

of our final end is indistinguishable from God's. Regardless of the existential status of our souls and/or bodies, our first-person standpoint and narrative sense of self are extinguished; "our" experience of immortality on this view is nothing more or less than God's own experience of eternity. As Porete writes of this stage, "And so nothing is, except He who is, who sees Himself in such being by His Divine Majesty through the transformation of love by the goodness poured out and placed in her. And thus also He sees Himself of Himself in such a creature, without appropriating anything from the creature. All is properly His own, and His own proper Self."[23]

Phrased this baldly, it's easy to see why this version of apophatic mysticism was often seen as falling outside Christian orthodoxy, for the sort of union it advocates with the divine blurs the Creator/created distinction to the point of erasure. Indeed, both Porete's and Eckhart's views underwent extensive doctrinal examination by the Inquisition, and both figures were condemned: Porete to the flames on June 1, 1310, and Eckhart posthumously on March 27, 1329. (The fact that the Pope took the trouble to issue an official condemnation of Eckhart's views after his death indicates the level of official ecclesiastical concern about them.[24])

Other less extreme versions of medieval apophaticism exist, but they share the belief that our final end involves transcending individual human experiences—particularly experiences that involve embodied sensations. Strongly influenced by Platonist prejudices against matter, apophatic texts such as Walter Hilton's *The Scale of Perfection* lay out detailed procedures for dealing with and overcoming attachment to the material world, including the need to move beyond 'false' mystical experiences that involve the body, such as "sounding of the ear, or savoring in the mouth, or smelling at the nose, or else any perceptible heat as

---

[23] *Mirror*, ch. 118, p. 194.
[24] A great deal of the Church's concern about these views stemmed from the way in which they appeared to undermine Church authority by claiming that laypeople could have a relationship with God unmediated by priests. Despite official attempts to stamp this idea out, it becomes a cornerstone of later medieval lay devotional movements and eventually the Protestant Reformation. For more on the politics of heresy in this period, see R. I. Moore's *The War on Heresy: Faith and Power in Medieval Europe* (London: Profile Books, 2012).

TRANSCENDING MATTER, BECOMING GOD 189

if it were fire, glowing and warming the breast."[25] In this, they affirm Eckhart, who repeatedly counseled his disciples that part of the process of detachment from self was detachment from sensory experiences, "tartly condemning those who want to see God with the same eyes with which they behold a cow."[26] The anonymous Middle English *Cloud of Unknowing* also advises us to move beyond consideration of created things—up to and including ourselves:

> So crush every thought of and feeling for every creature, especially thoughts and feelings for yourself. That's the linchpin. Your awareness of everything else is contingent on your awareness of yourself. Your reward for forgetting yourself is that you can then forget all other creatures easily. So try losing your self-consciousness. Test my advice, and you'll discover something remarkable. When you succeed in forgetting all creatures and their works and even your own life and all you've done, you will be left alone with God to experience a stark awareness of your own existence. But even this must go. Yes, you must lose the naked feeling of who you are. It must be destroyed, if you wish to experience the perfection of contemplation, or love.[27]

A conception of the final end of human life as selfless union with God constitutes one end of the medieval 'experiential continuum of immortality'—namely, immortality understood as endless undifferentiated experience of the divine and/or loss of any sort of individuated conscious experience whatsoever. (Not surprisingly, given the phenomenological loss of self to which this tradition aspires, the prospect of the bodily resurrection or continued physical existence in the

---

[25] Hilton, *The Scale of Perfection*. Hilton's target here is Richard Rolle, who in his influential *Fire of Love* describes mystical experiences that include a 'glowing' or warmth in the breast, a taste of unimaginable sweetness, and the sound of celestial music; Rolle explicitly understands these embodied experiences as a foretaste of the life to come.

[26] Bernard McGinn, Introduction to *Meister Eckhart: The Essential Sermons, Commentaries, Treatises, and Defense*, ed. E. Colledge, OSA, and B. McGinn (Mahwah: Paulist Press, 1981), p. 61. The sermon referenced is Sermon 16b in *Meister Eckhart. Die deutschen Werke, Vol. 1. Herausgegeben im Auftrage der Deutschen Forschungsgemeinschaft* (Stuttgart and Berlin: W. Kohlhammer, 1936–), p. 272.

[27] *The Cloud of Unknowing: with the Book of Privy Counselling*, trans. Carmen Acevedo Butcher (Boulder, CO: Shambhala Publications, 2009), ch. 43, p. 98.

190 IMMORTALITY AND THE AFTERLIFE

afterlife is not a subject of much discussion.) In Section 6.3 I examine the other end of this continuum: union with God that involves not self-annihilation but self-*fulfillment*, where the self is taken to include body as well as soul.

6.3 Embodied Immortal Experience

In contrast to the annihilative understanding of our final end, most medieval accounts of immortality and the afterlife include expectations not only for individual conscious experiences but for individual *embodied* experiences. The doctrine of the bodily resurrection maintains that we are resurrected physically at the Last Judgment and possess everlasting, incorruptible bodies in the afterlife. Although (as we saw in Subsection 6.1) this doctrine generates a number of metaphysical questions, it also supports a picture of the afterlife that resonates deeply with a number of thirteenth–fourteenth-century contemplatives who stress the importance of the Incarnation.

On this view, Christ did not just *become* human; Christ *remains* human, and Christ's ascension into heaven was bodily as well as spiritual, assuring us that our immortal existence will not be that of disembodied angels but that of flesh and blood creatures—albeit flesh and blood that have been transformed into incorruptibility.[28] Christ's current heavenly status thus becomes a subject of frequent contemplative attention and is seen as prefiguring our own experience of heaven. Mechthild of Magdeburg, for instance, writes in *The Flowing Light of the Godhead* that, "When I reflect that divine nature now includes bone and flesh, body and soul, then I become elated in great joy, far beyond what

---

[28] From at least Augustine's *The City of God* onward, these heavenly bodies were understood to possess four new qualities: 'clarity' (which includes a certain amount of shininess), 'agility' (the ability to move our bodies instantly and completely at will), 'impassibility' (the inability for our bodies to be injured or suffer pain), and 'greater dignity of human nature' (usually understood as our bodies becoming the best possible versions of themselves). The best literary example I know of for capturing what these new bodies might be like, from the inside as well as the outside, are the vampires in Stephenie Meyer's Twilight series, particularly Bella's description of her experience waking up as a vampire in the second part of the series' final book, *Breaking Dawn*.

I am worth.... The soul with its flesh is mistress of the house in heaven, sits next to the eternal Master of the house, and is most like him."[29] When Mechthild goes on to describe our immortal existence in both spiritual and bodily terms—"There, eye reflects in eye, spirit flows in spirit, there, hand touches hand, there, mouth speaks to mouth, and there, heart greets heart"—she is not speaking metaphorically.

Reference to Christ's resurrected body and its implications for our own experience of the afterlife appear in any number of contemplative texts at this time, crossing geographical regions and religious orders. In Catherine of Siena's *Dialogue*, for instance, God reminds her: "I have told you of the good the glorified body will have in the glorified humanity of my only-begotten Son, and this is the guarantee of your own resurrection."[30] Not only is Christ's resurrection a promise of our future resurrection, it is also the model. As the passage continues, "You will all be made like him in joy and gladness; eye for eye, hand for hand, your whole bodies will be made like the body of the Word my Son. You will live in him as you live in me, for he is one with me. But your bodily eyes, as I have told you, will delight in the glorified humanity of the Word." (See Figure 6.1, which depicts the joy of the resurrected greeting each other in Paradise.)

The humanity of Christ also plays an important role in the mystical experiences of Angela of Foligno, a late-thirteenth-century Franciscan tertiary and influential mystic. Angela speaks often of the Second Person of the Trinity as the "God-man" as a way of emphasizing Christ's two natures: human and divine. These two natures feature in the two sorts of mystical union Angela reports as well. The first involves Christ's humanity. After one experience, for instance, where she "saw and felt that Christ was within me, embracing my soul with the very arm with which he was crucified," Angela reports that she is filled with joy and now understands what "this man, namely Christ, is like in heaven, that is to

---

[29] IV.14, *Mechthild of Magdeburg, The Flowing Light of the Godhead*, trans. Frank Tobin (Mahwah: Paulist Press, 1998), pp. 157–8.

[30] *Catherine of Siena: The Dialogue*, trans. Suzanne Noffke, OP (Mahwah: Paulist Press, 1980), ch. 41, p. 85.

Figure 6.1 *The Last Judgment*, detail of *Paradise*, Giovanni di Paolo, c.1460–5, Pinacoteca Nazionale di Siena.

say, how we will see that through him our flesh is made one with God."[31] Again, meditation on Christ's continued humanity in heaven makes Angela stress it is our *flesh* as well as our soul that is made one with God in the life to come.

Catherine of Siena makes a similar point, writing: "When my Son was lifted up on the wood of the most holy cross, he did not cut off his divinity from the lowly earth of your humanity. So, though he was raised so high, he was not raised off the earth. In fact, his divinity is kneaded into the clay of your humanity like one bread."[32] Again, Christ's status as fully human and fully divine offers us a way of understanding how our experience of immortality could involve embodied spirituality. As we saw in Section 4.2, the wildly popular devotional genre of meditations in the later Middle Ages encourages people to imagine themselves physically present at key moments of Christ's life and to cultivate emotions appropriate to their participation in those scenes (wonder at the birth of

---

[31] Ch. VI, 4th Supplemental Step, from the *Memorial*, in *Angela of Foligno: Complete Works*, p. 175.
[32] *Dialogue* 26, p. 65.

EMBODIED IMMORTAL EXPERIENCE   193

Jesus; anger at his betrayal by Judas; sympathy for Mary watching her son's execution, etc.). The purpose of meditating in this way is to generate a vivid sense of human connection and a more passionate love for God. Rather than counseling practitioners to withdraw from one's attachment to the self and its experiences, this tradition advocates 'leaning in' to certain affective experiences as a way of developing an appropriate sense of self in relation to God.

Strong emotion was seen in this tradition as opening the subject to the divine presence, as were visions, auditions, smellings, and tastings. As God assures Margaret Ebner, a fourteenth-century German Dominican, "I am no robber of the senses, I am the enlightener of the senses."[33] It's not clear from this passage whether Ebner is referring here to the 'inner' or the 'outer' senses, but since the apophatic tradition calls for transcending both, the claim that God enlightens the senses is enough to distinguish this view from apophaticism.[34] Furthermore, the inner and outer senses were seen as intrinsically connected, and both the mystical experiences these contemplatives report and the language they use to describe them often move seamlessly from one to the other, as when Mechthild of Magdeburg writes, "I do not know how to write, nor can I, unless I see with the eyes of my soul and hear with the ears of my eternal spirit and feel in all the parts of my body the power of the Holy Spirit."[35] Many of the contemplatives in this movement also frequently describe mystic union in terms of self-loss and dissolution, but unlike figures in the apophatic movement they do so without downplaying or denigrating the significance of affective and embodied unitive experiences.

This acceptance of embodied mystical states, I would argue, actually constitutes the most important distinction between the apophatic and affective mindset. Figures like Porete, Eckhart, and Walter Hilton acknowledge that unusual embodied states such as visions and auditions

---

[33] *Margaret Ebner: Major Works*, trans. and ed. Leonard Hindsley (Mahwah: Paulist Press, 1993), p. 100.

[34] For more on the inner and outer senses, see Niklaus Largier's "Inner Senses – Outer Senses: The Practice of Emotions in Medieval Mysticism," in *Emotions and Sensibilities in the Middle Ages*, ed. C. Jaeger and I. Kasten (Berlin and New York: de Gruyter, 2003), pp. 3–15.

[35] *The Flowing Light of the Godhead*, IV.13, p. 156.

194 IMMORTALITY AND THE AFTERLIFE

occur regularly in the contemplative life, but they portray them as experiences to be ignored or suspicious of, and as part of a stage that needs to be moved past. In contrast, other figures such as Angela of Foligno and Hadewijch, both of whom are often labeled 'apophatic mystics,' regularly describe both experiences of self-loss *and* self-fulfillment in mystical union.[36]

In a letter to a fellow beguine, for instance, Hadewijch describes experience of mystical union with God both in terms of a loss of self via complete intermingling *and* in terms of an eternal self-awareness that includes physicality as well as spirituality:

> Where the abyss of his wisdom is, God will teach you what he is, and with what wondrous sweetness the loved one and the Beloved dwell one in the other, and how they penetrate each other in a way that neither of the two distinguishes himself from the other. But they abide in one another in fruition, mouth in mouth, heart in heart, body in body, and soul in soul, while one sweet divine nature flows through both and they are both one thing through each other, but at the same time remain two different selves—yes, and remain so forever.[37]

The portrayal of the "one flesh" scriptural metaphor for marriage here is striking; in speaking of God and the human being (God's Beloved) in these intimate terms, Hadewijch stresses the beauty of both spiritual and physical union.[38]

Importantly, this sort of unitive mystical experience is also what we are told we will enjoy in the life to come. Catherine of Siena, for instance, is told by God that the upward spiral of love and knowledge in which souls are carried off in the fire of God's charity culminates in "that

---

[36] The fact that apophatic mystical experiences have generally been portrayed as superior to or purer than affective and embodied experiences is no doubt part of the motivation for labeling Angela and Hadewijch as apophatic mystics, as a way of legitimizing their insights; for more on this, see Chapter 1, particularly Section 1.1.

[37] Letter 9, in *Hadewijch: The Complete Works*. ed. and trans. Mother Columba Hart, OSB (Mahwah: Paulist Press, 1980), p. 66.

[38] As Mary Suydam notes, "There is absolutely no indication, either here or anywhere else in her writings, that this embodied experience represents a 'lower' stage of religious experience" (16); "The Touch of Satisfaction: Visions and Religious Experience According to Hadewijch of Antwerp," *Journal of Feminist Studies in Religion* 12 (Fall, 1996), pp. 5–27.

eternal vision of me in which they will see and taste me in truth when soul is separated from body [i.e., after death]. This is the superb state in which the soul even while still mortal shares the enjoyment of the immortals."[39] Angela of Foligno, for instance, reports after a mystical experience of 'unspeakable good' that "This is the same good and none other than that which the saints enjoy in eternal life, but there the experience of it is different. In eternal life, the least saint has more of it than can be given to a soul in this life before the death of the body."[40] There is sometimes self-loss or being 'taken out of' oneself in this tradition, but there is also always a return to oneself. Angela also describes moving between profoundly apophatic experiences and deeply personal experiences that involve the embodied Christ. In the following passage, she explains how, as an experience of unspeakable 'darkness' and indistinguishable union ebbs away, she still remains intimately connected with the God-man:

> When I am in that darkness I do not remember anything about anything human, or the God-man, or anything which has a form. Nevertheless, I see all and I see nothing. As what I have spoken of withdraws and stays with me, I see the God-man. He draws my soul with great gentleness, and he sometimes says to me: "You are I, and I am you." I see, then, those eyes and that face so gracious and attractive as he leans to embrace me.[41]

Here again we see the sort of mystical identification of human being with God discussed in Section 6.2: "You are I, and I am you." Yet here it appears in a setting in which the second person of the Trinity is speaking those words to Angela with a human mouth and looking at her with human eyes, *after* her experience of darkness, not *during* it.

Angela immediately goes on to explain how her two sorts of mystical experiences are related to each other:

---

[39] *Dialogue* 85, pp. 157–8.

[40] *Memorial*, in *Angela of Foligno: Complete Works*, trans. Paul Lachance (Mahwah: Paulist Press, 1993), p. 217.

[41] *Memorial* IX, p. 205.

196 IMMORTALITY AND THE AFTERLIFE

In short, what proceeds from those eyes and that face is what I said that I saw in that previous darkness which comes from within, and which delights me so that I can say nothing about it. When I am in the God-man my soul is alive. And I am in the God-man much more than in the other vision of seeing God with darkness. The soul is alive in that vision concerning the God-man. The vision with darkness, however, draws me so much more that there is no comparison. On the other hand, I am in the God-man almost continually. It began in this continual fashion on a certain occasion when I was given the assurance that there was no intermediary between God and myself. Since this time there has not been a day or night in which I did not continually experience this joy of the humanity of Christ.[42]

It is hardly obvious how to read the claims made here—and, indeed, we've already seen Angela herself exclaim how poorly words capture her experiences. At the same time, although she says that she vastly prefers her experience of God's inexpressible darkness, her union with the God-man is already unmediated, and there is no indication that her experience of Christ's humanity is anything but an appropriate source of delight.

One reason this point is worth stressing is that the primary motivation for focusing on Christ's humanity within the affective tradition was precisely to counter the sort of gnostic tendencies which run through apophaticism. Rather than hoping to move beyond contemplation of Christ's humanity to an experience of divinity, the affective movement saw human beings as most closely joined with Christ's divinity *through* his corporeity.

This 'both/and' approach has been all-too-frequently overlooked in philosophical discussions of mysticism, but it proves crucial for understanding medieval expectations for immortality. The following vision reported by Hadewijch, for instance, beautifully captures this 'both/and' depiction of mystical union. First, she describes Christ as satisfying the "desire of my heart and my humanity" via a physical embrace during the celebration of the Eucharist:

---

[42] *Memorial* IX, p. 205.

EMBODIED IMMORTAL EXPERIENCE   197

With that he came in the form and clothing of a Man, as he was on the day when he gave us his Body for the first time; looking like a Human Being and a Man, wonderful and beautiful, and with glorious face, he came to me as humbly as anyone who wholly belongs to another. Then he gave himself to me in the shape of the Sacrament, in its outward form, as the custom is; and then he gave me to drink from the chalice, in form and taste, as the custom is. After that he came himself to me, took me entirely in his arms, and pressed me to him; and all my members felt his in full felicity, in accordance with the desire of my heart and my humanity. So I was outwardly satisfied and fully transported.[43]

Here, Christ is repeatedly referred to as a Man, and as such speaks to Hadewijch's human nature.

After this, however, Christ "dissolves" so that they became "one without difference"—an experience Hadewijch relates to the physical mystery of the Eucharist (via the metaphor of digestion): "So can the Beloved, with the loved one, each wholly receive the other in full satisfaction of the sight, the hearing, and the passing away of the one in the other." This 'passing away' then turns into an apophatic experience of complete self-loss: "After that I remained in a passing away in my Beloved, so that I wholly melted away in him and nothing any longer remained of myself; and I was changed and taken up in spirit, and there it was shown me concerning such hours."[44] As with Angela of Foligno and Catherine of Siena, embodied experience of Christ's humanity forms a crucial component of Hadewijch's mystical union with God. It's not self-annihilation *as opposed to* affective experience on this view, but something much more complex—and complex in a way that recognizes the importance of body as well as soul.

As Julian of Norwich writes, using a careful combination of physical and spiritual images,

We will long for our Beloved until the day we die. And on that day we will merge with our Beloved, knowing ourselves clearly and possessing

---

[43] Vision 7, *Hadewijch*, p. 281.   [44] Vision 7, *Hadewijch*, p. 282.

198 IMMORTALITY AND THE AFTERLIFE

God completely. We will be endlessly hidden in God, seeing him truly and touching him fully, spiritually hearing him, deliciously smelling him, and sweetly tasting him. Ultimately, we shall see God face-to-face, and he will be completely familiar when we meet him. Then the created creature shall fully behold God her Creator and eternally contemplate him.[45]

We see here again the language of merging mixed with the language of continued identity—and it is also significant that Julian portrays this everlasting union with God as not just preserving but perfecting self-knowledge. (For more on self-knowledge in the contemplative tradition, see Chapter 2.)

In general, the thirteenth–fourteenth-century emphasis on the Incarnation and Christ's humanity (including the fact that Christ was believed to have ascended physically into heaven, where he waits for the rest of us to join him) provided an embodied model of union with God that was enthusiastically explored by contemplatives from a wide variety of backgrounds. If we think of apophaticism's emphasis on phenomenological de-emphasis or erasure as one endpoint of the experiential continuum of immortality, then, affectivism's emphasis on embodied fulfillment can be seen as the other endpoint. In Section 6.4 I discuss how scholastic views map onto this continuum; perhaps surprisingly, the most relevant factor for where a figure falls is not religious affiliation (that is, whether the author is Carthusian, Dominican, or Franciscan, etc.) but, rather, whether the body is seen more as hindering or helping us connect with God.

6.4 Intellective Union and the Scholastic Tradition

We've seen that medieval expectations of immortality range widely, from loss of individual experience in union with God to a self-preserving

---

[45] *Showings*, ch. 43, p. 108. She continues: "No one can see God in this way and survive – not in moral form. Yet when, in his special grace, he wishes to show himself to us here on earth, he strengthens the creature beyond her own natural power, and he measures out the revelation according to his own will, so that she can handle it and it does her the most good."

INTELLECTIVE UNION AND THE SCHOLASTIC TRADITION   199

connection with God; to demonstrate the breadth of this range, I have drawn in Sections 6.2 and 6.3 on contemplative literature from a variety of literary genres and languages. In this final section I discuss where on this continuum to place two major figures in the Latin scholastic tradition: Robert Grosseteste and Thomas Aquinas. One common way of dividing up scholastic views of the afterlife is according to whether they stress the primacy of intellect or will in our final end—that is, whether the view maintains that we will be united with God via knowledge first and foremost or via love. When it comes to our experience of the afterlife, however, this distinction proves much less helpful, for an emphasis on intellective vs. volitional aspects of eternal union turns out not to map neatly onto the experiential continuum discussed above. What *does* help situate scholastic (and contemplative) accounts along that continuum, however, are the author's attitudes towards embodiment and the nature of union with God more generally.

Throughout this book (see particularly Chapter 4), for instance, we have encountered contemplatives who agree that love is our final end, but who nevertheless present widely divergent conceptions of our experience of that final end. Marguerite Porete stresses the importance of total self-annihilation in Love, whereas Hadewijch also emphasizes love's unifying power, but in such a manner that God and the Beloved "remain two different selves—yes, and remain so forever." Mechthild of Magdeburg in turn sees our final end as loving union with God, but she rejoices in the thought that the soul "with its flesh" will literally sit next to the resurrected Christ). Clearly, emphasis on the will and love does not lead to one particular view of our experience of immortality.

In the remainder of this section I show that an emphasis on intellective union also allows for a range of different expectations of immortality, focusing on the accounts of Robert Grosseteste and Thomas Aquinas. The human desire for knowledge runs throughout medieval discussions of immortality. In fact, the 'naturalness' of our desire for both abstract knowledge and immortality is appealed to by Augustinian illuminationists, Neoplatonists, and Aristotelians alike as an indication that human beings are meant for more than just material existence. Yet, to return to one of the central questions from Section 6.1, are we immaterial souls who need to transcend our corrupt bodies, or are those bodies an integral part of who we are?

200 IMMORTALITY AND THE AFTERLIFE

6.4.1 Robert Grosseteste

An important response to this question appears in Robert Grosseteste's early-thirteenth-century commentary on Aristotle's *Posterior Analytics*—a work that is especially significant because it represents the Latin university system's first attempt to address Aristotle's system in what had been largely a Platonic world. Rather than take sides in what in the ensuing century becomes a highly acrimonious debate, Grosseteste's central project is synthetic in nature; he incorporates Platonic ideas, Neoplatonic emanation, Aristotelian universals, *and* divine illumination into his complex framework. Although how best to understand details of the resulting framework remains controversial, what is clear is that on his view the highest forms of cognition involve separation from matter.[46] In his own words, "Knowledge is most complete in these things that lack senses."[47]

Grosseteste, a master at Oxford University, generally applies an Aristotelian epistemic framework to human cognition here on earth. His discussions of the levels of cognition, however, emphasize that cognition which depends on sense perception and phantasms (mental images that stored in the imaginations), is the lowest sort. The higher the intellect, the less dependent on the senses and phantasms it is. Employing Platonist language of purity, Grosseteste explains that "for the intellect that is pure and separated from phantasms—able to contemplate the first light, which is the first cause—the principles of cognizing are the uncreated ideas (*rationes*) of things that exist from eternity in the first cause."[48] In fact, "when the pure intellect is able to fix its sight on them, it cognizes created things in them as truly and clearly as possible—and not only created things, but also the first light itself in

---

[46] For discussion of both the controversies involved in interpreting Grosseteste's position on universals (with extensive bibliography) and my own interpretation, see my "The Truth, the Whole Truth, and Nothing but the Truth: Robert Grosseteste on Universals (and the *Posterior Analytics*)," *Journal of the History of Philosophy* 48/2 (2010), pp. 153–70.

[47] *Commentary on the Posterior Analytics* I.14; translation mine. References are to the Latin text of Pietro Rossi's critical edition, *Commentarius in Posteriorum Analyticorum Libros* (Florence: Leo S. Olschki, 1981).

[48] *Commentary* I.7, pp. 100–6.

INTELLECTIVE UNION AND THE SCHOLASTIC TRADITION   201

which it cognizes other things."[49] As becomes clear through the commentary, Grosseteste believes that we can gain true knowledge of God only when we have separated our intellects completely from their dependence on the body and its phantasms—that is, only after death. There is no mention of a positive role for the body here. Indeed, although we appear to retain a sense of individuality in the afterlife on this view, it is not because we are essentially embodied. We must draw our mental gaze away from corporeal matters, for "divine things are more visible to the mind's vision that is healthy and not clouded by phantasms." Grosseteste goes so far as to refer to the mind's vision, "while we are burdened by the weight of the corrupt body and the love of corporeal things," as *unhealthy*.[50] Our love for the material world is essentially a sickness that interferes with our ability to know both abstract truths (for which Grosseteste's favorite example is mathematics) and God. "The reason why the soul's sight is clouded by the weight of the corrupt body," he writes, "Is that the affection and vision (*affectus et aspectus*) of the soul are not distinct, and the soul attains its vision only by means of that by which it attains its affection or its love."[51] So long as the soul loves the body and its "enticements," the soul's vision is turned away from the source of its natural light. Our goal as human beings is to turn our love towards God, so that our minds can follow suit.

The vision of immortality that emerges from Grosseteste, then, is one in which our connection with physicality is tenuous at best. If (as Christian doctrine maintains) we spend the afterlife joined to incorruptible bodies, those bodies appear to play no role in our experience of our final end. Grosseteste's afterlife is one of Platonic intellective fulfillment, which in turn fulfills our wills as well. We may retain individual existence, but our primary experience of that individuality will come via our experience of God as our First and Final Cause.

[49] *Commentary* I.7, pp. 106–11.   [50] *Commentary* I.17, pp. 353–63.
[51] *Commentary* I.14, pp. 279–86. See ch. 18, conclusion 28, for further discussion about love and desire moving the soul.

202 IMMORTALITY AND THE AFTERLIFE

6.4.2 Thomas Aquinas

Robert Grosseteste's view is significant because it represents an early attempt in the Latin West to reconcile Aristotelian with Platonic intuitions; the resulting account, however, takes a decidedly Platonist perspective on the body. Thomas Aquinas, on the other hand, is known for advocating a thoroughly hylomorphic, Aristotelian account of human nature. On his view, the human being is a composite of form and matter, and cognition is an activity that requires us to use our bodies as well as our rational capacities. To make an extremely complicated story short, human beings have the weakest intellects in the hierarchy of being,[52] and so the typical process of human cognition moves first from sense experience to phantasms, and then from phantasms to intelligible species (the proper objects of abstract thought). Furthermore, in this life, any time we're thinking, our intellects must refer back to the phantasms that ground the intelligible species that serve as the objects of our thought.

This general account of cognition makes it look as though Aquinas's account of immortality should be robustly embodied, with us using our glorified sense perception as well as our rational capacities to better know and love God. Aquinas's actual depiction of our final end, however, emphasizes its intellectual, contemplative nature and explicitly denies that sense perception plays a role in that act of contemplation. As he writes in his Treatise on Happiness in the Summa theologiae, "In that perfect happiness in heaven to which we look forward…the operation by which the human mind is joined to God will not depend on the senses."[53] The reason for this is that Aquinas believes that the primary activity of the life to come is direct (unmediated) contemplation of God's essence—an activity we share with God and the angels, who are

---

[52] See, e.g., the extended discussions of human cognition in comparison to other intellects in *Summa theologiae* Ia 84–9, *Summa contra gentiles* II 94–101, III 37–60, *Quaestiones de anima*, and *De veritate* VIII–X.

[53] ST IaIIae 3.3.co. In his early *Sentences Commentary*, Aquinas mentions our seeing Christ's resurrected body and the glorified bodies of the martyrs as enhancing our experience of the Beatific Vision, but in his later works he omits any reference to this possibility and claims that our vision of God's essence will be entirely intellective, rather than also including a literal component. (See, e.g., *Summa contra gentiles* III.51.)

INTELLECTIVE UNION AND THE SCHOLASTIC TRADITION   203

wholly immaterial. In this life, we require mutable bodies for gathering information from the world around us; in the life to come, we will still have sense perception, but there will be no *need* for it.[54] Human beings attain the beatific vision only when God gives us his essence as intelligible form and then illuminates our intellects so we are capable of cognizing it to the degree that we love it.[55] God is the First and the Final Cause in this cognitive story: "In such a vision, the divine essence must be both *what is seen* and *that by which* it is seen."[56]

Our experience of immortality on Aquinas's view differs radically from our experience of mortal life, for it also involves a drastic shift in our experience of time. In this life, human beings employ discursive reasoning, moving from premise to premise to conclusion, rather than instantly comprehending an argument in its entirety. Aquinas argues that in the life to come, however, we will exist in a state of perfection in which motion ceases: "Each thing rests when it reaches its ultimate end, since all motion is for the sake of acquiring that end, and the ultimate end of the intellect is vision of the divine substance, as was shown above. Therefore, the intellect which is seeing the divine substance does not move from one intelligible thing to another."[57] Our contemplation of God's eternal and unchanging essence is "one continuous and sempiternal activity."[58]

Aquinas is also clear, however, that our rational souls will be joined to resurrected material bodies, which will be "brighter, more firmly impassible, much more agile, and with a more perfect dignity of

---

[54] See also *Summa contra gentiles* III.62, where Aquinas explains that the enjoyment of the beatific vision never ends, for our intellects will not tire in their contemplation (with God's assistance), "and no act which is carried out through a physical organ coincides with this vision."

[55] We've seen this quote from Catherine of Siena's *Dialogue* in previous chapters, but her depiction of the interplay between love and knowledge is worth quoting here again: "I have told you this, my dearest daughter, to let you know the perfection of this unitive state in which souls are carried off by the fire of my charity. In that charity, they receive supernatural light, and in that light they love me. For love follows upon understanding. The more they know, the more they love, and the more they love, the more they know. Thus each nourishes the other. By this light they reach the eternal vision of me in which they see and taste me in truth when soul is separated from body." *Dialogue* 85, pp. 157–8.

[56] *Summa contra gentiles* III.51.

[57] *Summa contra gentiles* III.60. Aquinas reiterates this point at length in his discussion of peace in his commentary on the Sermon on the Mount.

[58] *Summa theologiae* IaIIae 3.2.ad4.

204 IMMORTALITY AND THE AFTERLIFE

nature."[59] These bodies are glorified by sharing in the perfect happiness our souls receive from their contemplation of God's essence. In fact, Aquinas claims, "there will be such an outflow to the body and the bodily senses from the happiness of the soul that they will be perfected in their operations."[60] The beatific vision is everlasting and unchanging, and our experience of it will be likewise. Whatever information the sense might provide us with will at best enhance that vision, rather than forming any constituent part of it.

Aquinas's intellectivist view of the phenomenology of immortality, then, significantly downplays the role of our bodies and our senses in comparison to some of his contemporaries' contemplative views. At the same time, Aquinas does not depict our bodies as a burden we need to transcend or as weighing down our intellects, as Grosseteste does. Intellectivist accounts of union with God thus also fall on different points along the experiential continuum. Again, it seems that what's most relevant for medieval expectations of immortality is not a stress on love versus knowledge but, rather, attitudes towards the body and its connection (or lack thereof) to experiences of God: Platonist inclinations push towards self-abnegation in union with a God perhaps beyond being itself; emphasis on our connection to God via Christ's humanity inclines towards mystical union with physical and emotional as well as intellective and volitional components.

6.5 Conclusion

Traditionally, philosophical discussions of immortality in the Middle Ages have focused on scholastic arguments for and against the survival of the rational soul and questions of personal identity through death

---

[59] *Summa contra gentiles* IV.86. These qualities are possessed only by the bodies of the blessed, however. The bodies of the damned Aquinas describes as dark, heavy, suffering, and degraded.

[60] *Summa theologiae* IaIIae 3.3.co. As Aquinas clarifies in *Summa contra gentiles* IV.83, although we will have bodies and sense perception, "All the occupations of the active life (which seem ordered to the use of food and sex and those other things that are necessary for corruptible life) will cease. Only the activity of the contemplative life will remain after the resurrection."

and the bodily resurrection. These views are important and certainly worthy of attention, but even the brief overview of contemplative positions I have been able to provide in this chapter shows that scholastic accounts fall far short of representing the full range of medieval thoughts about immortality and the afterlife—even just in the Rome-based Christian tradition, and even just in the thirteenth–fifteenth centuries. My hope is that the 'experiential continuum of immortality' I have presented and motivated here will provide a useful framework for more holistic understandings of medieval views on immortality and the afterlife—a framework that should also prove of use to philosophers of mind, philosophers of religion, theologians, and scholars of the afterlife more generally.

Afterword

It is a strange and momentous time to be a medievalist. We are currently living through what many people are calling "the new Dark Ages,"[1] due in part to the horrific rise of white supremacist groups (many of whom claim to be drawing inspiration from medieval ideology and practices[2]) and the outbreak of a worldwide pandemic which has inspired any number of references to the Black Death.[3] 'Medieval' has become a synonym for backwardness and ignorance, and the Middle Ages an entire millennium of human experience considered worth noting only as a cautionary tale against "religious extremism, anti-science sneering, conspiracy theories and ill-conceived, ragtag, speak-and-pole crusades."[4]

This characterization has, for better or worse, inspired a fresh wave of interest in these so-called Dark Ages—a wave that a host of medievalists are cresting with their forefingers held high and the words "Well, actually!" burning on their lips. From Matthew Gabriele and David Perry's complete flip of the trope in *The Bright Ages: A New History of Medieval*

---

[1] See Petula Dvorak's "We're living in the new Dark Ages – and it's time to turn on the light," which appeared in the *Washington Post* on December 30, 2021 (https://www.washingtonpost.com/dc-md-va/2021/12/30/dark-ages-medieval-middle-ages/). In his introduction to *New Dark Age: Technology and the End of the Future* (New York: Verso Books, 2018), meanwhile, James Bridle makes explicit reference to the fourteenth-century *Cloud of Unknowing*.

[2] For a refutation of white supremacist claims to medieval backing, see Amy Kaufman and Paul Sturtevant's *The Devil's Historians: How Modern Extremists Abuse the Medieval Past* (Toronto: University of Toronto Press, 2020).

[3] The main website for the Centers for Disease Control and Prevention attributes both the name and the practice of quarantine to fourteenth-century efforts "to protect coastal cities from plague epidemics": https://www.cdc.gov/quarantine/historyquarantine.html.

[4] Dvorak, "We're living in the new Dark Ages"; Dvorak also calls our current economic structure "feudalism redux" in an approving reference to Joel Kotkin's 2020 doom-and-gloom-filled book, *The New Feudalism: The Coming Global Return to the Middle Ages*. See also Joel Kotkin's "The new Dark Ages: The woke assault on Western civilisation is taking us backwards," in *Spiked*, which describes "the memes of feudal times" as "driven by illiteracy, bias, and a rejection of the West's past" (https://www.spiked-online.com/2021/12/15/the-new-dark-ages/).

Europe[5] to Andrew Albin (et al.)'s *Whose Middle Ages? Teachable Moments for an Ill-Used Past*,[6] new scholarship continues to challenge the idea that the worst of today's present mirrors the best of the Middle Ages' past. This cutting-edge scholarship brings the rich complexity of the global Middle Ages to light, whether by drawing attention to the importance of Saharan Africa for medieval trade (as in Kathleen Bickford Berzock's *Caravans of Gold, Fragments in Time: Art, Culture, and Exchange across Medieval Saharan Africa*[7]), by re-examining accepted meanings of iconography (as Sara Lipton does in her *Dark Mirror: The Medieval Origins on Anti-Jewish Iconography*[8]), or by digging out the medieval roots of contemporary racism (as in Geraldine Heng's *The Invention of Race in the European Middle Ages* and Cord Whitaker's *Black Metaphors: How Modern Racism Emerged from Medieval Race-Thinking*).[9]

This book constitutes one very small step in the same direction—that is, towards a more accurate representation of an intellectual, cultural, political, and religious landscape that is often maligned and/or dismissed on the basis of events that didn't even happen during its thousand-year span. (Witch trials, for instance, really took off in the sixteenth and seventeenth centuries—the period known as the Scientific Revolution, and the scope of legal rights of women actually became *more* restricted in France, England, and other European countries in what's often called the Enlightenment and following centuries. Jane Austen's Mrs. Dashwood and her three girls in *Sense and Sensibility* would have had more and better options available to them in the England of Eleanor of Aquitaine than they did in their own age of primogeniture and entailed estates.) While many if not most disciplines in the humanities and liberal arts have spent the past thirty years and

---

[5] Matthew Gabriele and David Perry, *The Bright Ages: A New History of Medieval Europe* (New York: HarperCollins Publishers, 2021).

[6] Andrew Albin, Mary Erler, Thomas O'Donnell, Nicholas Paul, and Nina Rowe, eds. *Whose Middle Ages? Teachable Moments for an Ill-Used Past* (New York: Fordham University Press, 2019).

[7] Kathleen Bickford Berzock, *Caravans of Gold, Fragments in Time: Art, Culture, and Exchange across Medieval Saharan Africa* (Princeton, NJ: Princeton University Press, 2018).

[8] Sara Lipton, *Dark Mirror: The Medieval Origins of Anti-Jewish Iconography* (New York: Metropolitan Books, 2014).

[9] Geraldine Heng, *The Invention of Race in the European Middle Ages* (Cambridge: Cambridge University Press, 2018); Cord Whitaker, *Black Metaphors: How Modern Racism Emerged from Medieval Race-Thinking* (Philadelphia: University of Pennsylvania Press, 2019).

208 AFTERWORD

more rediscovering and incorporating the contributions of women to their fields, this trend is still just beginning to reach 'mainstream' philosophy (which is to say, philosophy as it tends to be understood by academics in philosophy departments). The idea that women produced work worthy of sustained philosophical attention is still quite novel to many of my fellow historians of medieval philosophy, let alone to the general field. (As I note in my Preface, we were all taught that women simply weren't allowed to do philosophy in the Middle Ages!) The fact that this work tends to appear in mystical and contemplative venues, and the idea that medieval contemplative traditions generally deserve more philosophical attention that they receive, are also not yet well appreciated. (Indeed, I hope that my focus on the Rome-based Christian contemplative tradition of the thirteenth–fifteenth centuries is enough to motivate others to look more closely at the mystical and contemplative traditions of other times and other places within the thousand years we call the medieval period, for there is fascinating work already being done on the medieval contemplative texts of Islamic, Jewish, Confucian, Buddhist, and Hindi traditions, and more.)

Let me close, then, by encouraging philosophers to look outside the scholastic tradition, both to form a more accurate picture of the range of medieval perspectives on 'classical' philosophical issues and to encounter a fresh set of questions voiced by traditionally marginalized groups. At the same time, I hope that historians, theologians, art historians, and those engaged in other disciplines that address the Middle Ages will appreciate the addition of philosophical perspectives to their conversations and perhaps even actively seek such perspectives out.

Medieval contemplative philosophy is vibrant, engaged, and surprisingly relevant to contemporary concerns about how to live. In this book I have been able only to highlight a few of the figures and ideas in this tradition that richly repay philosophical attention; my goal has been to provide a variety of conceptual hooks that allow people within philosophy to connect with relevant conversations in this tradition, while also giving medievalists in other disciplines a fresh lens through which to view familiar mystical and contemplative texts. This is perhaps the first book-length reintegration of the medieval contemplative tradition into discussions about medieval philosophy; I am hopeful that it will not be the last.

Bibliography

Primary Sources

Primary Sources in English Translation

Angela of Foligno. *Angela of Foligno: Complete Works*, trans. Paul Lachance. Mahwah: Paulist Press, 1993.

Anon. *The Cloud of Unknowing: with the Book of Privy Counselling*, trans. Carmen Acevedo Butcher. Boulder, CO: Shambhala Publications, 2009.

Aquinas, Thomas. *Thomas Aquinas, The Treatise on Happiness: Summa theologiae IaIIae 1–21*, trans. Thomas Williams, commentary by Christina Van Dyke and Thomas Williams. Hackett Aquinas Series. Indianapolis: Hackett Publishing Co., 2016.

Bonaventure. *Bonaventure: The Soul's Journey into God; The Tree of Life; the Life of St. Francis*, trans. Ewert Cousins. Mahwah: Paulist Press, 1978.

Bonaventure. *The Works of Bonaventure, Vol. 1: The Journey of the Mind to God, The Triple Way or Love Enkindled, The Tree of Life, The Mystical Vine, On the Perfection of Life, Addressed to Sisters*, trans. J. de Vinck. Mansfield Centre: Martino Publishing, 2016.

Catherine of Siena. *Catherine of Siena: The Dialogue*, trans. Suzanne Noffke. Mahwah: Paulist Press, 1980.

Chrétien de Troyes. *The Complete Romances of Chrétien de Troyes*, trans. David Staines. Bloomington: Indiana University Press, 1990.

Clare of Assisi. *Francis and Clare: The Complete Works*, trans. Armstrong, Regis J., and Brady, Ignatius C. Mahwah: Paulist Press, 1986.

de Lorris, Guillaume, and Jean de Meun. *The Romance of the Rose*, trans. Charles Dahlberg. Princeton: Princeton University Press, 1971.

de Pizan, Christine. *The Book of the City of Ladies*, trans. Earl Richards. New York: Persea Books, 1982, rev. 1998.

de Pizan, Christine. *A Medieval Woman's Mirror of Honor*, trans. Charity Cannon Willard. New York: Persea Books, 1989.

Ebner, Margaret. *Margaret Ebner: Major Works*, trans. and ed. Leonard Hindsley. Mahwah: Paulist Press, 1993.

Eckhart, Meister. *Meister Eckhart: The Essential Sermons, Commentaries, Treatises, and Defense*, ed. and trans. Edmund Colledge and Bernard McGinn. Mahwah: Paulist Press, 1981.

Eckhart, Meister. *Meister Eckhart: Teacher and Preacher*, ed. B McGinn, trans. McGinn, F. Tobin, and E. Borgstadt. Mahwah, NJ: Paulist Press, 1986.

Eckhart, Meister. *The Complete Mystical Works of Meister Eckhart*, trans. Maurice O'C. Walshe. New York: Crossroads Publishing Co., 2010.

210 BIBLIOGRAPHY

Francis of Assisi. *Francis and Clare: The Complete Works*, trans. Armstrong, Regis J., and Brady, Ignatius C. Mahwah: Paulist Press, 1986.

Gertrude of Helfta. *Gertrude of Helfta: The Herald of Divine Love*, trans. and ed. Margaret Winkworth. Mahwah: Paulist Press, 1993.

Guigo II. *The Ladder of Monks and Twelve Meditations*, trans. Edmund Colledge, OSA, and James Walsh, SJ. Kalamazoo: Cistercian Publications, 1978.

Hadewijch. *Hadewijch: The Complete Works*. ed. and trans. Mother Columba Hart, OSB. Mahwah: Paulist Press, 1980.

Hilton, Walter. *The Scale (or Ladder) of Perfection*, ed. Serenus Cressy. Monee, IL: Scotts Valley California, 2010.

Hrotsvit of Gandersheim. *Hrotsvit of Gandersheim: A Florilegium of Her Works*, trans. with an introduction, essay, and notes by Katharina Wilson. Cambridge: D. S. Brewer, 1998.

Julian of Norwich. *Julian of Norwich: Showings*, trans. Edmund Colledge and James Walsh. Mahwah: Paulist Press, 1978.

Julian of Norwich. *The Showings of Julian of Norwich: A New Translation*, trans. Mirabai Starr. Charlottesville, VA: Hampton Roads Publishing Co., 2013.

Kempis, Thomas à. *The Imitation of Christ*, trans. William C. Creasy. Notre Dame, IN: Ave Maria Press, 2017.

Locke, John. *Essay Concerning Human Understanding*, ed. Peter Nidditch. Oxford: Oxford University Press, 1975.

Marguerite d'Oingt. *The Writings of Margaret of Oingt, Medieval Prioress and Mystic (d. 1310)*, trans. with an introduction, essay, and notes by Renate Blumenfeld-Kosinski. Cambridge: D. S. Brewer, 1990.

Mechthild of Hackeborn. *Mechthild of Hackeborn: The Book of Special Grace*, trans. Barbara Newman. Mahwah: Paulist Press, 2017.

Mechthild of Magdeburg. *Mechthild of Magdeburg, The Flowing Light of the Godhead*, trans. Frank Tobin. Mahwah: Paulist Press, 1998.

Meditations on the Life of Christ, trans. F. X. Taney, Anne Miller, and C. Mary Stallings-Taney. Asheville, NC: Pegasus Press, 2000.

Meditations on the Life of Christ: The Short Italian Text, trans. Sarah McNamer. Notre Dame, IN: Notre Dame University Press, 2018.

Porete, Marguerite. *Marguerite Porete. The Mirror of Simple Souls*, trans. E. L. Babinsky. Mahwah: Paulist Press, 1993.

Pseudo-Dionisius. *Pseudo-Dionisius: the Complete Works*, trans. Colm Luiheid. Mahwah: Paulist Press, 1987.

Richard of St. Victor. *Richard of St. Victor: The Twelve Patriarchs, The Mystical Ark, Book Three of the Trinity*, trans. Grover Zinn. Mahwah: Paulist Press, 1979.

Richard of St. Victor and Anon. *The Pursuit of Wisdom and Other Works by the Author of the Cloud of Unknowing*, ed. and trans. James Walsh. Mahwah: Paulist Press, 1988.

Rolle, Richard. *The Fire of Love*, trans. Clifton Wolters. New York: Penguin Classics, 1972.

Rolle, Richard. *Richard Rolle: The English Writings*, ed. and trans. Rosamund Allen. Mahwah: Paulist Press, 1988.

BIBLIOGRAPHY 211

Ruusbroec, Jan. *John Ruusbroec: The Spiritual Espousals and Other Works*, ed. and trans. John A. Wiseman. Mahwah: Paulist Press, 1985.

Primary Sources in the Original Language

Angela of Foligno. *Angela da Foligno, Memoriale. Edizione crita a cura di Enrico Menestò*. Spoleto: Fondazione Centro Italiano di Studi sull'alto Medioevo, 2013.

Anon. *The Book of Privy Counselling*. MS: British Library Harley 674 (H), fols. 92r–110v.

Anon. *The Cloud of Unknowing*. MS: British Library Harley 674 (H), fols. 17v–31v.

Bernhard of Clairvaux. *Sermones in Cantica Canticorum*, in Patrologiae Cursus Completus, Vol. 183, ed. J.-P. Minge. Turnhout: Brepols, 1969.

Catherine of Siena. *Caterina da Siena. Libro della divina dottrina volgarmente detto Dialogo della divina Provvidenza*. http://www.bibliotecaitaliana.it/testo/si074, 2018.

Eckhart, Meister. *Die deutschen und lateinischen Werke. Herausgegeben im Auftrage der Deutschen Forschungsgemeinschaft*. Stuttgart and Berlin: W. Kohlhammer, 1936–.

Grosseteste, Robert. *Commentarius in Posteriorum Analyticorum Libros*, ed. P. Rossi, Florence: Leo S. Olschki, 1981.

Hadewijch. *Hadewijch: Brieven*. 2 vols, ed. Jozef Van Mierlo. Louvain: Vlaamsch Boekenhalle, 1924–5.

Hadewijch. *Hadewijch: Visioenen*. 2 vols, ed. Jozef Van Mierlo. Louvain: Vlaamsch Boekenhalle, 1924–5.

Hilton, Walter. *The Scale of Perfection*. MS: Cambridge University Library, MS Add. 6686.

Julian of Norwich. *The Writings of Julian of Norwich: A Vision Showed to a Devout Woman and A Revelation of Love*, ed. Nicholas Watson and Jacqueline Jenkins. University Park, PA: Pennsylvania State University Press, 2006.

Margaret Ebner. *Margaretha Ebner und Heinrich von Nördlingen. Ein Beitrag zur Geschichte der deutschen Mystik*, by Philipp Strauch. Freiburg i. B. and Tübingen: J. C. B. Mohr, 1882.

Marguerite d'Oingt. *Les Oeuvres de Marguerite d'Oingt*, ed. and trans. Duraffour, A., Gardette, P., and Durdilly, P. Publications de l'Institut de Linguistique Romane de Lyon, 21. Paris: Belles Lettres, 1965.

Meditationes Vitae Christi, Corpus Christianorum Continuatio Mediaevalis (CCCM 153), ed. Mary Stallings-Taney. Turnhout: Brepols, 1997.

Porete, Marguerite. *Le Mirouer des simple âmes*, ed. Romana Guarnieri. Turnhout: Brepols, 1986.

Richard de St. Victor. *De Trinitate: texte critique avec introduction, notes et tables*, ed. Jean Ribaillier. Paris: J. Vrin, 1958.

Ruusbroec, Jan. *Werken*, ed. Ruusbroecgenootschap. 4 vols. Mechelen: Het Kompas, 1932–4; 2nd rev. ed., Tielt: Uitgeverij Lannoo, 1944–8.

Tauler, John. *Die Predigten Taulers*, ed. Ferdinand Vetter (Berlin: Wiedmann, 1910; photomechanical repr., 1968).

von Bingen, Hildegard. *Analecta Sanctae Hildegardis*, ed. J. B. Pitra. Monte Cassino, 1882.

212 BIBLIOGRAPHY

von Bingen, Hildegard. *Epistolarium*, ed. Lieven Van Acker. CCCM 91–91a. Turnhout, 1991, 1993.

von Bingen, Hildegard. *Liber divinorum operum*, ed. Albert Derolez and Peter Dronke. CCCM 92. Turnhout: Brepols, 1996.

Windeatt, Barry, ed. *English Mystics of the Middle Ages*. Cambridge: Cambridge University Press, 1994.

Secondary Sources

Adamson, Peter. *Medieval Philosophy: A History of Philosophy without Any Gaps, Vol. 4*. Oxford: Oxford University Press, 2019.

Albin, Andrew, Mary Erler, Thomas O'Donnell, Nicholas Paul, and Nina Rowe, eds. *Whose Middle Ages? Teachable Moments for an Ill-Used Past*. New York: Fordham University Press, 2019.

Allen, Prudence. *The Concept of Woman*. Grand Rapids: Wm. B. Eerdmans Publishing Co., 1997, 2006.

Alston, William. *Perceiving God: The Epistemology of Religious Experience*. Ithaca: Cornell University Press, 1991.

Andersen, Elizabeth, Henrike Lähnemann, and Anne Simon, eds. *A Companion to Mysticism and Devotion in Northern Germany in the Late Middle Ages*. Leiden: Brill, 2014.

Badea, Gabriela. *Allegories of Selfhood in Medieval Devotional Literature*. Doctoral Thesis, Columbia University, 2018.

Bagger, M. *Religious Experience, Justification, and History*. Cambridge: Cambridge University Press, 1999.

Beal, Jane. "The Unicorn as a Symbol for Christ in the Middle Ages," in *Illuminating Jesus in the Middle Ages*, ed. J. Beal. Leiden: Brill, 2019, 154–88.

Beckwith, Sarah. *Christ's Body: Identity, Culture, and Society in Late Medieval Writings*. London: Routledge, 1993.

Bell, Rudolph. *Holy Anorexia*. Chicago: University of Chicago Press, 1985.

Berges, Sandrine. "Teaching Christine de Pizan in Turkey," *Gender and Education* 25/5 (2013), 595–605.

Berzock, Kathleen Bickford. *Caravans of Gold, Fragments in Time: Art, Culture, and Exchange across Medieval Saharan Africa*. Princeton, NJ: Princeton University Press, 2018.

Blumenfeld-Kosinski, Renate, and Timea Szell, eds. *Images of Sainthood in Medieval Europe*. Ithaca: Cornell University Press, 1991.

Blumenthal, David. "On the Intellect and the Rational Soul," *Journal of the History of Philosophy* 15 (1977), 207–11.

Borland, Jennifer. "Unruly Reading: the Consuming Role of Touch in the Experience of a Medieval MS," in *Scraped, Stroked, and Bound: Materially Engaged Readings of Medieval Manuscripts*, ed. Jonathan Wilcox. Turnhout: Brepols, 2013, 97–114.

Bornstein, Daniel. "Women and Religion in Late Medieval Italy: History and Historiography," in *Women and Religion in Medieval and Renaissance Italy*, ed.

BIBLIOGRAPHY   213

D. Bornstein and R. Rusconi, trans. Margery Schneider. Chicago: University of Chicago Press, 1996, 1–27.

Bos, E. P. *Medieval Supposition Theory Revisited*. Leiden: Brill Publishing, 2013.

Boulter, Stephen. *Why Medieval Philosophy Matters*. London: Bloomsbury Academic, 2019.

Brower, Jeff. *Aquinas's Ontology of the Material World: Change, Hylomorphism, and Material Objects*. Oxford: Oxford University Press, 2014.

Browne, Borden Parker. *Personalism*. Boston: Houghton Mifflin Co., 1908.

Buber, Martin. *Ich and Du (I and Thou)*, trans. Ronald Gregor Smith. Edinburgh: T&T Clark, 1987, 2nd ed.

Burns, J. H., ed. *The Cambridge History of Medieval Political Thought c.350–c.1450*. Cambridge: Cambridge University Press, 1988.

Bynum, Caroline Walker. *Jesus as Mother: Studies in the Spirituality of the High Middle Ages*. Berkeley: University of California Press, 1984.

Bynum, Caroline Walker. *Holy Feast and Holy Fast: The Religious Significance of Food to Medieval Women*. Berkeley: University of California Press, 1988.

Bynum, Caroline Walker. *Fragmentation and Redemption: Essays on Gender and the Human Body in Medieval Religion*. New York: Zone Books, 1991.

Bynum, Caroline Walker. *The Resurrection of the Body in Western Christianity, 200–1336*, New York: Columbia University Press, 1995.

Bynum, Caroline Walker. *Wonderful Blood: Theology and Practice in Late Medieval Northern Germany and Beyond*. Philadelphia: University of Pennsylvania Press, 2006.

Caciola, Nancy. *Discerning Spirits, Divine and Demonic Possession in the Middle Ages*. Ithaca: Cornell University Press, 2003.

Campbell, Joseph. *The Hero with a Thousand Faces*. New York: Pantheon Books, 1949.

Celano, Anthony. *Aristotle's Ethics and Medieval Philosophy: Moral Goodness and Practical Wisdom*. Cambridge: Cambridge University Press, 2015.

Cornet, Ineke. *The Arnhem Mystical Sermons: Preaching Liturgical Mysticism in the Context of Catholic Reform*, Leiden: Brill, 2019.

Cory, Therese Scarpelli. *Aquinas on Human Self-Knowledge*. Cambridge: Cambridge University Press, 2014.

Crosby, John. "The Incommunicability of Human Persons," *The Thomist* 57/3 (1993) 403–42.

Cusato, Michael. "Poverty", *The Cambridge History of Medieval Philosophy*, eds. R. Pasnau and C. Van Dyke. Cambridge: Cambridge University Press, 2009, pp. 577–92.

Dales, Richard. "The De-Animation of the Heavens in the Middle Ages", *Journal of the History of Ideas* 41/4 (1980), 531–50.

Dales, Richard. *The Problem of the Rational Soul in the Thirteenth Century*, Leiden: Brill, 1995.

Daly, Mary. *The Church and the Second Sex*, Boston: Beacon Press, 1985.

Davis, Emmalon. "Typecasts, Tokens, and Spokespersons: A Case for Credibility Excess as Testimonial Injustice", *Hypatia* 31/3 (2016), 485–501.

de Beauvoir, Simone. *The Second Sex*, trans. by H.M. Parshley. New York: Vintage Books, 1989.

214 BIBLIOGRAPHY

de Certeau, Michel. *La Fable mystique: XVI–XVII siècle.* Paris: Gallimard, 1982.

de Certeau, Michel. *Heterologies.* Manchester: Manchester University Press, 1986.

Denise, Sister Mary. "The Orchard of Syon: An Introduction," *Traditio* 14 (1958), 269–93.

de Rijk, Lambertus Marie. *Logica Modernorum—A Contribution to the History of Early Terminist Logic,* composed of *On the Twelfth Century Theory of Fallacy* (Assen: Van Gorcum, 1962) and the two-part *The Origin and Early Development of the Theory of Supposition* (Assen: Van Gorcum, 1967).

de Töth, Pietro Tommaso. *Storia di S. Chiara da Montefalco secondo un antico documento dell'anno 1308.* Siena: tip. pont. S. Bernardino, 1908.

DeYoung, Rebecca Konyndyk, Coleen McCluskey, and Christina Van Dyke. *Aquinas's Ethics: Metaphysical Foundations, Moral Theory, and Theological Context.* Notre Dame, IN: University of Notre Dame Press, 2009.

Ebbersmeyer, Sabrina, and Gianni Paganini, eds. *Women, Philosophy, and Science: Italy and Early Modern Europe.* (Women in the History of Philosophy and Sciences, Vol. 4.) Cham: Springer Nature Switzerland AG, 2020.

Fanous, Samuel, and Vincent Gillespie, eds. *The Cambridge Companion to Medieval English Mysticism.* Cambridge: Cambridge University Press, 2011.

Fibla, Sergi Sancho. "Colors and Books in Marguerite d'Oingt's *Speculum.* Images for Meditation and Vision," *Commitments to Medieval Mysticism within Contemporary Contexts,* Bibliotheca Ephemeridum Theologicarum Lovaniensium. Leuven: Peeters, 2017, 255–71.

Flora, Holly. *The Devout Belief of the Imagination. The Paris Meditationes Vitae Christi and Female Franciscan Spirituality in Trecento Italy. Disciplina Monastica,* Vol. 6, Turnhout: Brepols, 2009.

Franke, W. *On What Cannot Be Said: Apophatic Discourses in Philosophy, Religion, Literature, and the Arts, Vol. 1: Classic Formulations.* Notre Dame, IN: Notre Dame University Press, 2007.

Frelick, Nancy, ed. "Introduction," in *The Mirror in Medieval and Early Modern Culture: Specular Reflections.* Turnhout: Brepols, 2016.

Fricker, Miranda. *Epistemic Injustice: Power and the Ethics of Knowing.* Oxford: Oxford University Press, 2007.

Frugoni, Chiara. "Female Mystics, Visions, and Iconography," in *Women and Religion on Medieval and Renaissance Italy,* ed. D. Bornstein and R. Rusconi. Chicago: University of Chicago Press, 1996, 130–64.

Furlong, Monica. *Visions & Longings, Medieval Women Mystics,* Boston: Shambhala Publications, 2013.

Gabriele, Matthew, and David Perry. *The Bright Ages: A New History of Medieval Europe.* New York: HarperCollins Publishers, 2021.

Gavrilyuk, Paul, and S. Coakley, eds. *The Spiritual Senses: Perceiving God in Western Christianity.* Cambridge: Cambridge University Press, 2012.

Gellman, Jerome. *Mystical Experience of God, a Philosophical Inquiry.* London: Ashgate Publishers, 2001.

Gellman, Jerome. "Mysticism," in *Stanford Encyclopedia of Philosophy,* ed. E. N. Zalta, https://plato.stanford.edu/entries/mysticism/. First pub. 2004; substantial rev. 2018.

BIBLIOGRAPHY   215

Gilbert, Bennett. "Early Carthusian Script and Silence." *Cistercian Studies Quarterly* 49/3 (Fall, 2014), 367–97.

Gilson, Étienne. "Le personnalisme chrétien," in *L'esprit de la philosophie médiévale*. Librairie philosophique. Paris: J. Vrin, 1932, 195–215.

Glanz, Elaine. "Richard Rolle's Imagery in Meditations on the Passion B: A Reflection of Richard of St. Victor's Benjamin Minor," *Mystics Quarterly* 22/2 (1996) 58–68.

Green, Karen. "Virtue Ethics and the Origins of Feminism: The Case of Christine de Pizan," in *Feminist History of Philosophy: The Recovery and Evaluation of Women's Philosophical Thought*, ed. E. O'Neill and M. Lascano. Cham: Springer Nature Switzerland, 2019, 261–79.

Greene, Logan Dale. *The Discourse of Hysteria: The Topoi of Humility, Physicality, and Authority in Women's Rhetoric*. Lewiston, NY: Edwin Mellen Press, 2009.

Grundmann, Herbert. "Die Frauen und die Literatur im Mittelalter: Ein Beitrag zur Frage nach der Entstehung des Schrifttums in der Volkssprache," *Archiv fur Kulturgeschichte* 26 (1936), 129–61.

Grundmann, Herbert. *Religiöse Bewegungen im Mittelalter: Untersuchungen über die geschichtlichen Zusammenhänge zwischen der Ketzerei, den Bettelorden und der religiösen Frauenbewegung im 12. und 13 Jahrhundert* (1935), trans. and repub. as *Religious Movements in the Middle Ages: The Historical Links between Heresy, the Mendicant Orders, and the Women's Religious Movement in the Twelfth and Thirteenth Century, with the Historical Foundations of German Mysticism*. Notre Dame, IN: University of Notre Dame Press, 1995.

Harris, Nigel. *The Thirteenth-Century Animal Turn: Medieval and Twenty-First-Century Perspectives*. Cham: Palgrave Macmillan, 2020.

Harvey, Susan Ashbrook. *Scenting Salvation: Ancient Christianity and the Olfactory Imagination*. Berkeley: University of California Press, 2006.

Heng, Geraldine. *The Invention of Race in the European Middle Ages*. Cambridge: Cambridge University Press, 2018.

Hindsley, Leonard. *The Mystics of Engelthal: Writings from a Medieval Monastery*. New York: St. Martin's Press, 1998.

Hollywood, Amy. *The Soul as Virgin Wife: Mechthild of Magdeburg, Marguerite of Porete, and Meister Eckhart*. Notre Dame, IN: University of Notre Dame Press, 1995.

Hollywood, Amy. *Sensible Ecstasy: Mysticism, Sexual Difference, and the Demands of History*. Chicago: University of Chicago Press, 2002.

Hollywood, Amy, and P. Dailey, eds. *The Cambridge Companion to Christian Mysticism*. Cambridge: Cambridge University Press, 2012.

Hughes, Aaron. *The Texture of the Divine: Imagination in Medieval Islamic and Jewish Thought*. Bloomington, IN: Indiana University Press, 2004.

Hughes-Edwards, Mari. *Reading Medieval Anchoritism: Ideology and Spiritual Practice*. Cardiff: University of Wales Press, 2012.

Hyman, Arthur, James Walsh, and Thomas Williams, eds. *Philosophy in the Middles Ages: The Christian, Islamic, and Jewish Traditions*, 3rd ed. Indianapolis: Hackett Publishing Co., 2010.

216   BIBLIOGRAPHY

Idel, Moshe, and Bernard McGinn, eds. *Mystical Union in Judaism, Christianity, and Islam: An Ecumenical Dialogue.* New York: Continuum, 1999.

Jaeger, C. Stephen. *The Origins of Courtliness: Civilizing Trends and the Formation of Courtly Ideals 939–1210.* Philadelphia: University of Pennsylvania Press, 1985.

James, William. *Varieties of Religious Experience: A Study in Human Nature.* Gifford Lectures held at Harvard, 1902.

Jantzen, Grace. *Power, Gender, and Christian Mysticism.* Cambridge: Cambridge University Press, 1995.

Johnson, Timothy. "Visual Imagery and Contemplation in Clare of Assisi's 'Letters to Agnes of Prague',' *Mystics Quarterly* 19/4 (1993), 161–72.

Jung, Jacqueline. *Eloquent Bodies: Movement, Expression, and the Human Figure in Gothic Sculpture.* New Haven and London: Yale University Press, 2020.

Karnes, Michelle. *Imagination, Meditation, and Cognition in the Middle Ages.* Chicago: University of Chicago Press, 2011.

Katz, Steven, ed. *Mysticism and Philosophical Analysis.* New York: Oxford University Press, 1978.

Kaufman, Amy, and Paul Sturtevant. *The Devil's Historians: How Modern Extremists Abuse the Medieval Past.* Toronto: University of Toronto Press, 2020.

Kent, Bonnie. *Virtues of the Will: The Transformation of Ethics in the Late Thirteenth Century.* Washington, D.C.: Catholic University of America Press, 1995.

Kieckhefer, Richard. "Mysticism and Social Consciousness in the Fourteenth Century," *Revue de l'Universite d'Ottawa* 48 (1978), 179–86.

Kieckhefer, Richard. "Holiness and the Culture of Devotion: Remarks on Some Late Medieval Male Saints," in *Images of Sainthood in Medieval Europe,* ed. R. Blumenfeld-Kosinski and T. Szell. Ithaca: Cornell University Press, 1991, 288–305.

Kim, Hannah. "Metaphors in Neo-Confucian Korean Philosophy," *The Journal of Aesthetics and Art Criticism* 2022, https://doi.org/10.1093/jaac/kpac030.

King, Peter. "Marguerite Porete and Godfrey of Fontaines: Detachable Will, Discardable Virtue, Transformative Love," in *Oxford Studies in Medieval Philosophy Vol. 6.* Oxford: Oxford University Press, 2018, 168–188.

Knowles, David. *The Religious Orders in England.* Cambridge: Cambridge University Press, 1948–9.

Knudson, Albert Cornelius. *The Philosophy of Personalism.* New York: Abingdon Press, 1927.

Kobusch, Theo. *Die Entdeckung der Person: Metaphysik der Freiheit und modernes Menschenbild.* Darmstadt: Wissenschaftliche Buchgesellschaft, 1997.

Kristeller, Paul Oskar. "The Dignity of Man," in *Renaissance Concepts of Man and Other Essays.* New York: Harper & Row, 1972, 1–21.

Lackey, Jennifer. "False Confessions and Testimonial Injustice," *The Journal of Criminal Law and Criminology* 110/1 (2020) 43–68.

Largier, Nicholas. "Inner Senses – Outer Senses: The Practice of Emotions in Medieval Mysticism", in *Emotions and Sensibilities in the Middle Ages,* ed. C. Jaeger and I. Kasten. Berlin and New York: de Gruyter, 2003, 3–15.

BIBLIOGRAPHY 217

Lerius, Julia. "Hildegard von Bingen on Autonomy" in *Women Philosophers on Autonomy: Historical and Contemporary Perspectives*, ed. S. Berges and A. Sinai. New York: Routledge, 2018, 9–23.

Lerner, Robert. *The Heresy of the Free Spirit in the Later Middle Ages*. Berkeley: University of California Press, 1972.

Lewis, Gertrud Jaron. *By Women, for Women, about Women: the Sister-Books of Fourteenth-Century Germany*. Toronto: Pontifical Institute of Mediaeval Studies, 1996.

Lima, Manual. *The Book of Trees: Visualizing Branches of Knowledge*. New York: Princeton Architectural Press, 2014.

Lipton, Sara. *Dark Mirror: The Medieval Origins on Anti-Jewish Iconography*. New York: Metropolitan Books, 2014.

Lochrie, Karma. *Margery Kempe and Translations of the Flesh*. Philadelphia: University of Pennsylvania Press, 1991.

LoLordo, Antonia, ed. *Persons: a History*. Oxford Philosophical Concepts Series. Oxford: Oxford University Press, 2019.

MacDonald, Scott. 'Theory of Knowledge', in *The Cambridge Companion to Aquinas*, ed. N. Kretzmann and E. Stump. Cambridge: Cambridge University Press, 1993.

McDonnell, Ernest. *The Beguines and Berghards in Medieval Culture: with Special Emphasis on the Belgian Scene*. New York: Octagon Books, 1969.

McGinn, Bernard. "Ascension and Introversion in the *Itinerarium mentis in Deum*," in *San Bonaventura 1274–1974 Vol. 3*. Grottaferrata/Rome: Collegio S. Bonaventura, 1974.

McGinn, Bernard. "Introduction," in *Meister Eckhart: The Essential Sermons, Commentaries, Treatises, and* Defense, ed. Edmund Colledge, OSA, and Bernard McGinn. Mahwah: Paulist Press, 1981, 1–61.

McGinn, Bernard, ed. *Meister Eckhart and the Beguine Mystics: Hadewijch of Brabant, Mechthild of Magdeburg, and Marguerite Porete*. New York: Continuum, 1994.

McGinn, Bernard. *The Flowering of Mysticism: Men and Women in the New Mysticism 1200–1350. Vol. 3 of The Presence of God: A History of Western Christian Mysticism*. New York: Crossroad Publishing Co., 1998.

McGinn, Bernard. *The Harvest of Mysticism in Medieval Germany 1300–1500. Vol. 4 of The Presence of God: A History of Western Christian Mysticism*. New York: Crossroad Publishing Co., 2005.

McGinn, Bernard. *Varieties of Vernacular Mysticism: 1350–1550. Vol. 5 of The Presence of God: A History of Western Christian Mysticism*. New York: Crossroad Publishing Co., 2016.

McNamer, Sarah. "The Origins of the *Meditationes Vitae Christi*," *Speculum* 84 (2009), 905–55.

Mancia, Lauren. *Emotional Monasticism: Affective Piety in the Eleventh-century Monastery of John of Fécamp*. Manchester: Manchester University Press, 2019.

Marenbon, John. *Medieval Philosophy: an Historical and Philosophical Introduction*. London: Routledge, 2007.

218   BIBLIOGRAPHY

Marin, Juan. "Annihilation and Deification in Beguine Theology and Marguerite Porete's Mirror of Simple Souls," *Harvard Theological Review* 103/1 (2010), 89–102.

Marrone, Steven. *The Light of Thy Countenance: Science and Knowledge of God in the Thirteenth Century*. 2 Vols. Leiden: Brill, 2001.

Marrone, Steven. "From Gundisalvus to Bonaventure: Intellect and intelligences in the late twelfth and early thirteenth centuries," in *Intellect and imagination dans la philosophie médiévale*, Vol. 2, ed. M. C. Pacheco and J. F. Meirinhos. Brepols: Turnhout, 2006, 1071–81.

Matter, E. Ann, and John Coakley, eds. *Creative Women in Medieval and Early Modern Italy: A Religious and Artistic Renaissance*. Philadelphia: University of Pennsylvania Press, 1994.

Mazzoni, Christina. "Angela of Foligno," in *Medieval Holy Women in the Christian Tradition c.1100–c.1500*, ed. A. Minnis and R. Voaden. Turnhout: Brepols, 2010, 581–600.

Mercer, Christia. "Descartes' Debt to Teresa of Avila, or why we should work on women in the history of philosophy," *Philosophical Studies* 174/10 (2017), 2539–55.

Mews, Constant, and Anna Welch, eds. *Poverty and Devotion in Mendicant Cultures 1200–1450*. London: Routledge, 2016.

Minnis, Alastair, and Rosalynn Voaden, eds. *Medieval Holy Women in the Christian Tradition c.1100–c.1500*. Brepols Collected Essays in European Culture 1. Turnhout: Brepols, 2010.

Mooney, Catherine. "The Authorial Role of Brother A in the Composition of Angela of Foligno's Revelations," in *Creative Women in Medieval and Early Modern Italy: A Religious and Artistic Renaissance*, ed. E. Ann Matter and John Coakley. Philadelphia: University of Pennsylvania Press, 1994, 34–63.

Mooney, Catherine, ed. *Gendered Voices: Medieval Saints and Their Interpreters*. Philadelphia: University of Pennsylvania Press, 1999.

Moore, R.I. *The War on Heresy: Faith and Power in Medieval Europe*. London: Profile Books, 2012.

Morgan, Ben. *On Becoming God: Late Medieval Mysticism and the Modern Western Self*. New York: Fordham University Press, 2013.

Mueller, Joan. *The Privilege of Poverty: Clare of Assisi, Agnes of Prague, and the Struggle for a Franciscan Rule for Women*. University Park: Penn State University Press, 2006.

Murk-Jansen, Saskia. "Hadewijch," in *Medieval Holy Women in the Christian Tradition c.1100–c.1500*, ed. A. Minnis and R. Voaden. Turnhout: Brepols, 2010, 663–85.

Neel, Carol. "The Origins of the Beguines," *Signs: Journal of Women in Culture and Society* 14/2, *Working Together in the Middle Ages: Perspectives on Women's Communities*, 1989, 321–41.

Newman, Barbara. "Hildegard of Bingen: Visions and Validation," *Church History* 54 (1985), 163–75.

Newman, Barbara. *From Virile Woman to Woman Christ: Studies in Medieval Religion and Literature*. Philadelphia: University of Pennsylvania Press, 1995.

BIBLIOGRAPHY 219

Newman, Barbara. ed. *Voice of the Living Light: Hildegard of Bingen and Her World.* Berkeley: University of California Press, 1998.

Newman, Barbara. *God and the Goddesses: Vision, Poetry, and Belief in the Middle Ages.* Philadelphia: University of Pennsylvania Press, 2003.

Newman, Barbara. "What Does It Mean to Say 'I Saw'? The Clash between Theory and Practice in Medieval Visionary Culture," *Speculum* 80/1 (2005), 1–43.

O'Neill, Eileen, and Marcy Lascano, eds. *Feminist History of Philosophy: The Recovery and Evaluation of Women's Philosophical Thought.* Cham: Springer Nature Switzerland, 2019.

Pasnau, Robert. "Medieval Social Epistemology: *Scientia* for Mere Mortals," *Episteme* 7/1 (2010), 23–41.

Pasnau, Robert. *Metaphysical Themes 1274–1671.* Oxford: Oxford University Press, 2011.

Pasnau, Robert. *After Certainty.* Oxford: Oxford University Press, 2017.

Pasnau, Robert, and C. Van Dyke, eds. *The Cambridge History of Medieval Philosophy.* Cambridge: Cambridge University Press, 2009.

Paulsell, Stephanie. "Writing and Mystical Experience in Marguerite d'Oingt and Virginia Woolf," *Comparative Literature* 44/3 (1991), 249–67.

Pawl, Tim. *In Defense of Conciliar Christology.* Oxford Studies in Analytic Theology. Oxford: Oxford University Press, 2016.

Payer, Pierre. "Prudence and the Principles of Natural Law: A Medieval Development," *Speculum* 54/1 (1979), 55–70.

Pegis, Anton. *St. Thomas and the Problem of the Soul in the Thirteenth Century,* Toronto: Pontifical Institute of Mediaeval Studies, 1943.

Perler, Dominik. "Self-Knowledge in Scholasticism," in *Self-Knowledge,* ed. U. Renz. Oxford Philosophical Concepts Series. New York: Oxford University Press, 2017, 114–30.

Pickavé, Martin, and Lisa Shapiro, eds. *Emotion and Cognitive Life in Medieval and Early Modern Philosophy.* Oxford: Oxford University Press, 2012.

Pike, Nelson. *Mystic Union: An Essay in the Phenomenology of Mysticism.* Ithaca, NY: Cornell University Press, 1992.

Poor, Sara. *Mechthild of Magdeburg and Her Book: Gender and the Making of Textual Authority.* Philadelphia: University of Pennsylvania Press, 2004.

Ragusa, Isa. "L'autore della Meditationes vitae Christi sedondo il codice ms Ital. 115 della Biblioteque Nationale di Parigi," *Arte medievale* 11 (1997), 145–50.

Renz, Ursula, ed. *Self-Knowledge.* Oxford Philosophical Concepts Series. New York: Oxford University Press, 2017.

Reuther, Rosemary Radford. *Sexism and God-talk: Towards a Feminist Theology,* Boston: Beacon Press, 1995.

Ritchey, Sara. "Spiritual Arborescence: Trees in the Medieval Christian Imagination," *Spiritus: A Journal of Christian Spirituality* 8/1 (2008), 64–82.

Roberts, Michelle Voss. "Retrieving Humility: Rhetoric, Authority, and Divinization in Mechtild of Magdeburg," *Feminist Theology* 18/1 (2009), 50–73.

Robertson, Elizabeth. "Medieval Medical Views of Women and Female Spirituality in the *Ancrene Wisse* and Julian of Norwich's *Showings*," in Feminist Approaches

220 BIBLIOGRAPHY

to the Body in Medieval Literature, ed. L. Lomperis and S. Stanbury. Philadelphia: University of Pennsylvania Press, 1993.

Robinson, Joanne. *Nobility and Annihilation in Marguerite Porete's Mirror of Simple Souls*. Albany: State University of New York Press, 2001.

Rudan, Paola. "Riscrivere la storia, fare la storia. Sulla donna come soggetto in Christine de Pizan e Margeret Cavendish," *Scienza e Politica. Per Una Storia Delle Dottrine* 28/54 (2016).

Schwietering, Julius. "The Origins of the Medieval Humility Formula," PMLA 69/5 (1954), 1279–91.

Scott, Karen. "'This is why I have put you among your neighbors': St. Bernard's and St. Catherine's Understanding of the Love of God and Neighbor," in *Atti del Simposio Internazionale Cateriniano-Bernardiniano*, ed. D. Maffei and P. Nardi (Siena: Accademia Senese degli Intronati, 1982), 279–94.

Shaffern, Robert. *Law and Justice from Antiquity to Enlightenment*. Lanham, ML: Rowman & Littlefield Publishers, 2009.

Silvas, Anna. *Jutta and Hildegard: The Biographical Sources*. Turnhout: Brepols, 1998.

Spade, Paul, and Thomas Williams. "Medieval Philosophy," *Stanford Encyclopedia of Philosophy*, https://plato.stanford.edu/entries/medieval-philosophy/.

Stace, Walter T. *Mysticism and Philosophy*. London: Macmillan & Co., 1960.

Steiner, Rudolf. *Mystics after Modernism: discovering the seeds of a new science in the Renaissance*, trans. Karl E. Zimmer. Great Barrington, MA: Anthroposophic Press, 2000.

Stump, Eleonore. *Aquinas*, New York: Routledge, 2003.

Suydam, Mary. "The Politics of Authorship: Hadewijch of Antwerp and the Mengeldichten," *Mystics Quarterly* 22/1 (1996), 2–20.

Suydam, Mary. "The Touch of Satisfaction: Visions and Religious Experience According to Hadewijch of Antwerp," *Journal of Feminist Studies in Religion* 12 (Fall, 1996), 5–27.

Tiereny, Brian. *Medieval Poor Law: A Sketch of Canonical Theory and Its Application in England*. Berkeley: University of California Press, 1959.

Toner, Patrick. "St. Thomas Aquinas on the Problem of Too Many Thinkers," *The Modern Schoolman* 89 (2012), 209–22.

Tóth, Peter, and Dávid Falvay. "New Light on the Date and Authorship of the *Meditationes vitae Christi*," in *Devotional Culture in Late Medieval England and Europe: Diverse Imaginations of Christ's Life*, ed. Stephen Kelly and Ryan Perry. Turnhout: Brepols, 2015, 17–104.

Trinkaus, Charles. *"In Our Image and Likeness": Humanity and Divinity in Italian Humanist Thought*. 2 Vols. Chicago: University of Chicago Press, 1970.

Turner, Denys. *The Darkness of God: Negativity in Christian Mysticism*. Cambridge: Cambridge University Press, 1995.

Underhill, Evelyn. *Mysticism: A Study of the Nature and Development of Man's Spiritual Consciousness*. Grand Rapids, MI: Christian Classics Ethereal Library, 1911.

Underhill, Evelyn. *The Essentials of Mysticism and Other Essays*. New York: Dutton, 1920.

BIBLIOGRAPHY 221

Van Ackeren, Marcel, ed. *Philosophy and the Historical Perspective. Proceedings of the British Academy*. Oxford: Oxford University Press (2018), 214.

Van Dyke, Christina. "Not Properly a Person: the Rational Soul and 'Thomistic Substance Dualism,'" *Faith and Philosophy* 26/2 (2009), 186–204.

Van Dyke, Christina. "Mysticism," in *The Cambridge History of Medieval Philosophy*, ed. R. Pasnau and C. Van Dyke. Cambridge: Cambridge University Press, 2010, 720–34.

Van Dyke, Christina. "The Truth, the Whole Truth, and Nothing but the Truth: Robert Grosseteste on Universals (and the *Posterior Analytics*)," *Journal of the History of Philosophy* 48/2 (2010), 153–70.

Van Dyke, Christina. "I See Dead People: Disembodied Souls and Aquinas's 'Two-Person' Problem," in *Oxford Studies in Medieval Philosophy Vol. 2*, ed. R. Pasnau. Oxford: Oxford University Press, 2014, 25–45.

Van Dyke, Christina. "Aquinas's Shiny Happy People: Perfect Happiness and the Limits of Human Nature," in *Oxford Studies in the Philosophy of Religion Vol. 6*, ed. J. Kvanvig. Oxford: Oxford University Press, 2015, 269–91.

Van Dyke, Christina. "Self-Knowledge, Abnegation, and Fulfillment in Medieval Mysticism," in *Self-Knowledge*, ed. U. Renz. Oxford Philosophical Concepts Series Oxford: Oxford University Press, 2017, 131–45.

Van Dyke, Christina. "'Many Know Much, but Do Not Know Themselves': Self-Knowledge, Humility, and Perfection in the Medieval Affective Contemplative Tradition," in *Consciousness and Self-Knowledge in Medieval Philosophy*: *Proceedings of the Society for Medieval Logic and Metaphysics Vol. 14*, ed. G. Klima and A. Hall. Newcastle upon Tyne: Cambridge Scholars Publishing, 2018, 89–106.

Van Dyke, Christina. "What Has History to Do with Philosophy? Insights from the Medieval Contemplative Tradition," in *Philosophy and the Historical Perspective*, ed. M. Van Ackeren. Proceedings of the British Academy. Oxford: Oxford University Press (2018), 155–70.

Van Dyke, Christina. "Medieval Mystics on Persons: What John Locke Didn't Tell You," in *Persons: a History*, ed. A. LoLordo. Oxford Philosophical Concepts Series. Oxford: Oxford University Press, 2019, 123–53.

Van Dyke, Christina. "The Phenomenology of Immortality (1200–1400)," in *The History of the Philosophy of Mind. Vol. 2: Philosophy of Mind in the Early and High Middle Ages*, ed. M. Cameron. London: Routledge, 2019, 219–39.

Van Dyke, Christina. "From Meditation to Contemplation: Broadening the Borders of Philosophy in the 13th–15th Centuries," in *Pluralizing Philosophy's Past—New Reflections in the History of Philosophy*, ed. A. Griffioen and M. Backmann. London: Palgrave Macmillan, forthcoming.

Van Dyke, Christina. "Lewd, Feeble, and Frail: Humility Formulae, Medieval Women, and Authority," in *Oxford Studies in Medieval Philosophy Vol. 10*. Oxford: Oxford University Press, forthcoming.

Van Steenberghen, Fernand. *Thomas Aquinas and Radical Aristotelianism*, Washington, D.C.: Catholic University Press, 1980.

Voaden, Rosalynn. *God's Words, Women's Voices: The Discernment of Spirits in the Writing of Late-Medieval Women Visionaries*. Rochester, NY: Boydell & Brewer, 1999.

222 BIBLIOGRAPHY

Voaden, Rosalynn. "Mechthild of Hackeborn," in *Medieval Holy Women in the Christian Tradition c.1100–c.1500*, ed. A. Minnis and R. Voaden. Turnhout: Brepols, 2010, 431–51.

Wada, Yoko, ed. *A Companion to Ancrene Wisse*. Cambridge: D. S. Brewer, 2003.

Wallace, David, ed. *The Cambridge History of Medieval English Literature*. Cambridge: Cambridge University Press, 1999.

Ward, Jennifer. *Women in Medieval Europe 1200–1500*, 2nd ed. London: Routledge, 2016.

Watson, Nicholas. "Introduction," in *The Cambridge Companion to Medieval English Mysticism*, ed. S. Fanous and V. Gillespie. Cambridge: Cambridge University Press, 2011, 1–28.

Watt, Diane. *Women, Writing, and Religion in England and Beyond, 650–1100*. Studies in Early Medieval History. London: Bloomsbury Academic, 2019.

Wei, Ian. *Thinking about Animals in Thirteenth-Century Paris: Theologians on the Boundary Between Humans and Animals*. Cambridge: Cambridge University Press, 2020.

Whitaker, Cord. *Black Metaphors: How Modern Racism Emerged from Medieval Race-Thinking*. Philadelphia: University of Pennsylvania Press, 2019.

Williamson, Beth. *The Madonna of Humility: Development, Dissemination, and Reception, c.1340–1400*. Bristol Studies in Medieval Cultures, Vol. 1. Woodbridge: Boydell & Brewer Press, 2009.

Winston-Allen, Anne. *Convent Chronicles: Women Writing about Women and Reform in the Late Middle Ages*. University Park, PA: University of Pennsylvania Press, 2004.

Wojtyla, Karol. "Thomistic Personalism," in *Person and Community: Selected Essays* (*Catholic Thought from Lublin*: Vol. 4), ed. Andrew Woznicki. New York: Peter Lang, 1993, 165–75.

Zheng, Robin. "What is My Role in Changing the System? A New Model of Responsibility for Structural Injustice," *Ethical Theory & Moral Practice* 21 (2018), 869–85.

Index

Note: Figures are indicated by an italic "*f*" following the page numbers.

For the benefit of digital users, indexed terms that span two pages (e.g., 52–53) may, on occasion, appear on only one of those pages.

affective experiences 2–3, 6–7, 9–11, 14–16, 18–20, 37–8, 114–15, 126–7, 156, 173, 192–3, 197–9
affective mysticism 14–19, 58–9, 153–4, 193–4, 196
afterlife 23–4, 26–7, 47, 179–85, 187–91, 198–9, 201–5
angels 59, 69, 149, 160–1, 181–3, 190–1, 202–3
Angela of Foligno 9–10, 15, 27–8, 47, 87–8, 151–3, 155–6, 167–8, 185, 191–7
annihilation, of self 5, 7–9, 12–14, 57–9, 88–9, 154, 185–90, 197, 199
Anselm of Canterbury 175–6
apophaticism and apophatic mysticism 11–15, 19, 22, 30–1, 57–8, 70–2, 86–7, 124, 154, 184–6, 188–9, 193–8
Aristotle 74–5, 90–1, 134–5, 135*f*, 200
Augustine 25–6, 55–6, 69–70, 84–5, 90–1, 106, 142–3, 168–9, 177, 181–2

beguinage 62–6, 64*f*, 65*f*
beguine 15, 25–9, 62–6, 85–6, 100, 130–1, 151–3, 159, 170–1, 194
Bernard of Clairvaux 25–6, 52–4, 117, 119, 131, 153
Birgitta (Bridget) of Sweden 9–10, 29, 30*f*, 32, 93–5
Boethius 142–3
   Consolation of Philosophy 32, 69–70, 79–80
   Definition of person 147, 149–50

Bonaventure 26, 37–8, 75, 80–1, 106, 110–13, 123, 147–9, 175–6
   Mind's Journey into God 26, 37–8, 112–13
   Mystical Vine 106
   Tree of Life 26, 110–11
Book of Privy Counselling 30–1, 35, 58, 76, 123

Canterbury Cathedral 96–7
Carthusian Order 15, 28, 112–13, 116, 127–9, 156, 176–7
charity (*caritas*), *see* love
Catherine of Siena 15, 29–30, 31*f*, 32, 36–7, 40–1, 44, 47, 49, 51, 54–5, 80–1, 83–6, 106, 109–10, 122–3, 137–8, 138*f*, 151–3, 160–1, 164–5, 167–70, 191–5
Chartres Cathedral 96–7
Christ
   as fully human and fully divine 15–18, 28, 58–61, 77, 85–6, 106, 140, 154–5, 159, 190–8
   as Second Person of the Trinity 59, 86, 91–2, 119–20, 125, 140, 146, 153–5, 162–5, 176–7, 191–2, 195
   imitation of 122–4, 163–4
   life and Passion of 15–16, 32, 43–4, 52–4, 53*f*, 54*f*, 102, 114–19, 115*f*, 121, 128*f*
Christine de Pizan 32, 41–2, 79–80, 80*f*, 160–1
City of Ladies, *see* Christine de Pizan

224 INDEX

Clare of Assisi 25, 43–6, 113–14, 122, 167, 174–6
Cloud of Unknowing 11–14, 22, 30–1, 58, 76, 91–2, 104, 108–9, 124, 188–9, 193–4
Consolation of Philosophy, see Boethius
contemplation (*contemplatio*) 23, 50, 54, 58, 76–9, 102–3, 107, 112–13, 116, 119–26, 129–30, 165–6, 173, 189, 202–4

Dante 26–7, 83–4
Dark Ages 206–7
De Imitatione Christi, see Thomas à Kempis
Decretum and *Decretals* (*see also* Gratian) 142–4
dialogue, as philosophical genre 27, 69–71, 73, 162, 164–5, 167–71, 173
Dialogue, see Catherine of Siena
dignity 23, 44–8, 61, 83–4, 124–5, 144–6, 150–1, 157–61, 172–3, 203–4
divine illumination 55–6, 78–9, 107–8, 177–8, 181–2, 199–200
Dominican Order 26–30, 65, 73, 75, 88–9, 93–5, 145–6, 150, 154–5, 187, 193, 198
Duns Scotus, *see* John Duns Scotus

faith 43, 67–8, 77–8, 84–5, 101
personification of 78, 101
feeling, *see* affective experience
Ficino, Marsilio 32, 105, 157–8, 160
fin'amour 71, 73, 81–2, 134, 136–7
Fire of Love, see Richard Rolle
Flowing Light of the Godhead, see Mechthild of Magdeburg
Franciscan Order 15, 25–9, 80–1, 114–15, 126–7, 145–6, 150–3, 175–6, 185, 191–2, 198
Francis of Assisi 25, 26*f*, 145–6, 153, 167, 175–6

Gertrude the Great, also Gertrude of Helfta 27, 47–8, 87, 131, 159–60
Guigio II 112–14, 116
Gratian 142–3

Hadewijch 15, 17–18, 25–6, 30, 35, 37–8, 46–8, 54–6, 80–3, 85–6, 125, 131, 136–7, 151–3, 156–7, 159, 161–2, 167–8, 170–1, 184, 193–4, 196–7, 199
heaven, *see also* afterlife 50, 60, 78, 85–6, 148–9, 160, 190–2, 198, 202–3
Henry Suso 29, 91–2
Herald of Divine Love, see Gertrude the Great
human beings
nature of 2–3, 14–18, 33, 45–8, 59, 68–9, 76–9, 81–6, 102–3, 106–8, 112–13, 130–1, 139, 142, 145–6, 148–9, 154–5, 157–64, 171–2, 181–4, 191–3, 202–3
restoration of through Christ 58–60, 159
ultimate or final end of 11–12, 14, 21–4, 56–61, 67, 70, 78, 125, 149–50, 170, 185, 189–90, 194–9, 201–3
humility 25, 32, 38–9, 43–51, 57–8, 61, 101, 123–5, 153, 159–60, 163–4, 166–8, 174–6
humility topos, as literary genre 127–9, 174–6, 178

imagination
as faculty of the rational soul 15–16, 21–3, 51–6, 68–9, 107–8, 110–14, 121–4, 149–50, 161, 200–1
in relation to intellect and reason 16–17, 21–3, 54–5, 68–9, 110–11, 113–14, 117–20
use in meditation and spiritual exercises 16, 23, 51–6, 102, 110–14, 123–4, 159
image of God (*imago dei*) 22, 37–8, 44–6, 67, 71–2, 84–5, 103, 122, 125, 127–9, 160–1, 164
imitation of Christ (for *Imitation of Christ, see* Thomas à Kempis) 122–4, 163–4
individuality 13, 23–4, 56–7, 73–6, 139–42, 147, 156–7, 162–3, 165, 172–3, 185–7, 201

INDEX 225

intellect
  as capacity of the rational soul 8–9,
    14–16, 22–3, 52–4, 57, 67–9, 73,
    78–9, 101, 103–4, 110–11, 113–14,
    119–20, 130–1, 149–50, 154–5, 158,
    164–5, 181–4, 198–204
  relation to imagination, *see*
    'imagination'
  role in union with God 54, 70, 78–9,
    149–50, 198–9, 202–4

James, Henry 2–3, 5–7, 10–11
Jan van Ruusbroec 25–6, 30, 44–5, 153,
    156–7, 184
Johannes Tauler 28–9, 49, 57–8, 62–3, 65,
    80–1, 105, 154–5, 163–4, 184, 187
John Duns Scotus 80–1, 150
John of the Cross 11–12
Julian of Norwich 32, 34–5, 44, 49–50,
    59–60, 80–1, 84–9, 106, 120–2, 125,
    153, 164, 167–8, 170, 174–5, 177–8,
    184, 197

knowledge, *see also* self-knowledge
    22–3, 33–4, 39, 41–2, 51–2, 54–5,
    57, 59–60, 67, 69–73, 75–7, 80–1,
    83–4, 86–8, 90–2, 104–5, 107–8,
    110–11, 135–6, 149–50, 162–5,
    187–8, 199–201
  of God 44–5, 47, 49–50, 55–6, 59–60,
    120–3, 126, 149–50, 170, 186–8,
    194–5, 200–1
  personified 45–6, 71–2, 101
  scientia 22–3, 67–8, 74–5, 90–2,
    135–6, 163–4
  role in union with God, *see* 'intellect,
    role in union with God'

Ladder of Monks (*see also* Guigio II)
    112–14, 116
lectio divina 112–14, 117–19, 121–2
Locke, John 23, 139–40, 171–2
love, *see also* will
  annihilation in 33–4, 73–5, 154–6,
    162–3, 168–9, 186–8, 197
  as primary component of mystical
    union with God 25–6, 58, 61,

70–1, 73–7, 80–4, 105, 123, 126,
    150, 161–2, 164–5, 198–9
  charity (*caritas*) 40, 43–5, 54, 61,
    83–4, 164–5, 177, 194–5
  fin'amor or courtly love 44, 81–3, 131,
    133–7, 135*f*, 136*f*, 153
  for and of God 18, 25, 46–8, 50, 73–5,
    77, 80–4, 102, 104–7, 112–15,
    117–22, 125–30, 136–8, 149–50,
    159–60, 164–5, 176–7, 192–3, 197,
    199, 201–3
  for neighbors 25, 36–7, 40,
    50, 117–19
  for self 37–40, 55–6, 61, 201
  importance in meditation and
    contemplation 23, 54, 102–3,
    112–15, 117–20, 122–4, 126–7,
    192–3
  personified 73–5, 81–3, 101, 134–5,
    162, 166, 168–9, 186–7

Margaret Ebner 28–9, 88–90, 129–30,
    151–3, 167, 193
Margery Kempe 88–9
Marguerite d'Oingt 15, 18–19, 28, 47–8,
    60–1, 98–100, 115–17, 127–30, 156,
    167–8, 174–7
Marguerite Porete 11–12, 28, 43, 57, 61,
    73–6, 91–2, 101–2, 123–4, 131,
    136–7, 151–4, 162, 166, 168–9,
    184–7, 199
Mechthild of Hackeborn 27, 47–8, 131,
    136–7, 167–8
Mechthild of Magdeburg 27, 38–9,
    41–6, 71–3, 92, 131, 133–4, 136–7,
    151–3, 156, 159–60, 168–70, 190–1,
    193, 199
meditation (*meditatio*) 15–16, 23, 52–4,
    102–3, 112–29, 173, 191–3
Meditations on the Life of Christ 52–4,
    114–15, 117–21, 123–4, 126–7,
    155–6
Meister Eckhart 2, 7–8, 11–14, 22,
    25–6, 28–30, 35, 38, 49, 57–8,
    62–3, 65, 75–6, 80–1, 88, 139–40,
    154–5, 162–3, 170, 184, 186–9,
    192–4

226 INDEX

memory as faculty of the rational
soul 37–8, 68–9, 84–5, 125,
149–50, 161
Mind's Journey into God, see Bonaventure
Mirror of Marguerite d'Oingt (*see also*
Marguerite d'Oingt) 28, 98–100
mirror, as literary genre 43–4, 47–8, 70
mirror, as metaphor for self-knowledge
37–48, 45*f*, 52–4, 58–9, 79–80,
122, 160–1
Mirror of the Blessed Life of Jesus Christ
(*see also* Nicholas Love) 117
Mirror of Simple Souls (*see also*
Marguerite Porete) 12, 22, 28, 57,
73–6, 91–2, 101–2, 123–4, 136–7,
151–4, 162, 166, 168–9, 185–6
miserabiles personae as legal
category 144–6, 145*f*
mystical experience 2–11, 13–17,
19–21, 28, 31, 58–60, 86–7, 129–30,
165–8, 185, 188–9, 191–6
mystical union (*see also* intellect, love,
and will) 7, 14–15, 18–19, 67–8,
86–9, 129–30, 147, 154–7, 170,
179–80, 191–2, 194–7, 204

Nicholas Love 117

oratio, see prayer
Oxford University 67–8, 70–1, 90–1,
147, 171, 200–1

person 23, 103, 139–43, 146–50, 154,
157–61, 171–3, 182–4, 195
personalism, as philosophical
theory 172–3
personification, as philosophical
tool 23, 69–70, 77–80, 152*f*,
162, 165, 168–71, 169*f*,
174–5, 175*f*
Pico della Mirandola, Giovanni 32,
157–8, 160
Piers Plowman 110–11, 165–6
pilgrims and pilgrimages 96–7,
144, 145*f*

Plato and Platonism 9, 11–12, 16, 32,
34–5, 55–6, 157–8, 168–9, 182–5,
188–9, 199–202, 204
practical wisdom 41–2, 42*f*, 78–9,
107, 161–2
prayer (*oratio*) 27, 62, 76, 112–13,
121–3, 125
prudence, *see* practical wisdom
Pursuit of Wisdom 30–1, 34–5, 44, 50

rational capacities (*see also* imagination,
intellect, memory, sensation, and
will) 23, 67–9, 76–81, 83–90, 103,
107–10, 149–50, 161–5, 202–3
rational soul 142, 148–50, 179–84, 203–5
rationality 23, 67, 130–1, 139–40, 147,
149–51, 161–5, 171–3
reason, *see also* 'imagination, relation to
intellect and reason', 'intellect',
'rational capacities', and 'rationality'
nature of 68–70, 203
personified 41–2, 69–70, 73–83, 80*f*,
101, 107, 160–2, 166, 168–9
Reims Cathedral 97
Revelation of Love, see Julian of Norwich
Richard of St. Victor 13–14, 25–6, 30–1,
55–6, 77–9, 107–8, 110, 124–5,
159, 165–6
Richard Rolle 13–15, 28, 31, 153, 156
Robert Grosseteste 200–2, 204

sapientia, see also wisdom 90–2
Scale of Perfection, see Walter Hilton
scholasticism 1–2, 22–4, 26, 28, 33–4,
67–8, 70, 74–5, 77–9, 105, 140,
143–4, 147, 151, 161, 163–6, 171,
179–81, 184, 198–9, 204–5, 208
Showings of Divine Love, see Julian
of Norwich
scientia, see 'knowledge, *scientia*'
self
annihilation of 5–9, 11–14, 18, 21–4,
56–9, 61, 70–1, 73–6, 88, 90, 124,
154–6, 162–4, 184–90, 193–5, 197,
199, 204

INDEX 227

fulfillment or actualization of 10,
18–19, 21–4, 56, 58–61, 88–90,
156–7, 184, 189–90, 192–5,
197, 204
knowledge of 21–2, 33–51, 54–9,
61, 79–82, 89, 122–4, 149,
153–4, 160–1, 165–6, 170,
175–6, 197
selfishness 37, 40, 51, 54–6, 61
sense of 165–78, 187–9, 192–5
sensation and sense appetite 4–6, 8–9,
13–16, 18–19, 23, 31, 51–2, 54–5,
59–60, 68–9, 75, 78, 86, 89, 102–3,
105–12, 114–15, 119, 121–4, 126–7,
130–1, 139, 162–3, 170, 188–9, 193,
198–204
Showings, *see* Julian of Norwich
Sister Catherine treatise 187
spiritual disciplines/exercises (see also
lectio divina, meditation, prayer,
and contemplation) 15–16, 23, 27,
45–7, 49–50, 102–3, 112–14,
117–22, 124–9, 161–2
spiritual vision 3–5, 8–9, 16–19, 25–7,
32, 47–8, 60–1, 70, 73–4, 78, 81–3,
85–6, 98–100, 121–2, 164–5, 167–8,
173, 193–7, 201–4
spirituality and spiritual life 9–10,
12–14, 21–2, 30–2, 34–5, 37, 40–1,
43–5, 47–8, 52–6, 85–6, 105–12,
123–5, 135–6, 142, 154, 164–6,
170, 175–6
St. Denis cathedral 96–7

Teresa of Avila 11–12
Thomas à Kempis 32, 91–2, 105, 153,
163–4
Thomas Aquinas 26–7, 77–9,
83–5, 103, 109, 147–9,
183–4, 202–4
tree, as metaphor for self 18–19, 47–50,
60, 83–6, 160
Tree of Life (*see* Bonaventure)
Tree of Life of the Crucified Jesus
(*see* Ubertino Casale)

Trinity and Trinitarian theology 30, 32,
59, 66, 84–6, 88, 91–2, 119–21, 125,
139–40, 142, 147, 153, 162–5,
176–7, 191–2, 195
The Twelve Patriarchs (*Benjamin
Minor*), *see* Richard
of St. Victor

Ubertino da Casale 146
Underhill, Evelyn 2–3, 5–7, 9–10
University of Bologna 142–3
University of Paris 26–7, 67–8, 70–1,
90–1, 163–4

vernaculars, development and
use of 70, 117, 136–7, 151–3
visions and visionary literature, *see*
spiritual vision
Vision Showed to a Devout Woman
(*see also* Julian of Norwich)
167–8
virtue 21–3, 40–7, 54–6, 77–9, 91–2,
101, 107, 109–10, 112, 117–19,
123–4, 133, 161–6, 174–5

Walter Hilton 13–14, 31, 188–9,
193–4
will (*see also* love)
as faculty of the rational soul 12, 23,
37–8, 51–5, 57, 68–70, 77–85,
102–11, 113–14, 117–20, 123–5,
129–30, 149–50, 154–5, 158, 162,
164–5, 177, 187, 198–9, 201
relation to sensation/sense appetite
107–10, 119, 126–7
role in union with God 73–5, 102–3,
105, 113–14, 121–4, 129–30, 150,
162, 187, 198–9, 201
wisdom 18, 54–5, 73, 76, 78, 81–4, 86,
88–95, 97, 101, 104, 125–6, 128f,
161–2, 164–5, 194
women
as authors 1–2, 65, 93–5, 93f, 94f,
100, 102–3, 126–7, 131–2, 151–3,
174–8

228   INDEX

women (*cont.*)
  as better at loving than men 23,
    102–3, 126–7, 130–1
  as contemplatives and philosophers
    1–2, 7–11, 23, 65–6, 97–100, 102–3,
    126–7, 130–2, 153, 174–8, 207–8

  as readers 65, 93–100, 95*f*, 96*f*, 98*f*,
    99*f*, 114*f*, 115*f*, 131, 132*f*, 153
  bodies and emotions as impeding
    intellection 3–4, 8–10, 126–7, 130–1
  self-denigrating rhetoric and
    internalized misogyny 174–8